SOCIOLOGISTS

IN *Action*

ON INEQUALITIES

This book is dedicated with deep love, admiration, and adoration to Jennifer Wollheim. Her life's work stood as testament to the power of individuals to create impactful social change. Though she was taken from us suddenly and far too early, she remains deep in our hearts always. We miss you and love you Jennifer, and we remain ever with deepest respect for all that you stood for and all of the beauty that you left in this world.

SOCIOLOGISTS

IN *Action*

ON INEQUALITIES

RACE, CLASS, GENDER, AND SEXUALITY

Shelley K. White
Worcester State University

Jonathan M. White
Bentley University

Kathleen Odell Korgen
William Paterson University

Los Angeles | London | New Delhi
Singapore | Washington DC

Los Angeles | London | New Delhi
Singapore | Washington DC

FOR INFORMATION:

SAGE Publications, Inc.

2455 Teller Road

Thousand Oaks, California 91320

E-mail: order@sagepub.com

SAGE Publications Ltd.

1 Oliver's Yard

55 City Road

London, EC1Y 1SP

United Kingdom

SAGE Publications India Pvt. Ltd.

B 1/I 1 Mohan Cooperative Industrial Area

Mathura Road, New Delhi 110 044

India

SAGE Publications Asia-Pacific Pte. Ltd.

3 Church Street

#10–04 Samsung Hub

Singapore 049483

Acquisitions Editor: Jeff Lasser

Editorial Assistant: Nick Pachelli

Production Editor: Kelly DeRosa

Copy Editor: Kimberly Hill

Typesetter: Hurix Systems Pvt. Ltd.

Proofreader: Dennis W. Webb

Indexer: Jean Casalegno

Cover Designer: Anupama Krishnan

Marketing Manager: Erica DeLuca

Printed in the United States of America

Library of Congress Cataloging-in-Publication Data

Sociologists in action on inequalities : race, class, gender, and sexuality / Shelley K. White, Jonathan M. White, Kathleen Odell Korgen.

pages cm
Includes bibliographical references and index.

ISBN 978-1-4522-4202-6 (pbk. : alk. paper) — ISBN 978-1-4833-1147-0 (web pdf) — ISBN 978-1-4833-2229-2 (epub)

1. Race. 2. Social classes. 3. Gender identity. 4. Sex.
I. White, Shelley K., editor of compilation.
II. White, Jonathan M. (Jonathan Michael) editor of compilation. III. Korgen, Kathleen Odell, 1967- editor of compilation.

HT1521.S5443 2014
305—dc23   2013045922

This book is printed on acid-free paper.

SUSTAINABLE FORESTRY INITIATIVE
Certified Chain of Custody
Promoting Sustainable Forestry
www.sfiprogram.org
SFI-01268
SFI label applies to text stock

14 15 16 17 18 10 9 8 7 6 5 4 3 2 1

Contents

Acknowledgments

We feel incredibly fortunate to have worked with two tremendous editors in creating this book. David Repetto began this adventure with us and supported us with unwavering enthusiasm, creativity, and warmth. We are so grateful for having had the opportunity to work with him. We also could not be more thrilled to work with Jeff Lasser, who has helped us seamlessly transition into our work with a new team and has supported us wholeheartedly in creating this new *Sociologists in Action* book. We are also fortunate to be working with our editorial assistant, Lauren Johnson, who has helped us with endless details along the way. As well, we are grateful to our production editor Stephanie Palermini and our copyeditor Kim Hill, and we remain ever grateful to our Marketing Manager Erica DeLuca for her constant support.

It is always a great pleasure to work with the SAGE team.

Shelley would like to thank her parents and siblings for their constant, loving support. I am also especially grateful to my nieces and nephews for keeping me playful even as I pursue my research and action on social injustices in the world. I am ever indebted to my grandparents for lending me the perspective and appreciation that long lives well lived afford. I also must thank my mentors who have supported and guided me on my path to understanding the marriage of scholarship and activism, including Charlie Derber, Eve Spangler, Bill Wiist, Pauline Hamel, Kris Heggenhougen, Monica Onyango, Bill Bicknell, Lucy Honig, and Bob Woods. I also must acknowledge the many inspiring young activists I have met through Free The Children, and through my work at Boston College, Simmons College, and Worcester State University, who in many ways teach me more than I could ever teach them! Finally, I feel so fortunate that my life partner is also my partner in changing the world. Thank you, Jonathan, for supporting me and journeying with me every day!

Jonathan owes a special debt of gratitude to his mentors and colleagues Charlie Derber, Eve Spangler, David Karp, Gordie Fellman, Irv Zola,

Morrie Schwartz, Karen Hansen, Sue Dargan, Lucille Lawless, Joe Bandy, Terry Arendell, Craig Kielburger, Marc Kielburger, and Fintan Kilbride, for their incredible guidance and support on his journey as a sociologist in action. I am especially grateful to my students and coworkers at Bentley University, Bridgewater State University, Colby College, and Framingham State University and to the Free The Children and Me to We staff and youth, past and present, who have inspired and continue to inspire me with their deep commitment to social change and social justice. I am eternally grateful to my family for their constant support and unconditional love. Especially, I could never express deeply enough how lucky I feel to have my wife Shelley by my side as my best friend and partner in life. Thank you, Shelley, for inspiring me with your passion for social justice and equity and for this incredible journey we are on together!

Kathleen is grateful to have earned her PhD in sociology at Boston College, where she learned that sociology can and should make a positive impact on the world. She thanks her family for their love, support, and patience. Mom, you will always be my #1 editor. Thanks for all you do. Julie and Jessica, the stories in this book will help you to understand more fully why your mom loves being a sociologist. You two make me so very proud to be your mom. Jeff, thanks for being such a wonderful motivator, source of inspiration, and all around incredible partner (and excellent dad).

Finally, we are enormously indebted to our contributors—an incredible array of inspiring *Sociologists in Action* and gifted writers. They make us proud to be sociologists!

Introduction

Sociology is an exciting subject to study! Sociologists have the ability to uncover and analyze the social problems that exist in our world, including those faced by people because of the social norms and values that guide us surrounding race, ethnicity, gender, class, and sexuality. But what makes sociology so exciting is that sociologists also possess the skills to create change, to work to make a difference on the very social problems they have identified!

Does this appeal to you? Have you ever . . .

- Wondered how you can make a positive impact on the world?
- Wished you could better understand *why* there remains so much prejudice and discrimination based on race, class, gender, and sexuality while also understanding *what* you can do to change this?
- Wanted to know how sociology can play a key role in giving you the tools to understand and create the change you want to see in the world?
- Wondered why sociologists are some of the most interesting and empowering people you've ever meet?

If so, you have started reading the right book! Throughout this book, you will be treated to dozens of pieces written by sociologists who are using their skills to have a positive social impact on a variety of issues related to diversity in our society and around the globe.

The book is broken into five chapters, closely related to courses on diversity as well as to many introductory sociology and social problems courses taught through the central lens of diversity. At the end of each chapter, you will find thought-provoking discussion questions aimed at challenging you to think more deeply about the issues being raised by the various authors. Each chapter also provides an extensive list of great resources that will help you to learn more about the social problems seen throughout the book and the many inspiring individuals and organizations working to create solutions.

All of the sociologists in this book follow in a long line of tradition, using their sociological tool belt to create solutions to the enduring prejudice and discrimination based on race, class, gender, and sexuality that is wrapped throughout our society. C. Wright Mills (1959) speaks of the responsibility of sociologists to connect personal troubles to public issues and Randall Collins (1998) teaches of the two core commitments of sociologists to (1) use their sociological eye to uncover societal injustices and (2) use their sociological skills to actively work to confront these injustices and to seek solutions. The contributors to this book are each a shining example of what Mills and Collins had in mind, and collectively they provide a powerful story about the unique ability of sociologists to change the world.

The three editors of this book feel honored to be able to bring this book to you, sharing the stories of dozens of our sociology colleagues. Combined with our sister book, *Sociologists in Action: Sociology, Social Change, and Social Justice* (2nd Edition, 2014), we feel more energized than ever about the potential for our discipline to create powerful social change. What a cool professor you must have for choosing to use a book that not only teaches you about the persistent and poignant issues of prejudice and dis- crimination in our world but also provides real-life examples of how you can become part of the solution. We hope you enjoy the book and that you are inspired yourselves to become sociologists in action, utilizing the tools that your professors are providing for you to create a more socially just world!

References

Collins, R. (1998). The sociological eye and its blinders. *Contemporary Sociology,* 27(1), 2–7.

Korgen, K. O., White, J. M., & White, S. K. (2014). *Sociologists in action: Sociology, social change, and social justice.* Thousand Oaks: Sage.

Mills, C. W. (1959). *The sociological imagination.* New York: Oxford University Press.

1

Race

R *ace* is a social construction with profound implications in our social world. While constructions of race vary across time and place, racial inequality remains a social problem throughout U.S. society and the world. Today, sociologists can often be found at the forefront of efforts to uncover patterns of racial inequality and discrimination and to promote racial justice. In this chapter, six sociologists in action describe how they have used sociological tools to better understand and address racial inequality and discrimination.

The chapter begins with, "Amplifying the Youth Voice of the Food Justice Movement with Film: Action Media Projects and Participatory Media Production." Author Mike Cermak vividly describes his work as a food activist and how he has collaborated with inner city youth of color to promote the food justice movement. Through participatory action research and an action media project, he and the young people have attempted to address "the racial bias in the environmental and food movements," which privileges the voices and perspectives of whites over others. In this process, Cermak took a back seat, allowing the youth to guide their own learning about patterns of food inequality and to put their knowledge to work educating others and transforming their neighborhoods in the process. In one culminating event of their work, Cermak describes how two of the youth presented their film, *Planting for Peace: Bury Seeds, Not Bodies* (2010), in front of an audience of over 300—and how they shone. Having grown as youth leaders in this movement, these young people gained the skills and confidence to deliver a presentation that moved and motivated their audience. For Cermak, this experience affirmed that "becoming a sociologist in action required that I use any medium at my disposal to amplify the voices that need to be heard."

Next, in "Place and Race: Cultural Democracy and Reclaiming Public Space," Diane Grams writes about her work in Chicago protecting and restoring cultural works in a traditionally African American community threatened with gentrification. As new investment flowed into Chicago's near south side, deemed the "Soul of Black Chicago," she and fellow activists had to grapple with the question, "how does one preserve yet change local culture?" Bringing her students into her community work, she was able to elucidate how cultural symbols can empower a neighborhood. In describing the research her class undertook, she states, "this process of documenting knowledge from oral histories and personal accounts and assembling them into reports and publications helped to demonstrate how local cultural sites are community assets to build upon, not erase. This kind of cultural work I identify as 'empowerment' because it seeks to restore cultural reserves of communities suffering from disinvestment." Grams' work shows how sociologists, by bringing attention to the importance of these symbols, can help save them from destruction and move communities toward the ideal of a cultural democracy.

In the third piece in this chapter, "Social Movements in Action: Combating Environmental Racism on a Native American Reservation," Brandon Hofstedt provides an example of the positive impact students can make. Students in his social movements class learn about these movements, why they matter, under what conditions they are successful, *and* how to create one. From the many impressive social movements students have started, Hofstedt describes the work of one group to address environmental racism in their community. This group effectively used the sociological tools they gained in their class to stall the efforts of a mining company to develop an iron ore mine in the Penokee Mountain range in northern Wisconsin. The mine would have resulted in environmental damage and health risks for the Native American nations in the area. The students' successful efforts to thwart that plan are an inspiring picture of sociology in action. As Hofstedt describes, "Using their sociological tools and their newly acquired understanding of social movements, students were able to organize a successful Social Movement Campaign and to make a real impact in confronting environmental racism in their own community!"

In "When Resilience Is Not Enough: Recovery, Privilege, and Hurricane Katrina," Pamela Jenkins shows how race, class, and power intersected in the Hurricane Katrina disaster in New Orleans. Through sharing her own experience living through Katrina and its aftermath, and her training as an activist and sociologist, Jenkins illustrates how issues of race and class can help determine who survives a disaster such as Katrina. She shows how those with higher racial and class statuses tend to have resources to call upon that give them an advantage over others in the same situation. Speaking of her own relative advantage, she states, "This privilege in the face of disaster placed me in a contradictory position of being 'part of' something yet 'standing apart' as well—the subject and observer of an event." As she observed the disaster and its aftermath unfolding, she reflected on how racism shaped media depictions of the chaos, stating, "The portrayal began to surface as some residents (usually white) were shown as 'taking' from stores and other individuals (usually poor and African American) were viewed as 'looting' from the stores. This stereotype of young African American men as looters did not show those men of color who saved people in neighborhood after neighborhood." Race also became an important factor in shaping the kinds of post-storm settlements families received, and Jenkins describes how groups and allies mobilized to address these inequalities.

Joshua Warren writes about how he used the sociological tools he gained as a sociology major at Bridgewater State University in "Living the DREAM: Race, Privilege, and DREAMs of a Brighter Future." Working with the DREAM program first in Vermont, and then in the Roxbury community in Boston, Warren helped connect children living in subsidized housing developments with college student mentors. Warren used sociological tools to understand why the DREAM program was a successful model in rural Vermont and how it could also be adapted successfully to urban Roxbury. He and the other members of the predominantly white DREAM program had to learn to recognize the lack of diversity on their staff and the issues that are raised when white staff and mentors work in a community of color. As they problem solved and negotiated these issues collaboratively with their partner communities, they also worked to encourage youth to recognize their potential and to achieve their goals. As Warren describes, "Youth who never before had access to college campuses now view higher education as a viable option. Many youth who may have joined gangs have made the decision not to. Instead, the program has created a positive peer group where youth are surrounded by friends and neighbors who are engaged in *constructive* [rather than destructive] risk taking."

In "Bridging the Campus and the Community: Blogging about the Asian American Experience," C. N. Le shares how he began to learn about and embrace his Vietnamese and Asian American heritage after he began to take some sociology courses in college. He decided to use his sociological knowledge to embrace the expectation that he would speak up for other Asian Americans. Through establishing his Asian-nation.org Web site and blog, Le has "portray[ed] Asian Americans as accurately and comprehensively as possible rather than let[ting] . . . other Americans rely on distorted portrayals and ignorant stereotypes about Asian Americans." In the mode of public sociology, he has made sure his postings are as jargon free as possible in order to bridge the campus and community divide. Le points out that, in

addition to educating the public at large, his Web site is "a source of information and learning for young Asian Americans, many of whom grow up
[as Le did] isolated from their history, culture, and collective experiences."
His Web site and blog are also a means "to mobilize [the Asian American]
community in times of crisis (e.g., responding to a high-profile incident of
racism)." Both are excellent examples of the use of sociological tools to
combat stereotypes, prejudice, and discrimination.

Amplifying the Youth Voice of the Food Justice Movement with Film: Action Media Projects and Participatory Media Production

Michael Cermak
Boston College

Michael Cermak is the founder and director of Environmental Justice
Action Media (EJAM), an organization dedicated to producing youth-
focused media on urban environmental issues. He is also a sociologist
and teacher at Boston College, where he completed his dissertation on
the role of hip hop and the arts in urban environmental education. His
food activism includes working in Boston-area K–12 schools where he
has set up numerous vegetable gardens and integrated them with science curriculum. His most recent work is as cofounder of The Green
Dragons, a food and fitness initiative that combines martial arts and
gardening education for youth.

There was a crowd of over 300 people filing into the room, and I was
starting to doubt my presentation plan. This would be the first test for two
urban teenagers who had little experience speaking in front of an audience,
even less so in front of 300 potentially restless and half-interested undergraduates. The youth were two of the stars of my film, *Planting for Peace:
Bury Seeds, Not Bodies* (2010), and we were to show the 20-minute piece
and then hear about their experience helping me make it. I wondered if
I was setting them up for failure. Sure, they were used to talking about their
unlikely love of urban agriculture to me and their boss, but in front of such
a large crowd the prospect was daunting. This would be an extension of a
program where I sought youth narratives about food justice and put them

into a film that was co-written, filmed, and edited by teens. The youth were getting paid well for this appearance but even that couldn't stave off the nervousness they felt as they watched the crowd amass.

My sociological research on race, nature, and media directly informed the process that led to my travelling exhibition with the youth. My research questions revolve around the racial bias in the environmental and food movements, what Julie Guthman calls the "unbearable whiteness of alternative food" (2011). As a scholar of color who cares deeply about urban sustainability and youth empowerment, I wanted to do more than just describe the racial bias in yet another progressive movement and intervene by working with a set of teens to create food media that represented more of their perspective. The standard eco-discourse (e.g., global warming, the ozone layer, greenhouse gases) is deeply wrought with scientific and hyperrational thinking. I had seen this turn off many of the youth with whom I worked. They had tired of hearing about the health content of foods, how everything they like is bad for them, and how organic is the way to go. Whatever the food message, the messengers were usually white scholars and writers (such as Michael Pollan, Frances Moore Lappe, Eric Schlosser, and Barbara Kingsolver) who are great but do not always tap into important justice and race-based frameworks for understanding food and culture. I wanted to engage young people in the production of their own narrative on food problems in their neighborhoods, and what *they* saw as the root of the issue.

The *Planting for Peace* (P4P) film project evolved from a methodology called Participatory Action Research (PAR). PAR is an approach to research and inquiry where the trained experts intentionally take a backseat to the community with whom they work. Instead of the researchers choosing the topic, they start with a meeting with community members to identify the most salient social problems. Instead of being the sole collector and cruncher of data, the researchers train and include the community in data collection and analysis. Last, PAR researchers make a commitment to help the community use the results of the field research to address the issues they have studied. PAR was born as a response to the nontransparent and noninclusive format taken by many researchers who study marginalized populations. As someone oriented to taking action, I also employ PAR because it gives me a chance to address the social problems I study side by side with the people who are the "subjects of research." This is what I was attempting to do by having the youth from the project present their film at the university.

Making this project into a film also helped me remedy the issue that much good PAR work gets done with such little documentation in popularly accessible media. Like PAR that critiques the standard research process, I extend this critique to the filmmaking process. We were starting to hear of media *about* food justice that features youth of color, but these were still accounts largely written, filmed, and produced by white filmmakers. One example of a great film about food justice issues is Scott Hamilton Kennedy's *The Garden* (2008). Kennedy's film chronicles a Latino community in South Central Los Angeles fighting to save the largest urban farm in the country. I decided to incorporate the practices of PAR in a similarly garden-focused project, but in contrast I decided to put the youth more in the "driver's seat" of the media produced about them. The result was a PAR project on food issues that was complemented by what I call an Action Media Project (AMP). An AMP is a framework that challenges PAR or community-based practitioners to create engaging media about their projects so that it may be effectively shared with others. It places the real community research and action of PAR into a media project, in this case a film, and requires that the youth from the community get behind the lens. As the acronym suggests, the goal is to "amp," or amplify, the voice of marginalized communities about social issues.

I have described the full process of this film elsewhere (Cermak, 2012), but what is relevant here is how my training as a sociologist helped us create a more participatory media and action outcome. In 2010, I received an artist in residence grant from a community organization with the challenge of making a film about food justice with a team of youth who had almost no experience thinking about food in a sociopolitical context. The team, who had worked on other projects prior to my arrival, consisted of ten black and Latino youth, some of whom had dropped out of high school and/or been involved with gangs. At the time, they could not have envisioned how they would eventually be presenting this film to groups all around the city, or in front of hundreds of people. They had good experience organizing around stopping violence in their community, but had not extended this to thinking about how this connected to food and sustainability.

We spent a full year doing a workshop at least once every other week, covering food issues for the first six months and then learning about how to produce a film for the second six months. Each workshop was focused on the intersection of food and social justice issues, framing growing food not as solely about health and nutrition but about identity, space, and power. We watched films like the aforementioned *The Garden* (2008) and learned about Guerilla Gardening, an urban movement where citizens populate any open space they can find with flowers or vegetables, even if the land is someone else's. We even went back in history and covered the Victory Gardens of World War II and the propaganda that said "our food is fighting," showing how growing food had a militant angle used to assert pride and ownership of land. We also engaged in real food growing by starting raised-bed gardens and growing cucumbers, peas, and tomatoes from seed. Next, we switched to workshops about filmmaking, covering everything from conducting interviews to using photography and videography. They learned how to create and conduct interviews on camera, and we traveled to other parts of the city to interview other urban teens doing urban gardening. This mix of content and skills helped develop the youths' perspective on food and their ability to coauthor this AMP.

The title of our film came from a script-writing workshop where I asked the youth to connect their framework of stopping violence to the food issues they were learning. David, a 16-year-old Puerto Rican teenager, said it best:

"To me it's about what we put in the ground . . . we need to bury more seeds than we do bodies."

His powerful phrase became the subtitle of the P4P film, *Bury Seeds, Not Bodies,* and the film calls for more paid opportunities to cultivate urban land and sell food at affordable prices at farmers' markets. These green jobs were also socially just because they would alleviate the unemployment of teens, a trend that is linked to higher crime rates as youth may turn to illegal work with gangs.

When the film was completed, I wanted to embody the AMP approach and do more than just distribute a DVD. The film could influence the way that people think about food justice with respect to race, class, and ethnicity, but a more interactive tour would help. I knew the youth would benefit from telling their story to a live audience, and I knew this would also enhance how the film was received. I decided to have a film tour that would employ the youth in the film by providing speakers' stipends, using the opportunity to create jobs and channel revenue back to the community. We began scheduling screenings with schools and other nonprofits. Sometimes only I would present the film, but eventually I trained two of the more vocal youth, Angel and Rigoberto (Riggy), to give a 5-minute introduction at the screenings and answer questions at the end of the film. It just happened that our first showing at Boston College, where I teach, attracted 300 people, vastly more than I anticipated.

Despite my worries, Angel and Riggy spoke from their hearts and quickly won over the audience. They spoke of the realities of living in their neighborhood, a so-called "food desert," that has only one grocery store for over 30,000 citizens and is inundated with fast food chains. They also spoke of what it was like for them, urban teens of color, to change their perspective from initially seeing gardening as a frivolous and relatively useless activity to seeing how growing food connected them to their community and provided one way to revitalize their local landscape. One young woman who watched our film and presentation sent me an e-mail:

I heard your presentation and watched your documentary at the teach-in yesterday. I just wanted to e-mail you because I can't stop thinking about it. I think what you're doing is so awesome. It seems like you have made a HUGE difference. Angel and Riggy were absolutely unbelievable. Riggy was so well spoken and did a great job getting the message across. Angel was adorable and SO positive. It seemed like every other word out of his mouth was "awesome." So, no need to e-mail me back or anything but I just couldn't not tell you how great I think what you are doing is.

The accolades were nice, but more importantly I saw how adding this educational piece to the production of our film empowered the youth involved in the project. By striving for an AMP approach, we made tangible changes in the opportunity structure for youth who had not previously seen food politics as a viable area of concern. Here is a short list of what we accomplished by having youth help create films that provide their perspective on food justice:

1. *We revised how education about food is conducted.* Switching the major frame of food from health and nutrition to jobs, justice, and antiviolence for violence-affected communities was a strong step in engaging the youth in this project. The workshops looking at food from a social justice perspective are still used in the trainings for new hires at the community organization.

2. *We created a documentary that can be used in classrooms and other venues across the nation.* This is a critical part of the AMP approach that creatively shows PAR projects in action. The film has been screened with a workshop over 75 times in the New England area for audiences ranging from middle school to graduate schools. I also use the film in my own undergraduate teaching.

3. *We created jobs.* Angel and Riggy still tour with the film, receiving pay for their work or a donation to their nonprofit organization that works on environmental justice and affordable housing. It is significant that both are youth of color from a low-income neighborhood. I also receive income from these screenings to supplement my income as a public speaker, and I share my views on the role of sociology for social and environmental change.

4. *We created a garden.* The film featured the evolution of our two raised-bed gardens where we grow produce and use it in recipes for some of our meals. This garden is still used and a strong symbol that youth of color are ready to participate in the food movement when it is tied more closely to the ownership of land in their communities.

The AMP approach has allowed me to take my sociological questions and turn them into tangible results at many levels. The journey started when I held my own work accountable with the simple statement: "Completing a paper and/or a documentary film is the beginning, not the end, of the empowering journey." As our culture becomes inundated with videos and websites for progressive causes, it is increasingly important to add real actions and job opportunities for those who are featured in these media. AMP helps remind me to continuously leverage my sociology and stay more accountable to the communities I study and serve. Angel and Riggy's beautiful presentation under pressure helped teach me of the power that intertwining creativity and sociology can bring. At the beginning of my sociology studies I would never have thought of myself as a filmmaker, but becoming a sociologist in action required that I use any medium at my disposal to amplify the voices that need to be heard. How can *you* put your sociology into a creative medium and then put it to work for those being studied?

References

Guthman, J. (2011). If they only knew: The unbearable Whiteness of alternative food. In A. Alkon & J. Agyeman, (Eds.), *Cultivating food justice: Race, class, and sustainability*. Cambridge: MIT.

Cermak, M. (Producer). (2010). *Planting for peace: Bury seeds, not bodies* [DVD]. United States: Environmental Justice Media.

Cermak, M. (2012). Nutritious media: Lessons from making a film about growing food with urban youth of color. *Media Fields Journal, 5*.

Kennedy, S. H. (Director). (2008). *The garden* [Documentary]. United States: Black Valley Films.

Place and Race: Cultural Democracy and Reclaiming Public Space

Diane Grams
Tulane University

Diane Grams is an Assistant Professor of Sociology at Tulane University in New Orleans. Her interest in cultural inequality began when she was Executive Director of The Peace Museum in Chicago (1992–1998), an activist museum providing community- and school-based violence prevention programs and exhibitions on peace, civil rights, and violence prevention movements. As the associate director of the Cultural Policy Center at the University of Chicago (2003–2007), she conducted research on the relationship of cultural institutions to local urban culture. Her current work focuses on public parading organizations in New Orleans.

Like many urban areas, Chicago's downtown has a concentration of business, government, and cultural institutions. From the earliest days of the city, the downtown had been surrounded by areas considered to be "inner city" areas of poverty. In the last quarter of the 20th century, the developers of the city center sought to expand into these areas long inhabited by foreign born immigrants and African Americans. In 2001, I began research in the African American community on Chicago's near south side. I was interested in how local activists challenged both historic segregation and contemporary gentrification efforts by asserting cultural ownership of this increasingly contested urban space. By claiming the area was the "Soul of Black Chicago," these activists were redefining the area once considered to be one of Chicago's most neglected ghettos as a place of importance to black culture and history. I joined their efforts as I believe that cultural democracy means broadening understanding of what a place dominated by African Americans might look like if we remove the label of "ghetto." These efforts to reclaim and redefine a place in Chicago, also gives new meaning to our sociological understanding of the relationship of race and place.

The problems of poverty and neglect, often associated with urban segregation, are the result of long-term urban processes stemming back to slavery. The term *segregation* is a 20th century term for what W. E. B. DuBois (1902), a prominent African American sociologist, referred to as "the color line." These social arrangements of racial separation, once mandated by the provision of separate drinking fountains, bathroom facilities, bus seats, and schools, continue to operate in urban areas through the positioning, resourcing, and privileging of one group over another and one culture over another. As a cultural sociologist, I sought to understand and highlight how cultural distinctions (Bourdieu, 1984) that assign value to a place, an object, a form of skill, or kinds of knowledge can perpetuate the inequalities of the color line or support cultural democracy.

Scholars of race and urban history consider discrimination and inequality embedded in symbols, policies, and practice as "structural racism" because they result in unequal access to resources, unequal opportunity, and privilege based on skin color. I wanted my research to help change this. I used the skills of a cultural ethnographer to become involved in the community I was interested in studying. As an activist scholar I hoped my work could affect the processes of urban development to benefit long neglected communities.

When my research began in 2001, the neoliberal housing policies which began during the Clinton Administration in the 1990s—known as the Hope VI—were in the latter stages of public/private housing redevelopment under the George W. Bush Administration. These policies sought to transform areas once dominated by government administered public housing projects for the poor into privately run, government funded, mixed-income developments.

When I first visited the near south side area, the Robert Taylor, Clarence Darrow, and Ida B. Wells Public Housing projects had been bulldozed, leaving large swaths of vacant land. Former residents moved into other communities near and far using public housing vouchers. The problem facing this community was no longer the problem sociologists refer to as *disinvestment*, the neglect evident when government and private business owners no longer reinvest in their properties and residents don't contribute as citizens of the community. Rather, a new problem emerged as money poured into the south side from local, state, and federal agencies: rapid change threatened to erase the history of black life and decimate a cultural history more than 100 years in the making. Community activists sought to ensure that investments to improve transportation, communication, institutions, and housing were designed to strengthen the black community and preserve its cultural history, not erase it.

The question then became how does one preserve yet change local culture? Through a series of studies, I was involved with an effort to inventory what was in the community (Grams & Warr, 2003). My interest continued through completion of my dissertation, teaching at a university in Hyde Park on Chicago's south side, the University of Chicago, and the publication of *Producing Local Color*, my book on the importance of local culture (Grams, 2010). Discussion of one project, "The Public Art of Bronzeville," on Martin Luther King Drive might best illustrate how this change took place. The project, initially criticized as part of the Mayor's beautification efforts because it was strategically completed in time for the 1996 Democratic Convention held in Chicago, came to symbolize long-term redevelopment of the area. The centerpiece of the artwork is a bronze map embedded in the median at 35th Street depicting the historic area. Harold Lukas and Paula Robinson, two longtime local cultural activists, led efforts to name the area depicted on the map and then ultimately rename the contemporary neighborhood, "Bronzeville." Few people, including some local residents, black activists, and other Chicago residents, understood Lukas's and Robinson's involvement or the purpose behind this effort.

Through my course "Excavating Cultural Policy" at the University of Chicago, my students and I interviewed people walking on Martin Luther King Drive where the "Public Art of Bronzeville" is located. We also interviewed a broad range of city workers and city policy makers to understand how this artwork came to be installed on King Drive. Our research traced the complex range of perspectives on the redevelopment of the neighborhood from within and outside the historic south side community.

For some, the term *Bronzeville* had racist connotations as it derived from a post-civil war era reference to a predominantly black community. Other local residents saw the name as a shallow promotional gimmick, as one artist remarked, "'Bronzeville' is an affectation by promoters. This is the South Side. When you say you are going to the 'South Side,' you don't mean Hyde Park, which is located on the South Side—you mean the black community." Others were afraid it was a racist effort to stereotype the black middle class or to divide the black community along class lines. As one community leader stated, "Some people have been referring to Bronzeville, marking out certain areas—this street and that street. I think wherever black folks live in Chicago is Bronzeville and is community."

If Lukas and Robinson were to be successful, the meaning of the term was to signify an area with rich cultural roots worthy of investment and preservation. Their efforts tapped into the history of the area, as "a city within a city," as it was referred to by sociologists St. Clair Drake and Horace R. Cayton (1945/1993, pp. 12), making Bronzeville "a place within a place" on Chicago's south side. After all, the south side of Chicago developed as a black area in the early twentieth century because restrictive policies barred black migrants from the southern United States from living in most neighborhoods, thus enabling this "Black Metropolis" to form. The area once thrived from the economic diversity of its black residents; the intention of the 21st century plan was to restore that economic diversity back to the area.

We often think of activism as carrying protest banners and doing sit-ins, but my research and that of my students sought to detail connections between works of "local heroes and she-ros" named on the Bronzeville Walk of Fame (terms local leader Sokoni Karanja used to highlight both men's and women's contributions) and the community they help build. Through such activism, my students and I tracked down people and events to build on local knowledge and broaden its reach.

We found, for example, historic homes of renowned African Americans who once lived in Bronzeville, such as activist and author of *Black Boy*, Richard Wright (1945), and journalist Ida B. Wells, who documented lynching in the south. The lives of these two historic figures continue to exemplify the kind of creativity, commitment to community, and social justice to be modeled by present and future generations. And, rather than whitewashing faded and pealing activist murals created in the 1960s and 70s on cement retaining walls, funds were raised for restoration because these artworks are significant local history. New cultural facilities were also built during this 20-year span. Among them, Little Black Pearl Workshop teaches young people entrepreneurial skills through artistry. New knowledge was passed on as elementary school teachers had their students visit the mile-long public art project to do rubbings from the bronze plaques naming current and former residents. Students then research the lives of the more than

200 people who are memorialized. Such projects place the cultural history of blackness into the public forum as a positive creative spirit.

This process of documenting knowledge from oral histories and personal accounts and assembling them into reports and publications helps demonstrate how local cultural sites are community assets (Kretzmann & McKnight, 1993) to build on, not erase. This kind of cultural work I identify as "empowerment" because it seeks to restore cultural reserves of communities suffering from disinvestment. Such efforts are distinct from the processes typical of "gentrification," which erase racial and ethnic cultural identity and replace it with the signs and symbols of a homogenous culture in order to attract wealthy white urban professionals.

This account shows how cultural democracy is an important part of the solution to the problems created by the history of segregation. Cultural democracy means cultural resources are not concentrated in a city center or only in a city's wealthiest communities and that local places are not marginalized or left without even the most basic cultural resources. After years of involvement to landmark and preserve individual properties, Lukas and Robinson have set their sights on having Bronzeville designated as a National Historical Area. The designation would be based on its historical and cultural significance as the only place black migrants to the city of Chicago could live during segregation and would symbolize and celebrate how a creative spirit, commitment to community, and social justice has enabled the survival of black communities throughout the United States.

References

Bourdieu, P. (1984). *Distinction: A social critique of the judgment of taste* (R. Nice, Trans.). Cambridge: Harvard University Press.

Drake, S., & Cayton, H. (1945/1993). *Black metropolis: A study of negro life in a northern city.* New York: Harper Row.

DuBois, W. E. (1903). *The souls of black folk: Essays and sketches* Chicago: A. C. McClurg & Co.

Grams, D. (2010). *Producing local color: Art networks in ethnic Chicago.* Chicago, IL: University of Chicago Press.

Grams, D., & Warr, M. (2003). *Leveraging assets: How small budget arts activities benefit neighborhoods.* Report for the Richard H. Driehaus Foundation and the John D. and Catherine MacArthur Foundation. Retrieved from http://www.luc.edu/curl/escd/discussions/links/gramssmall_budget_arts_activities.pdf

Kretzmann, J. P., & McKnight, J. L. (1993). *Building communities from the inside out: A path toward finding and mobilizing a community's assets.* Evanston, IL: Institute for Policy Research.

Wright, R. (1945). *Black boy, a record of childhood and youth.* New York: Harper & Brothers.

Social Movements in Action: Combating Environmental Racism on a Native American Reservation

Brandon Hofstedt
Northland College

Brandon Hofstedt is Assistant Professor of Sustainable Community Development at Northland College. His research and expertise is in applied, community-based research with a focus on social movements, community/civic participation, political sociology, community development, rural/urban studies, and land use planning and policy.

As an undergraduate student studying sociology, I found the most rewarding and memorable learning experiences came when theory met practice. Today, as a professor, I find myself constantly returning to these transformative experiences and trying to find ways to recreate these opportunities for my own students. When I first taught a course on social movements in the fall of 2008, I took the opportunity to integrate the academic literature with real life experiences and hands-on, applied learning projects. To bring the literature on social movements to life, I required students to work with a group of their classmates on an issue that they all found to be interesting and exciting. I called these projects Social Movement Campaigns (or SMCs). As part of their SMCs, I asked students to create, organize, market, and carry out their campaign during the semester. Over the last 4 years, I have worked with over 20 student groups on topics ranging from combating environmental racism on a local Native American reservation, to securing local food sources and alleviating local class inequalities, to reducing domestic violence and providing domestic partner benefits for all campus employees. Through these projects, students have felt the power of sociology, as they have become active participants in their communities and in their democracy.

Social Movement Campaigns in Theory

Before delving into the SMCs, we spend class time discussing how social movements matter and how they operate. I will do the same here.

How do social movements matter?

Broadly speaking, social movements matter in three ways: politically, socially, and culturally. Politically, social movements are seen as making a difference when they achieve acceptance or new advantages (Gamson, 1975). By *acceptance,* we mean that social movement leaders are recognized by other formal political establishments and are given a seat at the table during the decision-making process. When they help set or sway the political agenda and shape public policy, this represents having achieved *new advantages.* Culturally, social movements matter when they help shape attitudes, opinions, values, and knowledge systems (Earl, 2004). In other words, social movements are successful culturally when they influence how the broader public thinks about a given issue. And socially, social movements matter when they influence the arrangement of social networks and the flow of social capital (Diani, 1997).

How do social movements operate?

Place, space, and time all affect how social movements emerge, how they mobilize, how they operate and, ultimately, whether or not the social movement is successful. To fully understand the possible trajectory of a social movement, as well as the likelihood for success, one must grasp two separate but related ideas.

The first idea deals with the internal makeup (i.e., organizations, leaders, and participants) and dynamics (i.e., decisions, goals, strategies, tactics, and resources) of the social movement. The organizations, leaders, and participants of social movements make decisions about the tactics and strategies to use. They help develop the goals of the movement. They make decisions on which resources (e.g., financial, human, or social capital) to tap into and which resources to ignore. They make decisions about how the organization should operate (e.g., top-down and bureaucratic versus bottom-up and flexible) and what message(s) they want to convey to their adversaries, their potential supporters, and to the general public. All these things, these internal characteristics of the social movement, influence the ultimate success or failure of social movement activity.

All these decisions, however, are also made inside a social context (the second idea). In social movement literature, we refer to some of these contextual factors as political opportunity structures (POS). Political opportunity is "the degree to which groups are likely to be able to gain access to power to manipulate the political system" (Eisinger, 1973, pp. 25). If a social movement operates in a democratic system where those in power allow for open and transparent dialogue, the likelihood for members of the social movement to voice their concerns and to have success increases. If the social movement has people in power who are sympathetic to their cause, the likelihood for success increases. In contrast, if a government does not allow or suppresses opposition to its policies, the likelihood for success decreases. It also decreases if the social movement lacks a sympathetic ear from powerful decision makers.

Social Movement Campaigns in Practice: Native American Perspectives on an Iron Ore Mine

After spending the first few weeks of class discussing these important theoretical ideas, my students then attempt to put this knowledge into practice.

There are many great examples of how students have used their SMC projects over the years to create measurable difference on a variety of issues. For this piece, however, I would like to share one particularly effective example. In 2011, a large corporation expressed interest in developing an iron ore mine in the Penokee Mountain range in northern Wisconsin. The initial plan was to extract over two billion tons of iron from the ground to be converted into taconite pellets. The proposed mine immediately sparked a statewide debate pitting jobs versus the environment. Since this was an issue regarding a public policy that threatened the environmental well-being of Native Americans—a racial minority in the United States—this debate was also about a phenomenon that sociologists call "environmental racism." The proposed mine was located adjacent to sovereign tribal lands, raising concerns about air and water quality and natural landscape destruction. The students decided to carefully assemble a campaign that recognized the delicate nature of the proposal and offered a forum for marginalized voices to be heard.

The campaign involved a number of strategies: petitions, outreach efforts, and an educational forum. The primary goals of the SMC were to educate the college and local community on the proposed mine and to offer a forum for the leaders from the local Native American community to voice their concerns, needs, and wants. A secondary goal of the group was to raise awareness related to the negative effects of the mine, especially those connected to environmental racism such as reduced water and air quality and habitat destruction near the local Native American reservation. As part of their forum, the students brought together well respected community members, including a tribal elder, a female spiritual leader, the tribal chairman, and a local fish and wildlife commissioner.

Although the group's efforts were just a very small part of a larger statewide movement in opposition to changing mining laws in Wisconsin and in favor of stopping the taconite mine, the students, using their sociological skills and analysis, played an important role in stalling the proposed mine. The group was able to collect hundreds of signatures supporting the protection of clean air and water for the local tribe. The educational forum attracted well over 100 people and the attention of the local media. A number of the members of the group went on to volunteer and support the tribe's efforts through community organizing and protest. Using their

sociological tools and their newly acquired understanding of social movements, students were able to organize a successful SMC and to make a real
impact in confronting environmental racism in their own community!

Bringing Sociological Theory to Life: How Social Movement Campaigns Matter

In addition to the above campaign, over the last four years, student
groups conducting SMCs have used their burgeoning understanding of
social movements to make a difference in a number of ways. These student
groups secured many tangible and measurable outcomes, including donations in the form of money, food, and clothing; participation by a large
number of people; and the creation of helpful documents, pamphlets, and
petitions. Since 2008, SMCs have attracted over a thousand people from
campus and the surrounding community through volunteering and event
attendance. Student groups have collected over $2,300 in donations for
organizations dealing with hunger, clothing, water quality, child abuse,
and gardening. Additionally, these groups have secured over 300 pounds
of food for the local food bank and have collected hundreds of signatures
on petitions supporting better paper procurement policies, clean water,
and environmental protection. Additionally, SMCs helped rejuvenate a
dormant slow food movement on campus, created a number of booklets
with information related to local food options and political involvement
opportunities, and sparked an interest in local backyard gardening adopted
by a local nonprofit.

Along with these measurable successes, I have received consistent
feedback from students related to the lasting impact of organizing these
campaigns. In the words of one of my students:

> When we started this project, I didn't think that we would be very successful.
> . . . But after seeing the number of people who showed up to the event and
> how interested the audience was . . . I realized that any "normal" person like
> myself can put together an event or start a group to make a difference in their
> community. For me, it was empowering to have this experience and to realize
> that I can be successful in doing something like this.

I have found acknowledgements of feeling empowered such as this to
be very common in student evaluations. I am not surprised, however,
considering that the social movement literature suggests individuals who
participate in social movements are greatly influenced by their experience
(Polletta & Jasper, 2001). In my opinion, the most important outcome
of the SMC projects is not the tangible changes in policy, money raised,
or number of participants. Rather, I think the greatest outcome is when
in the process of putting together a campaign, students feel empowered.

I want them to gain the confidence and come to the realization that change can occur when they are involved and act in their communities and in their democracy. I have found inspiration in my students' projects and have identified a way to help them in the process of becoming sociologists in action by bridging theory and practice through the utilization of sociological ideas. Being a sociologist in action, I will continue to look for and implement ways to incorporate sociological concepts in meaningful, transformative ways.

References

Diani, M. (1997). Social movements and social capital: A network perspective on movement outcomes. *Mobilization, 2*(2), 129–147.

Earl, J. (2004). The cultural consequences of social movements. In D. A. Snow, S. A. Soule, & H. Kreisi (Eds.), *The Blackwell companion to social movements.* Malden, MA: Blackwell Publishing.

Eisinger, P. K. (1973). The conditions of protest behavior in American cities. *American Political Science Review, 67,* 11–28.

Gamson, W. A. (1975). *The strategy of social protest* (1st ed.). Homewood, IL: Dorsey Press.

Polletta, F., & Jasper, J. (2001). Collective identity and social movements. *Annual Review of Sociology, 27,* 283–305.

When Resilience Is Not Enough: Recovery, Privilege, and Hurricane Katrina

Pamela Jenkins
University of New Orleans

Pamela Jenkins, PhD, is a Research Professor of Sociology and faculty in the Women's Studies Program at the University of New Orleans. She is a founding and associate member of UNO's Center for Hazard Assessment, Response and Technology. Before Katrina, her research interests were diverse but focused on how communities respond to a variety of problems. Her research interests post-Katrina include documenting the response to Katrina as part of a national research team on Hurricane Katrina evacuees. At a community level, she is involved in several projects that work directly with best practice for violence prevention, including domestic and community violence.

"1400 people died so you could take this picture."

— *graffiti sprayed on an abandoned house in the*
Lower 9th Ward, New Orleans.

This phrase was directed to the thousands of people who came to New Orleans on disaster tours who rode in buses and cars to visit the destruction of a city. The storm in the Gulf and failure of the levees revealed long-standing racial and class inequalities at the same time that it showed the ability of communities and families to step up and attempt to recover. The term *resilience* often refers to an individual's ability to withstand and thrive from adversity; this essay discusses how resilience in a catastrophe depends on the context, not the individual.

I did not set out to be a sociologist. As with so many working class women of my generation, I "fell" into the field. It was the sixties—there was always something to protest. One day, we would be going to an antiwar protest, then boycotting grapes for farmworkers, and then standing with the unemployed. But it was my work with the Welfare Rights Organization in Waterloo, Iowa, that taught me about inequality and resilience. To get to know women who had few economic resources but had the ability, as Mills (1959) would say, to place their own biography in history was what I refer to as "my first degree." When we would sit in a welfare office to protest conditions, it was those women who understood about the length and depth of the struggle. They knew from their lived experiences that inequality harms the self on all levels, and that resilience in the face of inequality is linked not just to a person but to a community. This tension between exploitation and agency captures the experience of life during and after a catastrophe. Learning from these women about how to both endure and fight the everyday exploitation and understand inequality led me to the university library to try to find concepts to match my experience. It was "finding" sociology that allowed me to add a theoretical analysis to the lived experience. From the beginning, my work in sociology is indebted to those first women I met living in Waterloo, Iowa. They taught me that the work had to be grounded in, and done with, the community. Those lessons would also serve me well when Hurricane Katrina made landfall east of New Orleans along the Mississippi Gulf Coast on August 29, 2005. Disasters give the appearance that they strike randomly, yet vulnerable communities and vulnerable people are often the hardest hit. My home, along with 80% of the city, flooded. As the waters receded, I and my family became, as did thousands of others, homeless and displaced. More than being homeless, I thought of myself as a wanderer. I landed first in Iowa, then California, back to Iowa, then to Baton Rouge, then to a friend's house in New Orleans, then a FEMA trailer, then an apartment, and finally home eighteen months later.

Most of the social scientists from the eight colleges in the New Orleans area were asked to speak about their experience; we presented at national meetings that came to New Orleans, at conferences around the country, and even internationally. When I would give a lecture about Hurricane Katrina in the first year after the storm, I would begin with "I lost everything, but I was lucky." After the first year, I would say, "I was lucky, but I lost everything." My house flooded on Tuesday afternoon after the levees began to fail on Monday morning. There was no flood surge that pushed my home off its foundation and no unmoored barge that crashed into my house (as in the lower 9th ward). Instead, there was the slow rise as the water in the city rose to meet the water in Lake Pontchartrain. When all your possessions are on the curb and your home is down to the studs, the outside walls, and the roof, it seemed like I had lost everything. Yet the second phrase captures how I stood in privilege after this catastrophe; I still had my job at the University of New Orleans, my friends, and a community across the country that opened their doors and resources to us. Moreover, opportunities to write about this storm and to be funded to study this storm emerged. This privilege in the face of disaster placed me in a contradictory position of being "part of" something yet "standing apart" as well, the subject and observer of an event.

Standing in privilege included my ability to garner the necessary resources for recovery. After the initial failure of the federal, state, and local governments, there came resources from FEMA monies, FEMA trailers, and the Louisiana Road Home program (a federally funded Louisiana housing program). Because we stood in privilege with education and knowledge, my family was able to access these resources. We could not access them quickly or without a struggle, but eventually we were successful. Accessing these resources required a kind of agency that meant that individuals had to advocate for themselves. Having spent years advocating for others, it was uncomfortable and unfamiliar to advocate for myself and my family (Fothergill, 2011). Nonetheless, as a sociologist I know about lumbering bureaucracies and unresponsive structures. As a person in crisis, I used that knowledge to persevere.

Standing in privilege reflects the complex issues of race and class. The issues of inequality soon resurfaced after the disaster. From the first narrative about rescue, the story quickly shifted to a law and order event. The portrayal began to surface as some residents (usually white) were shown as "taking" from stores and other individuals (usually poor and African American) were viewed as "looting" from the stores. This stereotype of young African American men as looters did not show those men of color who saved people in neighborhood after neighborhood.

Race and class collided with issues of availability and accessibility of aid when evaluating, for example, the Louisiana Road Home Program implemented in Louisiana after Hurricane Katrina. The Road Home program, funded by the U.S. Department of Housing and Urban Development (HUD) for 10.5 billion dollars, is the largest housing redevelopment program in the history of the United States. Road Home began solely as a program to help homeowners rebuild after the storm but it was eventually extended to cover rental property. The Road Home began accepting applications in July 2006 and stopped new applications on July 31, 2007. More than 186,000 homeowners applied for grants through the program (Eden & Boren, 2008).

In 2008, the Greater New Orleans Fair Housing Action Center, National Fair Housing Alliance, and five African American homeowners filed a class action lawsuit against HUD and the Louisiana Recovery Authority (LRA). The suit alleged that the LRA's Road Home program discriminated against African American homeowners in New Orleans. The suit stated that the formula to calculate grants created by ICF International (approved by the Louisiana Recovery Authority and U.S. Department of Housing and Urban Development) used the pre-storm value of a resident's home rather than an actual estimate of rebuilding costs. As a consequence, black moderate and low-income homeowners received less money than their counterparts who were mostly white, living in comparably built and equally damaged but higher valued homes. The suit stated that the grants from Road Home should be based on rebuilding costs rather than the pre-storm value of the homes. In July 2011, the federal government approved a settlement that awarded 62 million dollars to Louisiana residents under its new Blight Reduction Grant Adjustment program. In addition, HUD and Louisiana changed the Road Home program grant formula to provide full relief to more than 13,000 homeowners. This settlement may help some homeowners in the area; it took nearly six years and a court case for the program to develop a formula that was equitable. In the meantime, homeowners made decisions about their homes and moved on with their lives (Fletcher, 2011).

While this action taken by a collaborative to challenge the injustice of the relief efforts was one of the largest and most successful, it was by no means the only effort. Acorn fought for homeowners in the Holy Cross section of the lower 9th ward to keep their homes; other activists fought unsuccessfully to save the four large public housing units. The struggle around land and recovery continues today.

My own story took many turns in light of the uneven events surrounding recovery. The last seven years is a blur of community meeting after meeting, rebuilding our home, and writing about the storm. In collaboration with both scholars and activists, I continue to attempt to understand how recovery is unequal. I work on and write about issues of the elderly, domestic violence survivors, community violence, nonprofits, and neighborhood recovery, and sociology provides a dynamic frame for this work, enriched and deepened by the community.

The flooding of New Orleans happened because the levees failed and the system failed. Because of that failure, people died in the immediate storm surge as they watched the water climb up their porches and into their houses. We all know people who did not leave and perished. Many were old, some were infirm and others too poor to leave. It is those who died who still haunt me. People died of exposure, dehydration, and shock throughout the city. Others drowned because they were so disabled or elderly, they could not get to their attics. Others died on what high ground they could find—overpasses, bridges, stretches of ground—because it took too long for someone to come rescue them from those pockets of high ground. Many of these deaths were preventable.

Those were the first round of deaths. In the aftermath of the storm, the recovery itself shortened lives. Somehow, we have stopped talking about those people who died. They have vanished quietly; there are few memorials to their struggles or their deaths. Seven years later, sociology still has much to say and sociologists still have much to do in understanding catastrophes and working proactively on the underlying issues of inequality that are exposed during times of catastrophe. Books such as *Displaced: Life in the Katrina Diaspora* edited by Lynn Weber and Lori Peek and *The Sociology of Katrina: Perspectives on a Modern Catastrophe,* edited by David Brunsman et al., are just some of the important sociological pieces giving depth of insight into this catastrophe. The struggle for recovery after a catastrophe is not separate from the struggle around inequality; they are linked. The most vulnerable of the storm, poor African Americans, are rebuilding their lives in reestablished patterns of inequality. Our job as sociologists is to continue to pull back the veneer of everyday life to expose the ongoing issues of race and class and to use the knowledge we gain through our analysis to make practical change for a more just society.

References

Eden, R., & Boren, P. (2008). *Timely assistance: Evaluating the speed of Road Home grantmaking.* Santa Monica, CA: Rand Corporation.

Fletcher, M. (2011, July). HUD to pay $62 million to La. homeowners to settle Road Home lawsuit. *The Washington Post.* Retrieved from http://www.washingtonpost.com/business/economy/hud-to-pay-62-million-to-la-homeowners-to-settle-road-home-lawsuit/2011/07/06/gIQAtsFN1H_story.html

Fothergill, A. (2011). *Heads above water—Gender, class & family in the Grand Forks flood.* Albany: SUNY Press.

Mills, C. W. (1959). *The sociological imagination.* New York: Oxford University Press.

Living the DREAM: Race, Privilege, and DREAMs of a Brighter Future

Joshua Warren
Massachusetts Association for the Blind and Visually Impaired

In 2004, **Joshua Warren** saw what was possible when children living in subsidized housing developments become connected with an abundant and often underutilized resource, college students. Working with the DREAM Program, Warren spent seven years collaborating with low-income communities in Vermont and Massachusetts, building communities of parents and college students that encourage and empower youth to recognize their options, make informed decisions, and achieve their dreams. An avid marathoner, he currently works with the Massachusetts Association for the Blind and Visually Impaired supporting blind and visually impaired endurance athletes from all over the world.

Nobody grows up with dreams of becoming a sociologist. Have you ever met a 10-year-old running around with a copy of George Herbert Mead's "The Social Self," tucked underneath her arm? Have you heard a child exclaim, "When I grow up, I'm going to be the next Emile Durkheim?"

How about you? Did you have posters of Karl Marx and Max Weber on your walls when you were in middle school?

Well, I was no exception. It wasn't until my junior year in college that I discovered the wonderful world of sociology through a required course. After I realized that the only books that I could bear to read cover to cover were for my sociology courses, I knew that this was the major for me! Now, despite the fact that the 10-year-old me never aspired to be a sociology major, it was the child inside of me that drew me to my work. You see, children tend to see things very concretely, almost as if the whole world is black and white. There's a right and there's a wrong. There's fair and there's unfair. When I was a child and I was cut in line, I felt cheated. When I had to stay indoors and miss recess but my peers were allowed to go outside I felt robbed. Sociology, however, helped me to gain the tools I needed to provide a critical lens I could apply to the social problems I see around me in the world. My inner child, for instance, just knows that homelessness isn't fair. But my sociological toolkit allows me to understand why people are homeless, what policies are involved, which demographic groups are most susceptible to homelessness and why, and especially what I can do to help create positive change.

As an undergraduate student studying a myriad of social issues, I was often frustrated, and even enraged, when reading about the prevalence of hunger and poverty in the United States, disease rates in developing nations, human rights violations worldwide, and sexism and racism throughout the world. But just as my coursework filled me with anger and frustration, my sociological training also equipped me with the tools and confidence to address those issues.

As a senior at Bridgewater State University, I began a sociology internship with The DREAM Program, a Vermont based mentoring program. Determined to break the cycle of poverty that often traps those living in subsidized housing, DREAM provides youth with long-term, one-to-one mentors from nearby college campuses and works closely with neighborhood parents, community partners, and local government officials to build a strong network of support committed to the youth and the entire neighborhood. For nearly a decade, DREAM had operated throughout rural Vermont, matching youth living in affordable housing neighborhoods with college student mentors. The results were astonishing. An early evaluation of DREAM's model, published in 2005, showed that a majority of youth participants felt that DREAM had given them a broader world view, expanded social horizons, increased social capital, increased self-reliance, created an expanded comfort zone, increased opportunities for constructive risk taking, and increased their aspirations and positive expectations for their lives.

My internship with DREAM took the form of a directed study under the guidance of one of my sociology professors, Dr. Jonathan White. DREAM had a vision of expanding beyond rural Vermont and into urban areas, and my research task was to take the DREAM mentoring model, which had only been rolled out in a rural, largely white population, and adapt it to a model that could be used in an urban, largely non-white setting. I set about conducting a large literature review that consisted of gaining deeper understandings of urban issues, race issues, and tackling the already existing literature on urban mentoring programs.

I began by trying to identify what facets of DREAM's mentoring model lent to the program's success by reviewing the internal and external evaluations of the organization as well as interviewing children, parents, and mentors. After a semester of research, I concluded that three basic tenets of DREAM's model may have held the key to its success. These tenets were: (1) a community-based approach to mentoring; (2) mentorship programming on a college campus; and (3) long-term, one-to-one mentoring relationships. Additionally, I explored the challenges that may be presented given the social issues that affect youth living in urban housing developments, including issues of race and racism.

By the end of the semester, I was excited to present my findings to the DREAM organization and proud that they felt I had helped create a revised version of their model that was ready to be tested in an urban setting. The culmination of my internship was a successful meeting with a Community Development Corporation in Roxbury, Massachusetts—part of Boston—to discuss the possibility of establishing DREAM in Roxbury.

As I prepared for that first big meeting in Roxbury, I refreshed myself on DREAM's mentoring model, program implementation, and successful track record in Vermont. I also reviewed my sociological research on the need for programs such as DREAM in urban communities with high concentrations of youth at risk. Entering the meeting, I felt confident that I had an understanding of the scope of many of the issues facing youth living in the communities that the Community Development Corporation represented and that, while DREAM may not offer a cure-all solution, it offered a very real means of engaging youth and curbing their engagement in risky behaviors.

Many of the challenges facing youth and families living in low-income housing developments in urban Roxbury mirrored the challenges facing those living in rural developments in Vermont, such as struggling school systems, high unemployment rates, low academic achievement rates, and alarming teen pregnancy rates. However, Roxbury was also plagued by two problems nearly nonexistent where we work in Vermont: gang violence and the historical legacies and current issues related to racism, including individual levels of racism (racism individuals face in their everyday lives) and institutional levels of racism (racism that is incorporated into power structures in society, such as within government, business, and education systems). Thus, as we ultimately moved our model to Roxbury, we noted some areas where race might be a factor. For instance, our mentors were mostly white college students going into a neighborhood comprised of 60–70% African Americans and 30–40% Latinos. It was an added layer trying to go into communities to tell them we have a great program for them, when ultimately we were a white staff pitching the idea of mostly white college students entering the community as mentors.

Moving to an urban setting raised the need for strong diversity trainings, something we hadn't had to do in Vermont. We called on the Community Development Corporations that manage the properties where our youth live to run these trainings, which became an essential cornerstone of our success in working with a more racially diverse population. These were intensive trainings, utilizing varying techniques, to help the mentors develop a heightened awareness of the role of diversity in the program, examine their own privilege, and have a better understanding of the ways that race and class affect their soon to be mentees. In the end, it did prove slightly harder for white mentors to gain trust from non-white youth than we had found in same-race mentoring relationships in Vermont, but one of the great things about kids is that if you're a fun adult and show you care and that you're there to stay, there is a lot of slack given. Ultimately, through a lot of hard work from mentors, mentees, and the skilled help of the community running their diversity trainings, race was a barrier we have been able to overcome in the formation of powerful, lasting mentoring relationships.

Another example that illustrates some of the important racial differences comes from the young people being mentored. Both in rural Vermont and in urban Roxbury, most of the young people didn't have high hopes of attending college. When we took the kids from Vermont to college campuses for their mentoring, they looked around and saw lots of other people who look like them, racially, and they could start to envision themselves going to college someday. When we took the kids from Roxbury, they looked around and saw mostly white students attending the colleges and it was harder for them to be able to say "this could be me, I could be a college student."

With gang activity being another hurdle in Roxbury, we felt the DREAM model would be a strong fit. Solutions to gang activity can be found in programs that are inclusive and create tight peer groups and family bonds, focused on healthy activities and socialization. For instance, one study indicates that "when Boston provided gang members with greater supervision, support, and services, youth homicides in that city dropped by two-thirds."[1] DREAM's program model creates many aspects of kinship that are lacking in many homes, and is able to replicate many of these attributes that often help youth avoid gangs.

In moving our program to Roxbury, we also learned more about ourselves as an organization. We realized that we had nearly no non-white staff throughout our program sites, and in analyzing this we came to understand that most of our staff were recruited from our mentors (who were mostly white) or from the college campuses with whom we were partnering (which also were largely white). We've undergone new strategies of creating a more diverse staff, and our community partners, parents and youth in Roxbury helped us identify this need.

Nearly three-and-a-half years after completing my senior sociology internship and that successful first meeting in Roxbury, DREAM has flourished in its new urban environment and expanded into other communities in the Greater Boston Area as well. DREAM programs currently support

---

[1] Caught in the Crossfire: Arresting Gang Violence by Investing in Kids, retrieved from the web; http://www.fightcrime.org/reports/gangreport.pdf

62 mentoring matches, partnering youth from four low-income housing areas and mentors from their neighboring college campuses: Harvard University, Boston University, Tufts University, and Northeastern University. The program has successfully transformed the lives of its participants. Youth who never before had access to college campuses now view higher education as a viable option. Many youth who may have joined gangs have made the decision not to. Instead, the program has created a positive peer group where youth are surrounded by friends and neighbors who are engaged in *constructive* risk taking such as hiking, skiing, and taking weekend adventures with their mentors.

The DREAM Program has also had a strong impact on the mentors. Many of the students who sign up to be mentors in our program express that living on campus and attending classes often feels like being trapped in a "bubble." Daily interactions often become limited to conversations with teachers, classmates, and others on campus, and theirs are campuses with rather homogenous racial and socioeconomic makeups. For many of our mentors, DREAM offers an escape from that "campus bubble," and a unique opportunity to have a positive impact on a community that they may have never before seen. One mentor summed this up well, stating "DREAM means a great deal to me because it has shown me an entire world that I had never experienced before; it threw me into the middle of it, and I came out knowing that I had a positive impact on it."

Having the opportunity to apply what I was learning in the sociology classroom and through my senior internship and research in sociology was a powerful experience for me. It showed me how the skills I was learning in the classroom could be directly applied to creating social change in the community. I've since transitioned to a new job, working for the Massachusetts Association for the Blind and Visually Impaired, where I continue to put my sociological skills of research and practice to work. The experience I gained with my work at DREAM changed my life, as it was likewise changing the lives of the youth and the mentors. In a survey conducted one semester after DREAM began programming in Orchard Gardens, one of the low-income housing communities in Roxbury, one participant shared, "I love that they (mentors) take me out of Orchard (Gardens) and I can see other parts of Boston. I also get to see what college is all about! I love the activities and I love hanging out with college kids!" Similarly, one young person shared, "I love hanging out with college students. I love playing with them and I love having fun with them! They want the best for me!" When asked, "Why is DREAM important for this community?" the youth shared, "They (mentors) don't want us to do drugs or to have guns! They believe that we can go to college!" Perhaps the most poignant sentiment was shared by a child who stated, "I can't wait to go to college!"

Bridging the Campus and the Community:
Blogging about the Asian American Experience

C. N. Le

University of Massachusetts Amherst

C. N. Le is a senior lecturer in sociology and is director of the Asian/ Asian American Studies Certificate Program at the University of Massachusetts Amherst. His work as a Sociologist in Action includes working for the National Asian Pacific American Bar Association, as director of education for the Asian Pacific Islander Coalition on HIV/ AIDS, and as a research associate for the Center for Technology in Government at the University at Albany SUNY. He also tries to put his academic, professional, and personal experiences to good use by blogging about issues related to Asian Americans and racial/ethnic relations at his Web site, Asian-Nation.org.

What do you do when you feel like you're the only one around? That's the question I frequently faced growing up in a predominantly white society. I had a lot of friends growing up, but almost always I was the only Vietnamese immigrant, the only Asian American, and the only person of color in my school and my neighborhood. I was expected to "represent" or be the spokesperson for these minority groups in a lot of situations. I didn't want that responsibility. Instead, I wanted to just blend in, to not stand out as being different or strange. In many ways, I wanted to be like my friends—to be white. Through those elementary, middle school, and high-school years, I did not really emphasize my minority identity, opting instead to deemphasize it as much as possible.

It wasn't until my junior year of college when I decided to minor in sociology and began taking classes on race and ethnicity, immigration, and Asian American studies that I finally began to learn about the history of people of color, immigrants, and Asian Americans in the United States. I learned how, in the face of injustices, inequalities, and oppression, people of color have not only survived but become stronger and more resilient through these experiences. I finally began to experience my Vietnamese and Asian heritage as a source of pride and confidence instead of shame and embarrassment. With this newfound understanding of myself and the world around me, I began to claim and embrace the expectation I had once shied away from: the responsibility of speaking up for others like me.

As I progressed through my research on various aspects of Asian American assimilation, the Internet revolution was well underway, and blogs, in particular, were becoming quite popular. I saw this as an opportunity to leverage the emerging power of the Internet by blogging to share what I was learning about the collective experiences of Asian Americans in particular (and immigrants and people of color more generally). It was my hope to portray Asian Americans as accurately and comprehensively as possible rather than let others portray my community however they want and have other Americans rely on distorted portrayals and ignorant stereotypes about Asian Americans.

With that in mind, I started my Asian-Nation.org Web site and blog in 2001. From the beginning, I wanted my site to be as accessible as possible. On my Web site and through my blog, I make "academic" research and data easy to understand. I also cover as many real-world issues and social problems in American society as possible. You might say that I have been able to bridge the gap that separates traditional academic articles from those published in magazines and newspapers—to connect the campus and the community.

I try to bridge these two aspects of society by first acknowledging that I am not always going to be completely objective or unbiased in my writing. As I tell my students, many academics claim to practice total objectivity in their research and teaching. Other professors think that it is virtually impossible to keep one's personal beliefs completely separate from one's research or teaching, and I happen to agree with the latter group. Biases can take many different forms: some may be quite blatant in terms of direct statements or writings, but other examples can be more subtle, such as when sociologists decide which questions to ask, which methods and data sources they'll use to answer those questions, and how they present their findings. In fact, as we see over and over again, the same statistical data can be used to support completely opposite interpretations and sides of a debate. With that in mind, I am up front with the students in my classes and the readers of my site and blog. I let them know that, based on both my academic training and my personal experiences, the political and social views I have tend to be liberal in nature. However, I also tell them that as a sociologist I am compelled to back up what I say and what I write with established theory, reliable data, and appropriate supporting examples.

I try to achieve a yin-yang balance between objectivity and subjectivity. Being an academic blogger means that people may pay a little more attention and perhaps give a little more credence to what I have to say because of my position as a professor. But with that added respect comes added responsibility. In other words, I can't get away with just ranting and raving about racial incidents or other injustices going on around me. Instead,

I understand that as an academic I have to support my opinions and back up my criticisms with valid theories, data, and intelligent analysis.

I think that sociologists are well-qualified to do this kind of work. I firmly believe that sociologists should apply their experiences and their expertise to educate as many people around them as possible (not just other faculty or college students) and apply their work to inform and influence social issues and policy to make sociology as "public" as possible. Sociologists can apply their research to lend some objectivity and empirical data to often emotional discussions and debates around controversial issues. I understand perfectly well that sound data and research may not ultimately sway people with passionate opinions, but I feel I've done my job if I help people look at issues more comprehensively and from different perspectives.

Beyond using my Web site and blog to educate the general public about the histories, experiences, and characteristics of Asian Americans, immigrants, and people of color, I also hope that my efforts can benefit the Asian American community specifically. That is, I hope that blogs like mine will be a source of information and learning for young Asian Americans, many of whom grow up isolated from their history, culture, and collective experiences, similar to what I went through when I was their age. I felt very satisfied when my site was mentioned in media outlets, such as *USA Today*, Yahoo News, the American Press Institute, the Library of Congress, PBS, and *The Washington Post*, to name a few. However, I am particularly gratified when I receive comments from ordinary readers, such as the following:

> Thank you for putting all this research together in one place! For most of my life, I haven't really paid much attention to Asian American issues. In school, I was always doing projects on the plight of the Native Americans, the Holocaust, or slavery, but I was never really encouraged to learn about Asian American History.

> I am so grateful that you are doing this. You have no idea how relieved I was to find this site. . . . I always realized the misrepresentation of Asian Americans in this country but had no idea just how far it extended.

> Yours is the best website that represents the Asian American community I have seen so far. It is very well-organized, informative, and most importantly, it has a certain candid and personal tone, which I feel makes it very distinctive from other sites.

Web sites and blogs also can help Asian Americans develop networks of people who share similar concerns, experiences, expertise, and so forth that can be used as a source of social support, but also to mobilize our community in times of crisis (e.g., responding to a high-profile incident of racism). A sampling of these responses in recent years includes Asian American blogs like mine joining with national advocacy organizations, such as the Asian American Justice Center, the Asian American Legal

Defense and Education Fund, the Media Action Network for Asian Americans, the Japanese American Citizens League, and the Organization of Chinese Americans, to protest racist and stereotypic media portrayals of Asian Americans in the 2009 movie *The Goods* and in the "Gay or Asian" column in *Details* magazine. We also took legal action to protect the rights of Asian American high-school students in Philadelphia, Pennsylvania, who endured a series of physical attacks in 2009, with school officials turning a blind eye to their repeated requests for help. Perhaps most famously, we advocated for nuclear physicist Wen Ho Lee who was falsely accused of espionage by federal authorities in 1999.

I think that Asian American Web sites and blogs like mine demonstrate that we want to be part of the American cultural mainstream and engage in the communication and democratic processes rather than secluding our-selves from the rest of American society as critics sometimes charge. Also, Asian Americans can use blogs and other emerging forms of Internet tech-nology, such as Facebook, Twitter, YouTube, and so on to be at the fore-front of technology and Internet culture—to be "cultural entrepreneurs," like our technological counterparts who are achieving success in Silicon Valley. Finally, these forms of technological expression give us a voice that we haven't had before—another mechanism to speak up and empower our-selves to overcome the ways in which we've been silenced through the years by the cumulative effects of racial stereotypes and discriminatory laws.

With these points in mind, my site and blog are basically extensions of my research and teaching—they are an integral part of who I am as a scholar and an Asian American. On top of that, the topics that I am most interested in— race relations, immigration, assimilation, politics, and the cultural effects of globalization—are some of the most controversial and important issues fac-ing American society today. Since these issues are still being played out and will continue to evolve for the foreseeable future, I anticipate having plenty of material to write about. For me, being a Sociologist in Action means fully expressing myself academically and personally, educating and empowering others, and contributing what I can to the larger human community.

Discussion Questions

1. According to Mike Cermak, how do Action Media Projects work to "amp" the voice of marginalized communities of color as they describe social issues? How do such projects relate to the goals of participatory action research?

2. Cermak managed to change the frame of the food issue "from health and nutrition to jobs, justice, and antiviolence for violence-affected communi-ties." How did his ability to do so work to engage youth from marginalized

communities? Are you a part of the food justice movement? If not, why not? What would (or did) compel you to join the food justice movement?

3. After reading Diane Grams's piece, how has your understanding changed of how cultural attributes of a neighborhood can be used to strengthen a racial or ethnic community? According to Grams, how is the "empowering" cultural work she undertook in Bronzeville different from "the processes typical of gentrification?"

4. Imagine, as in Bronzeville, that your own community faces an influx of wealthier people from a different race or ethnicity. How might you and other members of your community work to protect and maintain the cultural symbols of your community?

5. How did Brandon Hofstedt's students help fight environmental racism? Think about one example of environmental racism you have witnessed or heard about. Describe what you can do to help address that injustice.

6. For Hofstetdt, what has been the most important outcome of the Social Movement Campaign projects? Why?

7. How did Pamela Jenkins's social context help her recover after Katrina? Why did she consider herself "lucky"? If a disaster were to displace you and your family, do you think you would be as "lucky" as Jenkins? Why or why not?

8. According to Jenkins, how were most black homeowners in New Orleans disadvantaged by the initial funding allotment for home repairs? How did race and power intersect in that decision?

9. What were some of the challenges Warren and his colleagues faced when they moved the DREAM program to Roxbury? How is a sociologist uniquely qualified to understand and deal with these challenges?

10. Who has been a mentor in your life? How has that person (or those people) helped to socialize you? Are you now or would you consider becoming a youth mentor? How could you use your sociological training to help a young person succeed in life?

11. What prompted C. N. Le to become interested in his Asian American background and to eventually create Asian-Nation.org? If you were asked to create a sociologically based blog, what would be your focus? Why?

12. How does Le's blog and Web site help to both inform and support the Asian American community? What other purposes does it serve? Why do you think this site is unique?

Resources

Asian Nation

Sociological exploration of the historical, demographic, political, and cultural issues informing today's diverse Asian American community.

Excellent resource section with links to Asian American related websites on culture, economy, history, politics, and current organizations.
http://www.asian-nation.org

Civil Rights Movement

History Channel site on the Civil Rights Movement. Includes videos, photos, speeches, interactive resources, timelines, chronologies of events, and links.
http://www.history.com/topics/civil-rights-movement

DREAM Village Mentoring Organization

Mentoring program that builds communities of families and college students that empower youth from affordable housing neighborhoods to recognize their options, make informed decisions, and achieve their dreams.
http://www.dreamprogram.org

Environmental Justice Resource Center

Research, policy, and information clearinghouse on issues related to environmental racism, environmental justice, race and the environment, civil rights, and human rights. Provides excellent bibliographies, resources, media, and archives on these issues and on the environmental justice movement.
http://www.ejrc.cau.edu

Hispanic and Latino Americans

Detailed history of Latinos in the United States.
http://en.wikipedia.org/wiki/Hispanic_and_Latino_Americans

Latino Americans

Companion site to the landmark PBS documentary on the history of Latinos in the United States. Site offers resources such as educator guides, video testimonials, and links to other resources and organizations.
http://www.pbs.org/latino-americans/en

Martin Luther King Jr. and the Global Freedom Struggle

Interactive encyclopedia with over 1,000 entries on various events, key people, and legislation surrounding the civil rights movement.
http://mlk-kpp01.stanford.edu/index.php/encyclopedia/encyclopedia_contents

MENTOR National Mentoring Partnership

National organization promoting and setting standards for mentoring programs in the United States. Provides resources, studies, toolkits, trainings, and webinars and serves as a clearinghouse for mentoring programs.
http://www.mentoring.org

Native Americans

PBS website on Native Americans with over 250 videos from the show *American Experience.*
http://www.pbs.org/wgbh/americanexperience/films/filter/native-american-history

Race: Are We So Different?

The Race Project from the American Anthropological Association combines history, science, and lived experience. Explains differences among people and discusses the myths and realities of race. Website has a virtual exhibit, along with resources for students and researchers.
http://understandingrace.org/home.html

Race: The Power of an Illusion

Complement website for the PBS video. Teacher and student resources, interactive quizzes, curriculum, website links, and excellent information.
http://www.pbs.org/race/000_General/000_00-Home.htm

Real Food Challenge

Leverages the power of youth and universities to create a healthy, fair, and green food system. Primary campaign is to shift $1 billion of existing university food budgets away from industrial farms and junk food and toward local/community-based, fair, ecologically sound and humane food budgets. Offers resources such as films, organizations, and reports.
http://www.realfoodchallenge.org

The Storm

PBS Frontline documentary on Hurricane Katrina, which includes the full documentary online. Provides educator resources, links to organizations and online resources, timelines, and interviews.
http://www.pbs.org/wgbh/pages/frontline/storm

We Shall Remain

Companion site to PBS documentary on Native Americans, which includes the full documentary online. Excellent educator resources, time-lines, bibliographies, resources to organizations, and a Native Now section with information updating progress and problems today.
http://www.pbs.org/wgbh/amex/weshallremain

White Privilege: Unpacking the Invisible Knapsack

Full text of seminal article by sociologist Peggy McIntosh discussing the visible and invisible privileges of race.
http://ted.coe.wayne.edu/ele3600/mcintosh.html

2

Class

In all societies, people are stratified, or ranked, on the basis of their access to and possession of what is valued in their culture. In U.S. society, class position is one key means of ranking. Sociologists tend to measure social class (lower, lower-middle, middle, upper-middle, and upper) by profession, education, and income. Those who have higher status professions, higher levels of education, and more income also tend to have more prestige and power in our society. They have the greatest ability to spend their time as they please, consume what they want, and have access to power. The essays in this chapter indicate just how much our social class position can influence our individual lives and our place in society—and demonstrate how sociologists in action can work to address these issues of stratification.

Kevin Bales opens the chapter with "Confronting Slavery with the Tools of Sociology." He explains how he first came to recognize modern day slavery and how he has used sociological tools to expose and combat it. He states of his work to uncover this modern-day phenomenon, "slavery was hidden under a thick blanket of ignorance, concealed by the common assumption that it was extinct." Slaves, those with the least power in society, come from the ranks of its most poor and vulnerable members—and suffer from the great lengths that their holders undertake to keep the slave trade clandestine. Thus, Bales embarked on a "large-scale research project . . . in search of modern slavery, traveling to India, Pakistan, Thailand, Mauritania, and Brazil—often going undercover [to study] slave-based businesses in each country." This research resulted in his book, *Disposable People: New Slavery in the Global Economy* (1999, 2004, 2012) and to his cofounding of an antislavery organization. In outlining his organizing and activist work, Bales powerfully reveals that slavery can be eradicated if we have the will and sociological tools to combat it effectively.

In the following piece, "From Magazine Publishing to Homelessness, From Public Housing Research to Congressional Testimony," Deirdre Oakley describes her work in the area of housing. Oakley describes how she became interested in housing inequality after she watched her poor neighbors of color become displaced from her neighborhood in the Alphabet City area of New York City. She states, "As someone who had not experienced poverty first hand, I began to question my now acknowledged privilege and occupation, and this questioning led me to go back to graduate school to study urban social inequality." When she later moved to Atlanta to teach at Georgia State University, she and a colleague embarked on a long-term study of the effects of displacement and relocation on poor residents of Atlanta. Despite resistances that she and her fellow researcher encountered from the Atlanta Housing Authority, the study was completed and received enough attention that she was ultimately invited to testify before members of Congress. Her work helps show that efforts to improve housing conditions for the poor must keep in mind the needs and desires of people in poverty. She and her colleagues help give voice to this marginalized group of people and help influence the debate and policy surrounding housing.

In "An Accidental Activist: My Stumble Upon Sociology," Bria Wilbur describes how, through her undergraduate sociology courses, she became invested in helping exploited members of society across the globe. Moving from an individualistic perspective, where she saw people's class positions as determined by their own individual efforts, to a sociological perspective recognizing the impact of social forces, Wilbur became committed to improving society. Putting her sociological tools to work, she and fellow students formed the Social Justice League, which tackled a variety of issues of inequality on her campus and beyond. In particular, the group raised awareness about the issues of sweatshop and child labor by creating a mock sweatshop in their campus center, and then worked with their university's administration to have their campus partner with the Worker Rights Consortium. As Wilbur explains, this organization "oversees the factories in which apparel is made to prevent the exploitation of workers." Since graduating, Wilbur has continued her efforts as a sociologist in action, working with the international children's rights organization Free The Children to help empower and free children from poverty and exploitation.

Susan Ostrander uses sociological tools to change perspectives on philanthropic giving and make it a more effective source for positive change. She describes how she does so in "Putting a New Theory of Philanthropy Into Practice: Challenges and Opportunities." Ostrander describes how a social relational view of philanthropy "helps us to think about how donors and recipient groups might *share* the power to decide how and for what purposes charitable dollars are used." She makes a convincing case that recipients of donations are best equipped to determine how to use donated funds and when given more of a voice in these decisions, often direct funds toward addressing the root causes of poverty and inequality. These root causes might otherwise be overlooked, a caution that Ostrander recalls from Dr. Martin Luther King, Jr., who stated, "Philanthropy is commendable, but it must not cause the philanthropist to overlook the economic injustice that makes philanthropy necessary." Putting her sociology into action, Ostrander has used her prestige as a widely recognized expert in the field to advocate for a change in the process of philanthropic giving. She has also translated her sociological findings into action, working with multiple donor organizations to model a social relational philanthropic approach.

In the next piece in this chapter, "Localizing International Human Rights: Engaging with the World Social Forum Process," Jackie Smith describes how she has used her sociological tools to help challenge the corporate dominated globalization process. Her participatory observation research on global activism has taken her from protests against the World Trade Organization (WTO) in the streets of Seattle to World Social Forums around the globe. Through this participatory research, she has helped activists from various backgrounds form collaborative relationships, fostered efforts to strengthen diversity and democracy within the global activist movement, and "promoted a different story about globalization—one that stresses the negative consequences of global markets for both working and unemployed families around the world." She notes patterns of increased economic inequality as multinational corporations have become ever more powerful players in the globalization process. Smith uses sociological tools to challenge the current process of globalization and give voice to the poor and less powerful. In the process, she has helped spread the word about, and inspired many others to join, the global justice movement.

Angela Aidala, like Smith, is an advocate for marginalized people. Her research has helped bring to light the need for secure housing for those living with HIV and AIDS. In "Housing and HIV/AIDS: A Tale of Academic, Provider, Advocacy, and Public Policy Collaboration," Aidala conveys how her work has highlighted the relationship between housing and HIV prevention and treatment, a connection that has been overlooked for many years. Through this work, she has also worked to challenge the "risky person" paradigm that is pervasive in health-related research, which emphasizes individual responsibility for health outcomes. In reframing this risk paradigm, she calls on her training, stating, "Sociologists have long argued that health is shaped by "upstream" or fundamental causes—macro (societal or global) economic, political, and social arrangements and resources that shape differential access to knowledge, money, prestige, and power, which can be used to avoid or buffer exposure to health risks." Her research, cited by members of Congress, has proven highly valuable in the efforts to advocate for housing supports for people living with HIV/AIDS—efforts which resulted in housing being highlighted as a key concern and priority in the latest National HIV/AIDS Strategy.

Confronting Slavery with the Tools of Sociology

Kevin Bales
University of Hull

Kevin Bales is Professor of Contemporary Slavery at the Wilberforce Institute for the Study of Slavery and Emancipation (WISE), University of Hull, and cofounder of Free the Slaves, Washington, D.C. His book *Disposable People: New Slavery in the Global Economy* was named one of "100 World-Changing Discoveries" by the Association of British Universities in 2006. The film based on *Disposable People,* which he cowrote, won a Peabody Award and two Emmy Awards. His 2007 book *Ending Slavery: How We Free Today's Slaves,* won the 2011 Grawemeyer Award. In 2008, with Zoe Trodd, he published *To Plead Our Own Cause: Personal Stories by Today's Slaves.* In 2009, with Ron Soodalter, he published *The Slave Next Door: Human Trafficking and Slavery in America Today.* He is currently writing on the relationship between slavery and environmental destruction and, with Jody Sarich, a book exploring forced marriage worldwide.

Becoming an abolitionist sociologist crept up on me. The first tiny prodding was a leaflet I picked up at an outdoor event in London. The front of the leaflet read "There are Millions of Slaves in the World Today." I was a university professor, and I confess to an unpleasant mixture of pride and hubris in my reaction to the bold title of the leaflet. Having been involved in human rights for many years, I thought, "How could this be true if I don't know about it already?" My ego was engaged. My heart and brain took a little longer to catch up.

I started reading the leaflet on the way home. Inside were anecdotes: the story of a child from Sri Lanka enslaved as a camel jockey in the United Arab Emirates, the tale of a woman trafficked into prostitution, and the account of a family trapped in hereditary slavery linked to a debt taken by an ancestor in rural India. These were moving stories, but where were the millions? As a social scientist, I wanted more than anecdotes. I wanted proof and data, not wild claims, and I nearly threw the leaflet away. But something began to itch in my mind . . . what if? What if there *were* millions of people in slavery? What if almost all of us—governments, human rights groups, the media, the public—were simply unaware? Could there really be millions of people in slavery without it being public knowledge? And if there were millions in slavery, how could they be so hidden, and what should be done to liberate them? After all, everyone knew that slavery had ended in the 19th century; maybe these were just a few rare cases, or poorly paid sweatshop workers dramatically relabeled as slaves. Millions of hidden slaves seemed unlikely, but my nagging thought was that if there *were* millions of people in slavery, then finding them was the job of a social researcher. And if there *weren't* millions of slaves, this type of literature needed debunking.

In the library, I searched the academic literature using the keyword "slavery." Within moments, I had more than 3,000 journal articles, many more than I had expected, and I sat down to the long slog of reviewing them. By the end of the day, I found there were thousands of articles on historical slavery but only two on contemporary slavery. Neither answered my question. Where were the millions of slaves?

I began to spread my net more widely: to human rights groups, government reports, and the United Nations. As one source led to another, I pulled in students to help dig and sift through information and paid one researcher to look further afield. As a faint picture of global slavery began to emerge, I came to understand why this issue was invisible.

Slavery was hidden under a thick blanket of ignorance, concealed by the common assumption that it was extinct. With slavery illegal in every country, criminal slaveholders kept their activities hidden. It is important to remember that, in the 1990's, most people were absolutely certain that slavery no longer existed. And since everyone *knew* that slavery only existed in the past, anyone who said otherwise was quickly labeled a crank. Even the word "slavery" was rapidly losing its meaning. Some claimed incest was slavery and others that home mortgages were a form of slavery. Some politicians were trumpeting that taxation was slavery. With the real thing long gone, with even the word up for grabs, real slavery was invisible.

It seems strange now to be exploring an issue as serious as slavery and being told again and again—"everyone knows it doesn't exist!" Even when presenting evidence to university research seminars, I was never able to get the audience past the stage of an intellectual free-for-all over how to define slavery. Soon I stopped trying and spent the next few years thinking through and arriving at an operational definition used to organize my research that, for the time being, I kept to myself.

As I built up a picture of slavery, every new set of facts generated new questions. I began to realize that a large-scale research project was needed and I went in search of modern slavery, traveling to India, Pakistan, Thailand, Mauritania, and Brazil—often going undercover as I studied slave-based businesses in each country. The result was the book *Disposable People: New Slavery in the Global Economy* (1999, 2004, 2012).

While *Disposable People* is full of sociological assertions, I did not write it in the style of a formal academic text. I knew that if I had done so, with assertions spelled out formally as theories and hypotheses, it could be deadly dull to most people. I hoped this book would be read by a much wider audience rather than simply a few scholars. Some readers took the assertions as facts, leaping beyond the discoveries and evidence on which they were based. That worried me, since good social science rests on data not guesses. An example of this was my belief that there had been a global collapse in the price of slaves after World War II. Some years later, I was able to build a database of slave prices over time that showed that slaves had been high-ticket capital purchase items in the past (even though occasional gluts caused prices to dip) and are normally low cost disposable inputs today. Since this distinction has important policy implications, it was crucial that it was founded on good information.

There were other assertions I made in *Disposable People*, that[1]: Current profit margins on slavery tend to be higher than in the past; the number of people who are available to be enslaved because of their vulnerability is greater today than in the past (though this is more a function of the population explosion than anything else); the length of a person's enslavement is usually shorter today than in the past; less care tends to be given to slaves by their slaveholders today because of their lower cost and easy replacement; and ethnic and racial differences are not as important as rationalizations and justifications for slavery as they were in the past. As a sociological work, these assertions described *trends*, not every individual case. After all, slavery is like all other human activity: It takes many forms in many different contexts.

There is one type of slavery that I purposely left out but could have, and probably should have, included. This was the slavery of forced marriages. The United Nations Convention on slavery includes forced marriage as a practice similar to slavery. Between the "marriages" of very young girls and the young women who are physically forced into marriages over which they have no choice, there could be millions of women enslaved in this way. But I

---

[1] Remember, a social theory is normally just an assertion about society; a hypothesis is an assertion about some specific thing in society.

knew that a public that didn't believe slavery still existed would have an even harder time accepting the idea that some marriages were fronts for slavery. It was one thing to resurrect the ghost of slavery; it was another to suggest that marriage could be a ceremony and practice tantamount to an auction block—though there were and are many women today who know this first hand.

——I'm still learning. I've only just come to understand the strange paradox of slavery's existence today and how this is a special moment in history. Today's 27 million slaves, while comprising the highest ever number of living slaves, in fact make up the smallest fraction of the total world population to ever live in slavery. The estimated $40 billion they generate as profits for slaveholders is tiny compared to other industries and is the smallest proportion of the global economy ever represented by slavery. With slavery illegal in every country and universal agreement on the human right of freedom, the stage is now set for complete eradication. Slavery has been pushed to the dark and hidden edges of our global society. It stands on the edge of its own extinction. Never has there been a better time to end it once and for all.

To accomplish that aim is only partially the work of sociologists. Practitioners in rehabilitation and social and economic development are needed, as well as specialists in every culture where slavery is found. Since slavery is illegal in every country, policy workers are needed to move governments to keep the promises they made when they abolished legal slavery. Altogether, this is the work of a nongovernmental organization. Therefore, in 2000, I, with three others, helped found Free the Slaves, the American sister-organization of Anti-Slavery International, the world's oldest (1787) and original human rights group. Free the Slaves works with local partners to liberate slaves around the world and change the systems that allow slavery to exist. In addition to addressing the crime of enslavement, this work often involves confronting gender inequality, racism, ethnic and religious discrimination, and the negative outcomes of global economic growth. We have learned that freedom and empowerment are viral, and that freed slaves will stop at nothing to stay free and help others to liberty.

Recently, a team from a Free the Slaves partner group was working in an enslaved village in northern India. It was still in the early days of its efforts there, but a rough and ready transitional school had been set up and many of the children were now spending more time learning than working in the stone quarry. The slaveholders were beginning to worry that something was going on. As the liberation workers taught the children and mixed with the families, thugs hung around making sure everyone knew they were being watched, letting people see their weapons. For the village women especially, who had already suffered a lifetime of rape and assault by these thugs, it was a grim and frightening moment. But something had changed, and, in spite of their fear and the risks they were taking, the women just kept pushing their men, their children, and their whole community toward freedom. One of the liberation workers asked, "How can you do it?" One woman, her face twisted with worry, choked back her fear and explained: "We have hope now. How can we not succeed when we know people like you on the other side of the world are standing with us?"

Not every part of liberation and reintegration requires sociological training, but it would be very hard to be successful without it. Without carefully constructed longitudinal surveys of villages in slavery, we could never have demonstrated the "freedom dividend," the powerful and positive economic change that comes to whole communities when slavery is abolished. Without training in the empathetic understanding of a social researcher, we could never have developed the "slavery lens," a way of seeing this hidden crime that the U.S. government now requires of all its foreign aid programs. Without learning about the complex interplay of culture, society, economics, politics, and social vulnerability, we would never be able to build the unique methodologies of liberation tailored to specific and culturally rooted forms of slavery. And there is nothing like the ugly reality of a crime like slavery to push young sociologists to do their best work—using solid social science to change the world.

References

Bales, K. (2007). *Ending slavery: How we free today's slaves.* Berkeley: University of California Press.

Bales, K. (2012). *Disposable people: New slavery in the global economy.* Berkeley: University of California Press.

Bales, K., & Soodalter, R. (2009). *The slave next door: Human trafficking and slavery in America today.* Berkeley: University of California Press.

Bales, K., & Trodd, Z. (Eds.). (2008). *To plead our own cause: Personal stories by today's slaves.* Ithaca, NY: Cornell University Press.

From Magazine Publishing to Homelessness, From Public Housing Research to Congressional Testimony

Deirdre Oakley
Georgia State University

Deirdre Oakley is an Associate Professor in the Sociology Department at Georgia State University. Her research, which has been widely published in both academic and applied venues, focuses primarily on housing, homelessness, and inner-city redevelopment. Most recently, she has been working on a collaborative project examining the impact of public housing elimination in Atlanta on former residents, funded in part by the National Institutes for Health (NIH), the National Science Foundation (NSF), and the University of Kentucky Center for Poverty Research (UKCPR). She is also the Editor of Social Shutter, a community and urban photo essay blog.

I worked in magazine publishing mostly as a copywriter (from mid-1980s to 1990) at venues such as *Vanity Fair, Family Circle,* and *Fortune.* I was an American History major at Bowdoin College and after finishing my degree landed in the New York City publishing arena. At the time I had no intention of studying urban social inequality, which in its most basic form is characterized by extreme racial and socioeconomic neighborhood segregation. But you do not make very much money working in magazine publishing, and many of us lived in the then-still-affordable Lower Eastside between Avenues B and C off of East Houston, an area more commonly known as Alphabet City. Back then it was still a very poor neighborhood, particularly on the south side of East Houston. In addition, on that side of East Houston there were very few white people like me. At the time, I sort of thought of it as an "other side of the railroad tracks" thing like I had seen on TV and in the movies as a kid but otherwise hadn't thought much about it.

I loved living there. Everyone seemed to look out for each other. Residents gave me advice about painting my bicycle with my own colors to avoid it being stolen, as well as telling me which subway stations to avoid. There was drug dealing—mostly pot and heroin as far as I could tell—but as long as you stayed out of it, no one bothered you. It was also a quiet place with a lack of police presence—perhaps kind of "off the map." But somewhere around 1987 things started to change—not my neighbors, but the upscale redevelopment that was beginning on the nearby north side of East Houston. It disrupted the organization of the neighborhood. My neighbors began complaining about being displaced and I would ask why and they'd say because *they* had limited income and were minorities. "You're white, you're educated, you don't have to worry," my older down-stairs gentleman neighbor would say. As someone who had not experienced poverty first hand, I began to question my now-acknowledged privilege and occupation, and this questioning led me to go back to graduate school to study urban social inequality. Ironically, when I went to the property management office to give them my notice, they told me they'd renew my lease at a lower monthly rent because they "liked having tenants like me." I went back once in the 1990s and saw some of my old neighbors who were still there. But after that, redevelopment of the area accelerated and the fabric, as well as the residents, changed dramatically. I went back in 2010, and was surprised to find luxury hotels, as well as a rather fine dining establishment right there on Norfolk Street where I had lived. There was no one around. I wondered how much my $600 per month studio would cost. It was sad.

But let's go back to the 1990s as I worked on my PhD at State University of New York at Albany and, to help pay the bills, also worked as a program evaluation coordinator for federally-funded prevention of homelessness programs at Policy Research Associates, traveling to cities all over the country. The social inequality I saw was blatant and depressing but added to my knowledge base. For a while after I received my PhD and was on faculty in the Sociology Department at Northern Illinois University, I was so burnt out on face-to-face interaction with good people living in poverty who constantly had to struggle against monolithic structural odds, I was only able to research archival and secondary data on social inequality.

But that all changed when I landed a position in the fall of 2007 in the Sociology Department at Georgia State University (GSU). It turned out that earlier in the year, the Atlanta Housing Authority (AHA) had announced plans to eliminate all the city's remaining project-based public housing. Matthew Cardinale, a graduate student who was very active in a grassroots effort to halt these demolitions, introduced me and some colleagues to the President of the Jurisdiction-Wide Public Housing Residential Advisory Board (RAB) (Oakley, Ruel, & Wilson, 2008). We told her that we could not do anything to halt the demolitions but that we could document residents' experiences before and after relocation. This would mean following residents over time as the AHA implemented its plan to relocate qualified residents with Housing Choice Vouchers (HCV) to private market rental housing.

After we met with the RAB, we began designing a longitudinal survey to capture residents' views about, and experienced impacts of, relocation. Drs. Lesley Reid, Erin Ruel, and I formed the GSU Urban Health Initiative to conduct this study. Ultimately, a sample of 311 public housing residents was collected from six Atlanta public housing communities (four family developments and three senior/disability high rises).

Unfortunately, the AHA didn't want us to conduct our study, realizing the possibility that it might shed an unflattering light on this harsh housing policy. A few days before we were going to conduct the first round of interviews at Bowen Homes, the AHA found out about our study and closed down all the community centers at all the public housing communities where relocation had yet to take place. We did not know about this until the day before our visit to Bowen when Shirley Hightower, Bowen's Resident President, called us. Because she had other office space, we were able to move the location of the interviews. However, when we arrived we were met by Atlanta police who demanded that Dr. Ruel turn over the survey instrument. She said no. And they said something to the effect of "be careful, this is not a safe place," threatening us implicitly. Nevertheless, we conducted the interviews we set out to do that day. The AHA continued to harass us and created a myriad of roadblocks throughout our research process. We were able to persevere, however, and surprisingly and courageously, none of the residents seemed angry with us that their community centers were closed.

In the subsequent year, residents were relocated and, by spring, the last residents were being moved out of the family complexes while relocation from the senior high-rises had just begun. Keeping in touch with everybody was a challenge until we received National Science Foundation (NSF) funding and were able to hire people from the community to help. We ended up with an 87% retention rate between baseline and 6-month follow up and a 91% retention rate between the 6- and 24-month follow ups. During this period we had no contact with the AHA. By the spring of 2010, everyone in our study had been relocated and demolition began.

We published an op-ed in the *Christian Science Monitor* about the end of public housing in Atlanta (Oakley, Ruel, & Reid, 2010a). We ended the piece with a policy plea of *mending not ending* public housing. Our op-ed was reposted on a number of grassroots websites and, ultimately, received the attention of Congresswoman Maxine Waters, who invited us to give Congressional Testimony before the Subcommittee on Housing and Community Opportunities, Committee on Financial Services, on April 28, 2010 (Oakley, Ruel, & Reid, 2010b). I gave the testimony. On my cab ride over to the Congressional Building, my cab driver asked me what I was doing at Congress. When I told him, he asked me what CSPAN channel I would be on. I had no idea there was more than one channel. Giving Congressional testimony for a "newbie" like me was nerve-wracking. You sit at this table with all the others giving testimony and there is this green-yellow-red light device in front of you. And you only have 5 minutes, so you need to stay focused. In the end, there were many questions from Congressional members, and my testimony was broadcast by Georgia Public Radio. The GSU library blog began following the proposed legislation so that undergraduate and graduate students could see how their work on the study was informing the discourse about this policy.

The week after the testimony we were contacted by the AHA to begin a dialogue. In the end, we were invited to present our findings and in turn they shared data with us. We certainly will never agree on many aspects of these public housing transformation efforts, but I think we have at least learned from each other and we continue our dialogue to this day.

And the residents—how did they fare? By and large the condition of their homes is an improvement over public housing, and neighborhoods they moved to have less poverty, but not low poverty, and are safer. Yet these neighborhoods are just as racially segregated as public housing. Older residents were more likely to report a loss of social support. None reported improved access to better economic opportunities. Thus, our findings reveal the complexities of relocation. It is difficult to predict much longer term impacts of relocation, and the subsidized relocated residents themselves have certainly lost some things but gained other things as well.

But we are sociologists and are doing what we do best: following the evidence on the ground. The underlying assumptions of the poverty decon-centration imperative are not supported by our study. More specifically, our study points to the importance of acknowledging that "one size does not fit all." Public housing transformation efforts utilizing relocation to the subsidized private rental market need to better accommodate the varying circumstances of the residents pre-relocation, as well as their relocation preference within the context of health conditions, disability, age, public housing tenure, and essential social supports. Our findings also speak to the importance of proactively including residents' voices in the relocation pro-cess and not simply assuming that they will be better off just because they are moving out of public housing and into neighborhoods with less poverty.

Our public housing study is a good example of using sociology to both study a marginalized and disadvantaged population and work toward change. The results aren't quite what I would have liked; for example, the legislation for which I provided Congressional testimony has not moved forward at the scale we anticipated. Yet, at the same time, we as sociolo-gists in action learned a great deal from the residents, and our students have become more aware of what it's like to be poor and to struggle to make ends meet on a day-to-day basis. We will continue to use our sociological research to work toward influencing policy and social change and would encourage you to as well.

References

Oakley, D., Ruel, E., & Reid. L (2010a, January 27). Public housing for the poor: Mend it, don't end it. *Christian Science Monitor*. Retrieved from http://www.csmonitor.com/Commentary/Opinion/2010/0127/Public-housing-for-the-poor-Mend-it-don-t-end-it

Oakley, D., Ruel, E., & Reid, L. (2010b, April 28). *Legislative proposals to preserve public housing*. Testimony to the U.S. House of Representatives Committee on Financial Services, Subcommittee on Housing and Community Opportunities, Washington, DC (Invited oral and written testimony). Retrieved from http://www.house.gov/apps/list/hearing/financialsvcs_dem/oakley_testimony_4_28_10.pdf

Oakley, D., Ruel, E., & Wilson, E. (2008). *A Choice with No Options: Atlanta Public Housing Residents' Lived Experiences in the Face of Relocation*. Atlanta: Georgia State University.

An Accidental Activist: My Stumble Upon Sociology

Bria Wilbur
Free The Children

Bria Wilbur is a recent graduate of Bridgewater State University (BSU) with a Bachelor of Arts in Sociology. As an undergraduate student, she cofounded the Social Justice League student group, was a mentor in the FAM for Change (Friends and Mentors for Change) partnership project between BSU and Brockton High School, and cofounded the BSU Chapter of Free The Children. Upon graduation, Bria moved to Toronto and later Minneapolis to become an Outreach Speaker for Free The Children, the world's largest organization of youth helping youth through education. She has spoken to over 45,000 youth and facilitates leadership trainings and youth volunteer trips with Me to We.

As a 19-year-old college student, the phone call from my parents telling me that I had to transfer schools, because of the financial burden of living on campus, and move back home was devastating. I was currently three hours from my hometown with all the freedom in the world. I saw moving home as a loss of that freedom, a crackdown on school work (which up until that point I slacked on), and the unfortunate likelihood of seeing one too many people from high school. Little did I know, transferring to Bridgewater State University (BSU) would change my life, my career path, and cause me to fall in love with learning, especially sociology.

It began with an 8:00 a.m. "Social Inequality" course. Up to this point, I had no idea what "social inequality" even meant; all I knew was it fulfilled a course requirement and it was unfortunately at 8:00 a.m. Growing up in a politically conservative family, I thought people's lives were the way they were because of their own choices. People who were homeless were homeless because they chose to be. People who were poor were poor because they made bad decisions with their money. And, of course, the list went on. When my uncle was found dead on a loading dock where he spent most of his nights, I was angry because, in my mind, he *chose* to be homeless. It wasn't until that 8:00 a.m. Social Inequality course that I learned about the social barriers in the world that influence our lives every day.

The more I learned in this course, the more I began to feel frustrated. I was learning about local and global issues, as well as my own impact on them, but I didn't feel as though I was learning *how* to overcome the issues. Just at the peak of my frustration, I found myself sitting with a classmate, discussing the lack of conversation on our campus about important issues of domestic and global social inequality. We decided to start a student club, the Social Justice League (SJL), in hopes of meeting other students who shared our views, educating our peers on campus, and creating lasting change at BSU and in the local and global communities outside BSU.

We held meetings, went through all the paperwork hurdles to become a recognized student group, found a faculty advisor (the same professor from our Social Inequality course), and started to recruit a small group of dedicated students who would be our core leaders. We decided that our first event would be "Tent City," a 5-day event in which students and faculty members sleep in tents on campus, eat in a mock soup kitchen in a campus cafeteria, and generally detach ourselves from our comfortable lives by leaving behind cell phones, laptops, iPods, and so forth. We would bring in guest speakers from various nonprofit organizations to speak at Tent City about homelessness and poverty. When we approached the campus administration with a proposal, we were told, literally, that clubs usually hold events such as bake sales for their first event and that we could not have Tent City. I and some others felt deflated and defeated, and we were on the verge of giving up, but some members of SJL and our faculty advisor insisted we rewrite the proposal and try again. Once we approached the administration a second time, and this time in a more organized way, with a stronger proposal, and with more committed support from some friends in the faculty and administration, we were granted permission to hold our event. But they told us we had one chance and, if anything went wrong, Tent City would never happen again.

Flashing forward, Tent City has now been an annual event at BSU for 6 years, and has become a part of the campus's cultural fiber. We, a small group of sociology students in action, created an event that has educated hundreds of students, garnered major media attention, helped with the creation of a new Homeless Taskforce at BSU, and started a social justice movement on a campus that had been without one.

I didn't realize it at the time, but in the planning stages of Tent City, I was also learning the ins and outs of social movement planning. As we would plan for meetings with campus administration, we always had our next steps ready: what we would do if they said yes, what we would do if they said no, and answers to any questions we thought they might possibly have. After Tent City, we began to realize that we could actually have an effect on our campus community. We felt empowered! We started throwing other events, ranging from biweekly movie nights to educate the campus on social justice issues; to an "Arts for Advocacy" event, combining multiple genres to teach and learn about issues of inequality; to a fair trade fair, which is now an annual event that brings in hundreds of BSU community members to learn about fair trade and to purchase fair trade goods from local vendors; to motivational speakers from international NGOs. And the campus culture started to change!

As I continued studying sociology, I found that Karl Marx's ideas on social class really resonated with me. It wasn't until I attended BSU that I learned about the issue of child labor in the world (why hadn't I learned about this before?!) and I began to understand social class, specifically Marx's idea of the bourgeoisie (the class that owns the means of production) and the proletariat (the working class), on a global scale. The Social Justice League researched the apparel in our school bookstore. When we discovered that our school apparel could be produced in sweatshops, we felt something had to change, and we jumped into action. We had no idea, though, that we were about to start a social movement at BSU.

Each member of the Social Justice League began extensively researching sweat-free clothing companies. Through this research, we learned of the Worker Rights Consortium (WRC), a third-party organization that oversees the factories in which apparel is made to prevent the exploitation of workers. After learning about the WRC, we began strategizing how to create a strong enough campus movement to get BSU to partner with the WRC. With student and faculty support, consistent and creative events on campus (such as holding a "mock sweatshop" simulation in the student center!), petitions, teamwork, and passion, BSU became an affiliated university with the Worker Rights Consortium. Through this movement, I found my passion for social movements and discovered the power young people have to create lasting, sustainable change in the world.

In my final semester at BSU, I decided to write my honors thesis about youth social movements and to analyze how three well-respected organizations empower youth to change the world. One of the organizations I researched was a Canadian-based nonprofit, Free The Children (FTC). Free The Children was started in 1995 by a 12-year-old boy, Craig Kielburger, after he read a Toronto Star article about Iqbal Masih. Iqbal had spent six years of his life working in a carpet factory to pay off a $16 debt his parents owed. Upon escaping the factory at 10 years old, he began traveling the world and speaking out against child labor. When he was just 12 years old, he was murdered for his actions. Free The Children has become the world's largest network of children helping children through education, with nearly two million shamelessly idealistic youth involved worldwide.

The mission of Free The Children is to free children around the world from poverty and exploitation and to free children in North America from the idea they are powerless to change the world. The first part of FTC's mission is accomplished through their sustainable development model, Adopt a Village, through which they help communities become sustainable by providing education, clean water, health and sanitation, sustainable agriculture, and alternative income projects. The first pillar to be implemented in any community is education, because it is the key factor in breaking the cycle of poverty.

The second part of FTC's mission, freeing young people from the idea they are powerless to change the world, is accomplished through youth empowerment and leadership within the organization. FTC provides resources and support so that youth can run successful fundraising and awareness-raising campaigns. With the support of FTC staff, student leaders, and educators, youth around the world volunteered over 1.6 million hours and raised $2 million for local causes and $3.4 million for global causes through events such as bake sales, school dances, and various FTC campaigns during the 2010–2011 school year. And they are continuing these efforts.

Throughout my years at BSU, and particularly when studying Free The Children in my courses with a professor involved in the organization, I fell in love with the work they do and the ways in which they do it. Upon graduation, I applied to be an "Outreach Speaker" and found myself moving from Massachusetts to Toronto and then Minneapolis. On a day-to-day basis, I have the privilege of traveling to various K–12 schools and delivering speeches about the work we do at Free The Children and how young people can become involved and find their spark to make a difference in the world. I get to meet youth who have already done amazing work within their local and global communities. I have also had the chance to bring young people to Kenya where they stay in a community in which Free The Children works, help build a Free The Children school, and participate in activities with the local community, such as going on a water walk with local mamas (to collect water from the local river for drinking, bathing, cooking and the like) and getting a small taste of what day-to-day poverty in rural Kenya feels like.

The sociology courses I took at Bridgewater State University and the social movement I was part of there led me to a career in which I help empower youth to change the world. Sociology has given me the ability to look beneath the surface of society and understand how social forces impact individual choices. It has also taught me that my own daily choices impact the world, and that I can use my sociological tools to create positive and sustainable change.

Putting a New Theory of Philanthropy Into Practice: Challenges and Opportunities

Susan A. Ostrander
Tufts University

Susan A. Ostrander is Professor of Sociology at Tufts University. She has published widely about philanthropy; nonprofit organizations; issues of class, race, and gender; and community organizing for social change. Her students have long had the option of doing projects in the community for course credit. She was involved for many years at the Boston Women's Fund and was on the board of the national Women's Funding Network, as well as being appointed to the Human Rights Commission in her home city of Cambridge, Massachusetts. She is now on the board of a Somerville immigrant advocacy organization, The Welcome Project, where she chairs the Fundraising Committee.

People in the United States give away a lot of money for charitable purposes. Total giving was $290.89 billion in 2010, or about 2 percent of GDP. The majority of that came from individuals, who gave $211.77 billion.[2] Have you wondered how money like this is used in the United States? While many countries use government resources to meet needs like health, higher education, childcare and eldercare, the United States has historically wanted to do this more with private money through what is called philanthropic giving.

In 1990, a colleague and I published what has become a mini-classic in the study of philanthropy (Ostrander & Schervish, 1990). We set out to frame a new theory, a *sociological* theory. Our theory focuses on the *social relations* between donors (individuals and organizations who give money away for charitable purposes) and recipients (those in need of support who receive the money). The concept of social relations is, of course, foundational in sociology. It calls attention to how human relationships and interactions occur in patterns. All together, these patterns create social structure, which means how society is organized.

---

[2] Giving USA Foundation, 2011. *Giving USA Annual Report on Philanthropy for the Year 2010.* Chicago: Giving USA Foundation; Joseph Rosenberg, Patrick Rooney, C. Eugene Steuerle, and Katherine Toran. *What's Been Happening to Charitable Giving Recently?* Washington, D.C. Urban Institute Center on Nonprofits and Philanthropy and Brookings Tax Policy Center, October 2011.

While the idea that philanthropy is some kind of relationship between donor and recipient is not new (Mauss, 1923)[3], a social relational notion of philanthropy goes further. It calls attention to who relative to the other—donor versus recipient—has the power to decide how charitable dollars are used, for what purposes, and in what ways. Is it, for example, better to use charitable dollars to provide people in need with *services* like shelters, soup kitchens, counseling, and other "helping" measures; or is it better to use those dollars to *advocate* for good wages, quality public education, affordable housing, and a voice in making social change so that people would not need so many services in the first place? Most of the time, people who give money decide questions like this on their own. The importance of funding *both* services *and* advocacy calls to mind Dr. Martin Luther King, Jr.'s famous quote: "Philanthropy is commendable, but it must not cause the philanthropist to overlook the economic injustice that makes philanthropy necessary."

A social relational view of philanthropy helps us think about how donors and recipient groups might *share* the power to decide how and for what purposes charitable dollars are used. Why is it important for recipient groups to have some say? Recipients of charitable dollars are most often nonprofit organizations who work closely with people in need to provide services and/or advocacy.[4] Because of this close relationship, recipient groups are particularly knowledgeable about what needs are most important and how best to address them, so it makes sense that they should have much more control than they do over how this money is used.[5]

I have for many years been actively involved in trying to actually bring about this kind of philanthropy where donors and recipients work together and recipients "call the shots." In the past 15 years or so, this has become especially challenging. It's become standard practice in the philanthropy world to attend almost exclusively to what donors want—to donor preferences and choices—as a way to get them to give more and more money. The influence and control of donors has increased enormously. Recipient

---

[3] Marcel Mauss. 1923. *The Gift.*

[4] Nonprofits include social and human service agencies, all kinds of health and education organizations, child and other advocacy organizations, anti-poverty groups, community development organizations, etc.

[5] Opponents of this view argue that the money donors choose to give for charitable purposes is *their money* and they should have the only say in how those monies are used. While there is certainly something to this argument, it is also true that charitable donations are tax deductible and those deductions constitute a loss to the public treasury that would otherwise be available for public use. This view suggests that private donors should perhaps *not* have sole control when they provide resources to address public needs, especially when there is some reason to believe that those donors may not be in the best position to judge what are the greatest needs and the most effective ways to address them (Ostrander, 2007).

groups have less and less say about what needs and issues are most important and how they can be addressed most effectively (Ostrander, 2007).

What got me initially interested in the world of philanthropy was the research I did for my first book *Women of the Upper Class* (1984). The book is, in part, a critique of traditional philanthropy. Based on in-depth qualitative interviews with women from old wealthy families, my book argues that their charity work—while it did some good—served mainly to maintain the power and privilege of their class. How? Two examples are by using charitable giving of money and time to justify huge wealth and privilege, and by doing charity work through organizations like the Junior League which was at that time only open to upper class women.

The Executive Director of a funding organization called the Boston Women's Fund read my book, and she contacted me thinking I might help raise money from wealthy women willing to support BWF's nontraditional way of doing philanthropy. While I had been thinking about alternative ways of giving away money, learning about BWF was probably the first time I heard about the kind of philanthropy that I later called social relational. When donors give money to BWF, they give up the power to decide which recipient groups should get their money and how they should use it, because at BWF committees of women from the recipient community, not donors, make the decisions about who gets the money. An article I published in the journal *Gender & Society* (2004) documents this practice.

In 1995, I published another book called *Money for Change,* which was a study of a charitable foundation in Boston called Haymarket People's Fund (HPF), which epitomized a philanthropy where recipient groups hold the power to determine how philanthropic dollars are spent.

At some point, as people became aware of my scholarly work, I began to be asked to join with other activists and activist organizations who were also trying to develop what they called social change/social justice philanthropy. A young woman of wealth in Boston wanted to persuade her family's foundation to have recipient groups join in the decision making about where to give the money. She set out to establish a new organization called Foundations for Change. Having heard of my research and writing, she asked me to be a member of the founding board. Over a period of several years, we worked hard to develop workshops and other materials for use by other young wealthy donors who shared our vision. We also provided advice and support to the young founder as she took on a high profile at conferences like the annual meeting of the Council on Foundations and wrote articles for the journals read by professional fundraisers and foundation executives. Eventually Foundations for Change became part of an organization called Resource Generation (RG). RG provides information to young people of wealth about how to do philanthropy which "focuses on the root causes of social, economic and environmental injustices" and (consistent with social relational philanthropy) "includes the people who are impacted by those injustices as decision-makers" in how the money is used (http://resourcegeneration.org/).

In 2000, I was invited to join the Board of Directors of the Women's Funding Network, the umbrella organization of then some 90 women's funds around the United States and a few outside the United States. Some of the women's funds, like the Boston Women's Fund with which I had long been involved, did their grant making in a method similar to Haymarket's, where people from the community close to recipient groups, not donors, made the decisions about what groups would get money.

More recently, I've moved some of my activist work from the funding side of the table to the recipient side. I serve on the board of an immigrant advocacy organization called The Welcome Project in Somerville, Massachusetts. A goal we have is to bring donors into closer relationship with the organization and its work so they can know more about how their money is being used. We want to build a community among our donors based on shared values and concerns and a shared commitment to the work of the organization. Have you ever raised money for an organization you care about? How did you help people see what the organization did and why it matters? Might you now think about how to get people more connected to the organization beyond simply giving money?

One thing we did at The Welcome Project was organize a small dinner with people who had been giving to this organization for several years. We wanted them to get to know each other and to hear what they thought about our new strategic plan. We wanted also to find out what we might do to engage them more in our work. After the dinner, one donor joined the board and the Fundraising Committee and another increased the size of his gifts. We've also worked to make the board more representative of the people the organization works with and to engage the board in connecting more with donors, such as in creating relationships between them. At house parties where we raise money and reach out to more donors, people we work with come to meet those potential donors.

As I write this, I've recently received two invitations to deliver talks at local universities on panels about this kind of philanthropy where I speak about why it matters for recipient groups to have more of a say in how charitable dollars are used. I also explain why donors who really want to have a positive impact should want to work with recipient groups and respect their knowledge about the issues philanthropy tries to address. Social change rarely comes easily and part of being a sociologist in action is to understand that and keep working at it over the long haul even when the results are not always immediately evident. When social change does happen, after all the hard work, it's exceptionally rewarding!

References

Ostrander, S. A. (1984). *Women of the upper class*. Philadelphia: Temple University Press.

Ostrander, S. A. (1995). *Money for change: Social movement philanthropy at Haymarket People's Fund*. Philadelphia: Temple University Press.

Ostrander, S. A. (2004, February). Moderating contradictions of feminist philanthropy: Women's community organizations and the Boston Women's Fund, 1995 to 2000. *Gender & Society, 18*(1), 5–28.

Ostrander, S. A. (2007, June). The growth of donor control: Revisiting the social relations of philanthropy. *Nonprofit and Voluntary Sector Quarterly, 36*(2), 356–372.

Ostrander, S. A., & Schervish, P. G. (1990). Giving and getting: Philanthropy as a social relation. In J. Van Til (Ed.), *Critical issues in American philanthropy*. San Francisco: Jossey-Bass.

Localizing International Human Rights: Engaging with the World Social Forum Process

Jackie Smith
University of Pittsburgh

Jackie Smith is Professor of Sociology at the University of Pittsburgh. She is active in Occupy Pittsburgh and in the U.S. Social Forum's National Planning Committee. She has authored, coauthored, or coedited several books on transnational social movements, including *Social Movements in the World-System: The Politics of Crisis and Transformation* (2012) (with Dawn Wiest), *Social Movements for Global Democracy* (2007), *Global Democracy and the World Social Forums* (2007) (coauthored with 11 others), and *Coalitions Across Borders* (2005) (coedited with Joe Bandy).

During my high school years in the 1980s, the U.S. government was escalating Cold War rhetoric and the nuclear arms race while engaging in deadly military interventions in Central America. In response, a wave of peace activism spread across the United States, and adults in my church and in my school helped introduce me to international peace and justice activism. I helped send supplies to Nicaragua and organize resistance to the nuclear arms race, and when I graduated high school I applied to universities with programs in peace studies. I wanted to use the tools of social science to understand the causes of violence and the sources of peace and social justice. In particular, I wanted to learn why the peace movement in the United States had little impact on U.S. foreign policy, despite having widespread popular support for many of its goals.

Since the time I began my research, and as the world has become increasingly globalized, many more social movements have become active in international contexts, and many more groups are organizing transnationally (across nations) to reduce economic inequality and advance human rights and environmental justice. In the late 1990s, I began using *participatory observation research* as a method to study the movements I wanted to better understand. I found that it was impossible to fully grasp the strategic thinking and the complex and dynamic aspects of transnational organizing without becoming more deeply involved in the work itself.

A participatory research approach has benefitted my research in numerous ways, and I often learn a great deal more from the activists and movements I study than I can from scholarly works alone. As they develop strategies of action, movement participants articulate their own theories of social change. By doing participatory research, we can bring these sources of knowledge into our scholarship while also bringing scholarly analyses, skills, and energy to the work of social movements.

Understanding how power operates requires an exploration of what voices are not expressed and what options are not explored. Why is it that certain groups tend to have their preferences realized while others do not? What is it about the visions or preferences of weaker groups that is incompatible with the interests of the powerful? Engaging our sociological imaginations when answering these questions can help us identify alternatives to existing practices that contribute to various social problems.

Participatory Research on Global Justice Activism

By late 1999, it was becoming clear to many activist groups that the World Trade Organization (WTO) and the larger processes of global economic integration it represented were huge threats to the environment, human rights, and democratic institutions. Countries joined the WTO and other international trade agreements to improve their position in the global economy, and by doing so they relinquished considerable authority in the realm of economic policy. Members of the WTO agree to enact policies that facilitate international trade and investment, even if these policies contradict national laws and preferences. WTO rules tend to favor the interests of transnational corporations and the most powerful states, because their large economies and economic resources allow them disproportionate influence (see Smith and Moran, 2000). This has meant that national regulations that privilege products for their health benefits, that are produced in ecologically-friendly ways or by local businesses have been deemed "illegal" under WTO rules. For example, the WTO rules undermine international codes against misleading baby food advertisements; overrule restrictions on trade in seafood that is caught in manners threatening to dolphins, turtles, and other sea life; and prevent local communities from passing laws banning trade with countries under authoritarian rule (Wallach & Woodall, 2004).

Many of the tens of thousands of activists who gathered in Seattle for the "Battle in Seattle" against the WTO in 1999 were critical of its undemocratic features and of its social and environmental consequences (see Smith, 2001). They called for a different kind of globalization that puts human rights and environmental sustainability above profit making, and they helped launch what has become a growing global justice or "alternative globalization" movement. A key complaint of people in this movement is class inequality linked to economic integration. They point out that, according to the U.N. Development Program, in 1960 the world's wealthiest 20% earned just 30 times the incomes of the poorest 20%. By the late 1990s, incomes of the richest 20% approached *80 times* that of the poorest 20%. This inequality is both a cause and an effect of the extraordinary role corporations and other financial players play in national and global politics. Because governments have been encouraged to focus on economic growth, they have tended to focus their support on the needs of businesses. Thus, while specific claims of people in this movement vary, most participants demand greater democracy and economic equality.

One of the first challenges the global justice movement faced was to convince the public that economic globalization, as framed by the WTO and economic elites, was neither inevitable nor natural. They needed to show that alternatives to industrial mass production and globalized trade were viable and able to meet people's needs. The mass protests in Seattle drew attention to how trade policies advanced a particular set of class interests, opening the way for people to question many basic assumptions about globalization (Smith & Moran, 2000). Many observers were surprised to see so many people in a country of such privilege resisting economic globalization. Thus, while it was not the first mass protest against a global financial institution, Seattle became a turning point in the history of global justice activism. Following the "Battle in Seattle," large numbers of activists began gathering more regularly to protest international meetings on global trade and finance.

I attended the protests in Seattle and subsequent demonstrations against the World Bank and Free Trade Area of the Americas in order to learn how activists from different countries and sectors (such as labor, students, Indigenous, antipoverty, feminist) were able to find a common sense of purpose and coordinate their actions. I worked with other scholar-activists to expand discussions of globalization on our campuses and in the larger community. We observed and reported on the ways people were challenging globalization and on how governments were responding to protests in increasingly repressive ways.

Many in the movement soon began speaking of the limits of "summit-hopping," and activists in Brazil and France called for people to come to Porto Alegre in Brazil to protest the World Economic Forum and put forward a new vision of globalization. Under the slogan "another world is possible," they convened the first World Social Forum (WSF) in 2001, attracting around 20,000 activists. The next year they drew 60,000 and the following year 100,000. At the same time, hundreds of local, national, and regional social forums were organized to connect conversations across global and local levels and to expand possibilities for people to participate in the WSF (see Smith & Wiest, 2012). Through my own participation in several World Social Forum meetings, European and U.S. Social Forums, and in local efforts in my community to relate to the World Social Forum process, I could see that activists were responding to a widespread desire to come together to share their experiences of economic globalization, develop analyses, and build collaborative networks based on a shared critique of economic globalization. More than 10 years later, the WSF continues to evolve and to inspire the imaginations of people seeking another world (Smith, Byrd, Reese, & Smythe, 2011).

The two most concrete results of the WSF process are the *networks* it has helped initiate and sustain and the *ideas* it has helped develop and spread. Groups with diverse aims and constituencies—from peasant farmers to Indigenous activists to scholar-activists—have built long-term collaborative relationships through the WSF process. These networks, in turn, helped generate new understandings and analyses, aiding the work of building broader alliances around more radically transformative demands. One prominent example is the emergence of a strong alliance supporting the call for food sovereignty which has been advanced by Via Campesina, a leading organization in the WSF process. Other examples are demands for global environmental justice responding to global climate change negotiations and the various alternative or solidarity economies—such as community currencies and community supported agriculture—which allow communities to meet their needs outside globalized markets.

The WSF is thus an important space for doing sociological research and putting sociological tools into action. As I've attended different local, national, and global forums and participated in organizing meetings of the

U.S. Social Forum, I have learned how people develop long-term working relationships that enable coalitions to survive over time. I also can see through this kind of research the ways people who are embedded in local organizing networks think about and relate to global networks and politics. This has helped facilitate the work of translating ideas between global policy arenas and local communities and across different national and global contexts.

One particularly useful example is the idea of *intentionality* (Juris, 2008). This idea recognizes that completely open spaces that prioritize participation can end up excluding many people according to race, class, and gender. So, in the U.S. Social Forum (USSF) process, my fellow USSF organizers have deliberately discussed how to ensure that leadership comes from those groups most harmed by global capitalism. This hasn't been easy, since people who have been marginalized by our economic system are not always able to come to meetings and to volunteer to do the organizing work—much less to take on leadership roles. In our meetings, we often need to take time to help newcomers learn about discussions we've had in the past and to facilitate participation by less experienced organizers. Intentionality means that more privileged activists are asked to step back to create space for these leaders and to work in solidarity to provide skills and resources that can support less privileged activists. The idea that the WSF is a *process* suggests that participants are learning new ways of working together and developing new kinds of relationships and identities. To learn how this process works and what its effects are, I have needed to engage in the participatory approaches I discussed above.

It is possible to identify some important accomplishments of the WSFs and the larger global justice movement, which I have tried to support in my own work and with the resources and skills I bring as a scholar-activist. First, the movement has promoted a different story about globalization— one that stresses the negative consequences of global markets for both working and unemployed families around the world. These include, for instance, growing inequality which has limited the political voice of working people and furthered growing economic insecurity by lowering wages and increasing the "precarity" of work—that is, the lack of job security and decent working conditions. By obstructing global trade negotiations, the movement highlights the conflicts and inequities surrounding globalization. It denies elites the ability to claim that globalization is unambiguously good and universally beneficial. Throughout the world, more and more people have found it harder to make ends meet, despite the vast amount of wealth in the global economy. This story demands a change in how our economy is organized, and it encourages more to resist. The other important part of this story is that many thousands of people around the world are coming together to resist their conditions. This is not a story the commercial media wishes to tell, and even very large social forums have been ignored by mainstream press. I have tried to overcome this media blackout by telling this story through my teaching, research, and public engagement.

For me, being a sociologist in action has been a way to help support and encourage the WSF process and other efforts to build broad and diverse movements among people with very different experiences. Because we learn as sociologists to think about how larger social structures shape people's identities, perspectives, and interests, I find that I can often be of assistance in helping groups see areas of shared interests or possibilities for cooperative alliances. Also, as a teacher and writer, I have been fortunate to be able to help communicate movement ideas to larger audiences who might not otherwise hear them. Writing for popular media and online media sources has allowed me to perform a role that many activists lack the time and energy for, and my university credentials can lend legitimacy to the movement. The longer I have been involved in this work, the more I discover new insights about the dynamics of social change and the ways people in all places of society—including universities—must be involved if we are to realize a more just and peaceful world.

References

Bandy, J., & Smith, J. (Eds.). (2005). *Coalitions across borders: Transnational protest and the neoliberal order.* Lanham, MD: Rowman & Littlefield.

Juris, J. (2008). Spaces of intentionality: Race, class and horizontality at the United States Social Forum. *Mobilization, 13,* 353–372.

Smith, J. (2007). *Social movements for global democracy.* Baltimore, MD: Johns Hopkins University Press.

Smith, J. (2001). Globalizing resistance: The Battle of Seattle and the future of social movements. *Mobilization, 6,* 1–20.

Smith, J., Byrd, S., Reese, E., & Smythe, E. (Eds.). (2011). *Handbook of world social forum activism.* Boulder, CO: Paradigm.

Smith, J., Karides, M., Becker, M., Brunelle, D., Chase-Dunn, C., della Porta, D., . . . Vazquez, R. (2007). *Global democracy and the world social forums.* Boulder, CO: Paradigm.

Smith, J., & Moran, T. P. (2000). WTO 101: Myths about the World Trade Organization. *Dissent.* Retrieved from http://dissentmagazine.org/article/?article=1498

Smith, J., & Wiest, D. (2012). *Social movements in the world-system: The politics of crisis and transformation.* New York: Russell Sage Foundation.

Wallach, L., & Woodall, P. (2004). *Whose trade organization?: A comprehensive guide to the WTO.* New York: The New Press.

Housing and HIV/AIDS: A Tale of Academic, Provider, Advocacy, and Public Policy Collaboration

Angela Aidala

Columbia University

Dr. Angela Aidala is a Research Scientist at Columbia University's Mailman School of Public Health, Department of Sociomedical Sciences. She has served as Principal Investigator or Co-PI for over 20 collaborative community health or services research projects. Her current work has focused on housing, homelessness, and health. Dr. Aidala has been recognized for her leadership in documenting the role of housing (lack of housing) within the HIV epidemic—applying sociological tools to show how housing occupies a central place in the causal chains linking poverty and inequality with HIV risk and outcomes of infection.

> *"[R]esearch without action is dusty books on a shelf . . . and action without research is simply a tantrum."*
>
> —*Shirlene Cooper, Opening Keynote Speech, Housing & HIV/AIDS Research Summit III, Baltimore Maryland, March 2008.*

Graduate sociology at Columbia University in the 1970s was a great opportunity to pursue my long-standing interest in the processes and mechanisms of inequality and social exclusion. It also gave me an opportunity to explore the potential for pushback against the systems that reproduce these inequalities—via public social movements and/or small scale social and cultural resistances in the private sphere (gender relations, family, community life), especially in urban settings. I learned field methods from iconic sociologist Herbert Gans, and survey methods and a set of conceptual tools important for understanding humans in social context at the Bureau of Applied Social Research. While people themselves are a very good (often the best) source of information about their lives, broader perspectives are also needed to understand the social, economic, and political forces that constrain personal agency and life outcomes.

I had an opportunity to bring together my enthusiasm for social theory, social methods, and social action in the early 1990s in response to a need for research to better understand and respond to the HIV/AIDS epidemic in

New York City (NYC). The Ryan White Comprehensive AIDS Resources Emergency (CARE) Act was passed in 1990, designed to improve the availability of medical care and supportive services for low-income, uninsured and underinsured persons living with HIV/AIDS (PLWHA) and their families. A unique provision of the CARE Act was the requirement that communities would have significant control over local spending, and funds could be used to support the community-based systems built up over the past decade (in response to what had been the limited response of public institutions to date). Local Planning Councils were established as a mechanism for securing input from PLWHA and their caregivers and had "determinative authority" over resource allocation and evaluation. Community representativeness was seen as a balancing force to local political and economic interests. But community members may not be equally well-positioned players in a complex planning process. Despite media attention to well-off professionals and celebrities, HIV has been primarily an affliction among individuals and communities with little economic, political, and social power.

Enter the Community Health Advisory & Information Network (CHAIN) Project. CHAIN is an ongoing program of research conducted by sociologists (Peter Messeri and myself) from Columbia University in collaboration with and under the auspices of the HIV Planning Council of NYC.[6] Its purpose is to assess the system of HIV care—both health and social services—from the perspective of people living with HIV/AIDS. Now in its nineteenth year, CHAIN has enrolled several cohorts of PLWHA who are interviewed yearly about their needs for health and social services, their service encounters, and their physical, mental, and social wellbeing. Research questions, data collection strategies, data collection tools, and the analysis and reporting of research findings are done (and redone) with input from care providers, persons living with HIV/AIDS, and others on the Planning Council as well as representatives from the Department of Health and other stakeholders.

From the first interviews with PLWHA and service providers in 1994, it was clear that housing (lack of housing) played a major role in the epidemic. Housing was consistently reported as the greatest unmet service need. Rates of housing need remain fairly constant over time, at 30%–40% of all PLWHA at any point in time—as some PLWHA get housing needs met, others develop housing problems. Unstable housing leads to discontinuous care and is a barrier limiting the use of lifesaving medications. Housing status is associated with poor health outcomes and early death.

---

[6] For further information about CHAIN methodology and research reports see http://www.nyhiv.org/data_chain.html.

The importance of housing—whether PLWHA have safe, secure housing in a positive residential environment—has also been apparent in a national multiple site effort to establish, evaluate, and disseminate information on model programs that integrate health care and other supportive services with housing assistance for PLWHA struggling with mental illness and/or substance abuse problems. This national study, the Multiple-Diagnoses Initiative (MDI), was a collaborative effort that brought together 34 community-based providers with Columbia serving as the coordinating and technical assistance center to facilitate 'practice-based' evidence and lessons learned.[7]

From 1994 through 2006 over 20 written reports and multiple presentations on housing and HIV were produced by CHAIN and MDI authors and widely disseminated among provider and stakeholder groups. Research findings were used for service planning but also for advocacy and legal battles to secure rights and funding to address housing issues among PLWHA. In the words of Virginia Shubert, lead attorney and advocate for many housing, health, and economic justice battles: "The 'credentialing' provided by the academic research has been critical to the combination advocacy strategy in NYC, including legislative, agency-level, litigation and direct action strategies to expand housing access." The significance of housing made sociological sense to me. Housing comprises more than just physical shelter. Where we live is where our social life and our economic life come together. It's easy to see how housing occupies an important place within a nested set of contexts, which shape vulnerabilities to HIV infection and poor outcomes among the infected.

The Institute of Medicine (IOM) and Congress were unconvinced. In 2006, the Ryan White Care Act was reauthorized based on an IOM study. Although the study urged a "holistic" approach to providing care for low income persons living with HIV/AIDS, housing was not mentioned among the recommendations. The reauthorized program required that agencies and programs that receive CARE Act funds use 75% of every dollar received for "core" medical services—primarily medical care and medications. This sharply restricted the ability of service providers to use funds for housing assistance and other supportive services central to the ability of disadvantaged PLWHA to maintain stability in their lives and manage their illness.

In response, a national and eventually international effort was undertaken to increase attention to the role of housing for HIV prevention, treatment, and care. The HIV/AIDS Housing Research Summit series was launched in

---

[7] For more information on this study, see "Facts from the Frontline: Successful Strategies for Working with Multiply Diagnosed Individuals." Invited presentation to the U.S. Department of Housing and Urban Development (HUD) Division of Community Planning and Development. Washington DC 2000. (Joint presentation with agency personnel from HUD-funded demonstration projects).

2005 by the National AIDS Housing Coalition (NAHC), bringing together researchers, providers, community members, and policy decision makers to exchange information and strategies on topics related to housing and HIV. Participants examine empirical data, discuss policy implications, and work collaboratively on development of collective strategies for ensuring a sound, data-driven public health response to the housing needs of persons living with HIV/AIDS and at high risk of infection. The Summit meetings are a time for colearning. As a convening researcher, I draw on my experience teaching methods to help community members understand medical and statistical research. In turn, community members help me interpret statistics and medical findings as they manifest in people's lives.

One difficulty that I and collaborators faced with what we learned from research into real programs and policies was that policy decision makers were aware of the associations between housing status and health but seemed stuck with assumptions about homelessness as an attribute of individuals rather than a situation or condition within which individuals may find themselves. This "risky person" paradigm predominates in much health-related research. Risky person arguments are also common in the deviance literature. This model assumes that for reasons of genetic predisposition, early socialization, or other influences resulting in enduring dispositions, some persons are led to drug use, risky sex and illegal activities, and so on, which would have both health (increased risk for HIV infection) and housing (limited economic resources to purchase conventional housing) consequences.

It was clear that some sociology lessons were in order. Sociologists have long argued that health is shaped by "upstream" or fundamental causes—macro (societal or global) economic, political, and social arrangements and resources that shape differential access to knowledge, money, prestige, and power which can be used to avoid or buffer exposure to health risks. My writing and talks at academic conferences and presentations to policy makers began to discuss how housing occupies a strategic position as an intermediate structural factor, linking these broader societal processes to the more immediate physical and social environments within which we carry out day-to-day life. The same fundamental causes put persons at risk for poor health and for unstable/inadequate housing: political contexts, inequality of opportunities and conditions, social processes of discrimination, and social exclusion. Persons who are homeless or unstably housed lack a protected space to maintain physical and psychological well-being; they find themselves consistently in stress-producing environments with consequences for mental health and immunological functioning. The homeless are not randomly distributed throughout a city but concentrated in neighborhoods of disadvantage and disorder. The press of daily needs can be a barrier to service use, even if services are available. Having a home structures the private sphere. The lack of housing, transient living conditions, and the communal sleeping arrangements in most homeless shelters pose a formidable barrier to forming or maintaining intimate partner relationships and conventional family life.

Evidence from studies of housing status and HIV prevention and treatment outcomes, including discussion based on my sociological analysis of 'risky contexts,' have been used by advocates to educate federal, state, and local policy makers. This research has been cited by members of Congress during debates on federal housing appropriations and in comments on proposed regulatory changes. Our research presentations and publications, which included not just the statistics but sociological interpretations of how to understand the statistics, were used to support successful advocacy to fund housing as an HIV prevention measure, and in at least one instance, to defeat a proposed statewide decrease in rental assistance for PLWHA.[8]

During 2009, the White House Office of National AIDS Policy (ONAP) held a series of town hall meetings to inform national strategy. Over and over again, people made the connection between housing and HIV prevention and between housing and effective HIV treatment. As a result, ONAP held a special meeting with researchers and key housing stakeholders where I presented my research, and others discussed cost and cost effectiveness implications. When the policy document was finalized, housing was featured as a critical issue of concern in the National HIV/AIDS Strategy (NHAS). A strategic policy goal was set to increase housing resources to serve an additional 22,000 persons living with HIV by 2015. Shortly thereafter, the U.S. House of Representatives and the Senate passed resolutions recognizing that the lack of adequate housing must be addressed as a barrier to effective HIV prevention, treatment, and care and requesting increased funding for housing assistance. The Housing Opportunities for Persons with AIDS (HOPWA) Program within the federal Department of Housing and Urban Development received a $5 million increase in 2011, at a time when many federal programs were faced with funding cuts.

I grew up with an understanding that it mattered to do something useful in the world. The application of sociological theory and methodological tools to understand mechanisms of disadvantage and injustice, and define practical points of intervention, has been my way to be useful.

---

[8] Specific examples and resources for evidence based housing advocacy are set out in NAHC's Policy Tool Kit at http://nationalaidshousing.org/policy-toolkit/

Discussion Questions

1. When Kevin Bales first started his research on slavery in the 1990s, why was modern day slavery so well hidden? Why did he feel he needed more than anecdotal evidence to believe that widespread slavery existed?

2. According to Bales, why would it be difficult to liberate slaves and reintegrate them into society without the tools of sociology? How have he and his colleagues used their sociological training to make modern slavery visible and help those enslaved become free? What can *you* do to combat slavery?

3. What led Deirdre Oakley to go to graduate school? What did she learn about her own privilege from her experience living in Alphabet City from the mid 1980s to 1990? In what ways are you privileged and how can that privilege be unwrapped so you can advocate for social justice?

4. How have Oakley and her colleagues given voice to a marginalized group of people through their work with individuals relocated by the Atlanta Housing Authority? Why is their doing so important?

5. How did you feel after reading Bria Wilbur's piece? Has your perspective on society changed, as hers did when she was a student at Bridgewater State University? Why or why not? How might you influence your own campus culture for the better?

6. Wilbur describes Free The Children's mission "to free children around the world from poverty and exploitation and to free children in North America from the idea they are powerless to change the world." Do you think that these two goals need to work in hand in hand? Why or why not?

7. According to Susan Ostrander, why is it important for recipient groups to have some control over how donations are spent? Do you agree? Why or why not?

8. When you or your family makes a donation, do you usually do so to provide a service or to promote advocacy? Why? After reading Ostrander's piece, are you more likely to consider giving money for advocacy? Why or why not?

9. What does Jackie Smith mean when she says "understanding how power operates requires an exploration of what voices are not expressed and what options are not explored?" How might you apply this perspective to researching the distribution of power at your school?

10. According to Smith, what are the major concerns of the "alternative globalization" movement? What evidence of economic inequality do you see a) on your campus, b) in your hometown, and c) in the United States? How can you, personally, work to mitigate some of the negative impacts of today's globalization process?

11. According to Angela Aidala, how do macro forces impact one's ability to have secure housing? How do such forces impact your own housing? Have

you ever been concerned about your or your family's ability to obtain safe housing? Why or why not? What can you do to help ensure that *you* have secure housing? What can you do to ensure that *everyone* has access to housing?

12. What are the connections between a) housing and HIV prevention and b) housing and HIV treatment? How has Aidala used sociological tools to make those connections clear?

Resources

ASA Inequality Poverty and Mobility Section

American Sociological Association section encouraging research and curriculum development on social class related issues.
http://www.asanet.org/sections/ipm.cfm

Center on Budget and Policy Priorities

Provides research and analysis to help shape public debate over proposed budget and tax policies. Works to ensure that policy makers consider the needs of low-income families and individuals. Research on the budget, climate change, the economy, food assistance, health, housing, poverty, social security, taxes, and welfare. Offers a "policy basics" section.
http://www.cbpp.org

Center for Popular Economics

Collective of over 80 economists advocating for new models of people-centered economics. Runs workshops and institutes. Has excellent resources, including Economics for the 99% booklet, a popular economics blog, the book *Field Guide to the US Economy*, and a regular newsletter.
http://www.populareconomics.org

Citizens for Tax Justice

Public interest research and advocacy organization focusing on federal, state, and local tax policies and their impact upon individuals and our economy. Works to give ordinary people a greater voice in the development of tax laws, hoping to create a more fair tax system and to reduce national debt.
http://www.ctj.org

Class Matters

New York Times resource with articles, data, stories, and interactive graphics and data.

http://www.nytimes.com/national/class

Dollars and Sense

Magazine presenting accessible economic news and analysis, reports on economic justice activism, primers on economic topics, and critiques of the mainstream media's coverage of the economy.

http://www.dollarsandsense.org

Economic Policy Institute

Think tank working to broaden discussions about economic policy to include the needs of low income and middle income workers. Working toward creating good jobs with fair pay, through research and policy advocacy. Offers a clearinghouse of research and publications on a large variety of economic equality issues, along with good resource links and an excellent interactive "Inequality Is" quiz.

http://www.epi.org

Feeding America

Nationwide network of food banks working to end hunger while advocating for policy change. Website offers a food bank network, good information and studies on hunger, and policy campaigns.

http://feedingamerica.org

Food Research and Action Center

Works to improve public policies and public-private partnerships to eradicate hunger in the United States. Works with hundreds of national, state, and local nonprofit organizations, public agencies, corporations and labor organizations to address hunger, food insecurity, and their root causes. Great information on federal food and nutrition programs and excellent updated data and information. Offers a variety of initiatives, actions, and publications.

http://frac.org

Free The Children

World's largest network of youth helping youth. Works to empower North American youth through leadership and education, and to empower youth in poor regions through development of schools, health, water, sanitation, and microdevelopment. Website offers excellent curriculum, resources and education on children's rights issues, and exciting campaigns such as We are Silent, Halloween for Hunger (We Scare Hunger), and the Year of Education.

http://www.freethechildren.com

Gapminder

Excellent resource with research and data on many class and inequality issues domestically and globally. Data are presented through graphs, charts, PowerPoints, and presentations.

http://www.gapminder.org

Inequality.org

Portal with information on wealth inequality, providing links to current research and top organizations working on these issues.

http://inequality.org

National Coalition for the Homeless

National network of people who are currently experiencing or who have experienced homelessness, activists and advocates, and community-based service providers. Works to prevent and end homelessness while ensuring the immediate needs of those experiencing homelessness are met and their civil rights protected. Excellent source for speakers, fact sheets, and other resources.

http://www.nationalhomeless.org

People Like Us: Social Class in America

Complement website to the seminal PBS documentary. Provides interactive quizzes, resources, stories, and curriculum.

http://www.pbs.org/peoplelikeus

Political Economy Research Institute

Leading source of research and policy initiatives on issues of globalization, unemployment, financial market instability, central bank policy, living wages and decent work, and the economics of peace, development, and the environment.

http://www.peri.umass.edu

State of Working America

Program offering a wide variety of data on family income, wages, jobs, unemployment, wealth, and poverty. Provides excellent charts, data, and fact sheets.

http://stateofworkingamerica.org

Wealth for Common Good

A network of business leaders and high-income Americans working together to promote shared prosperity and fair taxation, with members who range from entrepreneurs and doctors to elected officials of all backgrounds and political stripes. Offers campaigns, a blog, videos, and policy initiatives.

http://wealthforcommongood.org

3

Gender

Gender, the social roles assigned to males and females, impacts every aspect of our lives. Today, gender inequality remains a social problem. Like race and class, our gender influences our social position in the world. Gender does much to shape how we view others and how we view ourselves. In the pieces in this chapter, sociologists in action discuss issues that are gender-related in their causes and consequences and present their approaches to working toward social change.

Amy Lubitow starts off this chapter with "Breast Cancer Activism: Learning to Write Collaboratively for Social Change." In this piece, she discusses how she was drawn to study the issue of *pinkwashing*. Pinkwashing occurs when "major corporations contribute to increasing rates of breast cancer through the sale of consumer products containing toxic chemicals *and* then sell pink-ribbon products as a means of demonstrating a commitment to fighting breast cancer." As Lubitow explains, such practices serve to distract the public by focusing our attention on "the cure" at the expense of considering the products and environmental toxins that actually cause cancer. Lubitow then vividly describes how, as a sociologist, she effectively addressed pinkwashing through her collaboration with an anti-pinkwashing activist. Building on their different backgrounds and approaches proved to be a great success; they wrote an influential journal article examining the environmental causes of breast cancer and leveraging a critique of pinkwashing practices that gained a great deal of media attention. Working together, they were able to build a campaign against pinkwashing that was scientifically sound and also clear and compelling to a large audience.

The second piece in this chapter focuses on an extreme manifestation of gender inequality: honor killings. Mazhar Bağlı uses sociological tools to educate the public about honor killings and how to address them. In "Honor Killings: Murder of Mores, Mores of Murder," he explains how, through interviewing nearly 200 men convicted of this crime in over 40 prisons in Turkey, he came to the realization that those who commit such acts are not deviants—a finding that ran counter to existing understandings of honor killings. As Bağlı explains, "The idea that perpetrators are clearly different from others led to the faulty understanding that this was an isolated problem. My research, however, revealed that the perpetrators existed in a much broader, societal context." In fact, not only are they not considered deviants but they are supported by those in their community for upholding the moral code of society, a code that is gender specific. These powerful findings indicate that effective policies to curb honor killings must address societal issues, rather than focus on individual problems. To stop honor killings, societies must stem gender inequality.

Next, Brian Klocke describes why he became a sociologist in action and a feminist in "Speaking Out for Social Justice: Sociology and Cultural Transformation." As he explains, his was an indirect path to finding sociology. After studying in other disciplines, he found himself working in college residence life and student activities and explains, "I reflected about how personal biographies and socialization intersect with social norms and culture within institutions to shape group behavior, from the banal and benign, to the life threatening, such as attempted suicides and alcohol poisoning that I had to respond to decisively and quickly in my job. Ultimately, it was not fulfilling, as I wanted to be less reactive and more proactive about making the world a better place." Thus, he went on to study sociology and has found many ways to put the tools of sociology into action. Through his work with the National Organization of Men Against Sexism and as an advisor to the No More! student club on his campus, he has worked to draw attention to and to curb male violence against women. He and his students have worked proactively to shape a campus and community environment that is equitable and violence free.

In the fourth piece in this chapter, "On Becoming a Public Sociologist: Amplifying Women's Voices in the Quest for Environmental Justice," Tracy Perkins describes how she uses photos, interactive theatre, and a website to bring the experiences and concerns of female environmental activists to the larger public. Her Voices from the Valley project effectively communicates environmental concerns and illuminates the struggles and triumphs these activists experience. While ups and downs are a part of any campaign for change, these women have had incredible successes in campaigning for the removal of a carcinogenic chemical from the market, suing the state of California over legislation on global warming, and helping pass the first state law ensuring a human right to water. While celebrating this activism for change, Perkins also helps to dismantle stereotypes about female environmental activists by showing that their motivations are more multifaceted than the typical portrayal of concerned mothers. Her work shows what is possible when public sociology is married with the creative arts.

For any social problem to be effectively addressed, it must first be acknowledged. Margaret Abraham describes, in "Talking the Talk and Walking the Walk: Linking Research and Action on Domestic Violence," how she has helped make the issue of domestic abuse in the South Asian immigrant community visible. She discusses how she has worked to bring these personal troubles into the public domain where they can be understood as social problems requiring action. Her research on this previously underrepresented issue has been influential, and she has also actively sought opportunities to engage outside of academia, speaking before the media, and giving talks to South Asian Women's Organizations, law enforcement agencies and medical organizations. Abraham has also engaged the judicial system at many levels, leading efforts to enhance the understanding of marital abuse in the South Asian immigrant context and to provide services, such as translators and training for community service providers, for immigrant women of color who suffer abuse.

Linda Olson is another inspiring example of a sociologist creating means to address a serious social problem, by focusing her attention on addressing a "rape culture" prevalent on college campuses. In "Transforming Rape Culture on a College Campus: Using Peer Advocacy for Social Change," she describes how a "rape culture normalizes sexual violence." She explains, "As a result, we don't take sexual violence seriously as a crime, or we tend to blame the victim for this type of violence." Furthermore, while few individuals perpetrate sexual crimes, a rape culture encourages many to become silent bystanders. Olson describes how she and a group of students created the CHANGE Initiative (Creating, Honoring, Advocating, and Nurturing Gender Equity) and PAC (Peer Advocates for CHANGE) "to actively change campus culture to reduce sexual and relationship violence while also creating a matrix of support for survivors of these issues." Their efforts and creative campaigns have helped change perceptions about rape and bystanding and have created a more positive and safe environment for all students on their campus.

Breast Cancer Activism: Learning to Write Collaboratively for Social Change

Amy Lubitow
Portland State University, Oregon

Amy Lubitow, PhD, is an Assistant Professor of Sociology at Portland State University where she teaches courses related to the environment, politics, and sustainability. Her scholarly endeavors explore issues of environmental justice, gender, and critical approaches to sustainability. She has worked with environmental health and environmental justice organizations across the United States for the past 5 years.

Rates of breast cancer in the United States have quadrupled over the past 40 years. This means that one out of every eight American women will be diagnosed with the disease in her lifetime (Gray, 2010). Notably, this increase cannot simply be attributed to better diagnostics or to increased life expectancy but is also related to a range of environmental exposures from the food we eat, the air we breathe, and the consumer products that we use on a daily basis (Gray, 2010; Knopf-Newman, 2004). The growing recognition among scientists, public health experts, and breast cancer researchers of these environmental links to breast cancer inspired me to begin asking sociological questions about the breast cancer experience in America.

In my effort to develop a clearer understanding of the environmental aspects of breast cancer, I initially sought out as much information as I could find. Scientific research articles and books were my first exposure to research on the topic, but I soon discovered that some of the most interesting and compelling research couldn't be found in a library database but originated from nonprofit organizations committed to working on environmental health issues. Specifically, I began to explore the work of the Silent Spring Institute in Massachusetts and the Breast Cancer Fund and Breast Cancer Action organizations in California. Their research studies made vitally important connections between breast cancer rates and everyday toxic chemical exposures from pesticides, personal care products, and food or water consumption. Reviewing this research, which deftly made important connections in a clear, accessible language, using great visuals and a related call to action for readers, served as one of those "A-ha" moments for me. I realized that this type of research could serve as a catalyst for social change efforts.

Following this revelation, I sought out local organizations in Boston (where I was completing my PhD in sociology) where I would be able to put my research endeavors to work for social or political change efforts related to the environment and breast cancer. After volunteering with several organizations, I landed with the Campaign for Safe Cosmetics because of their commitment to raising awareness and changing federal policies regarding the regulation of cosmetic products. I learned that most of these products remain unregulated by the Federal Government and many contain ingredients linked to a host of reproductive ailments and cancers, including breast cancer (CSC, 2012; Kay, 2005). Through the Campaign for Safe Cosmetics, I was able to connect my understanding of the scientific aspects of environmental health concerns (including breast cancer) with practical ideas for solutions. These solutions include policy change efforts, consumer-driven campaigns to pressure companies to reformulate personal care products, and awareness-raising events to help educate people about the environmental links to disease and the health risks associated with an unregulated personal care products industry.

Through these hands-on volunteer experiences, my knowledge regarding the political, social, and environmental links to the breast cancer epidemic continued to grow. I was able to speak at public events, help publicize campaign initiatives, and develop relationships with environmental health activists. Such relationship building allowed me to develop an important collaboration with one particular activist named Mia Davis, who at the time served as the National Grassroots Organizer for the Campaign for Safe Cosmetics. In particular, we spent a great deal of time discussing the lack of research that explores the role of major corporations in complicating and confusing the public's understanding of breast cancer causes. As the activist campaign "Think Before You Pink" highlights, breast cancer fundraising efforts may be misleading. Major corporations contribute to increasing rates of breast cancer through the sale of consumer products containing toxic chemicals *and* then sell pink-ribbon products as a means of demonstrating a commitment to fighting breast cancer. This contradiction, known as pinkwashing, is the practice whereby breast cancer symbolism is co-opted by corporate actors who stand to profit from the use of breast cancer awareness imagery. Through this practice, companies and groups "position themselves as leaders in the struggle to eradicate breast cancer while engaging in practices that may be contributing to rising rates of the disease" (Malkan, 2007, pp. 75).

Once we had identified that there was a gap in the academic literature and pinkwashing remained undertheorized, we decided to develop a research article for publication in a peer-reviewed journal. In choosing to bridge our different backgrounds, Mia and I had to negotiate a great deal with one another. As a trained sociologist, I tended to want to write at length on theoretical concepts and use sociological terminology. Mia, a trained activist, wanted to intersperse calls to action more readily. In writing collaboratively, we had to agree on when to include sociological insights, when to encourage our readers to take action, when to use passionate language, and when to let theoretical insights take center stage. Merging our two different backgrounds together proved to be both thought provoking and challenging, and ultimately generated a more nuanced and accurate understanding of pinkwashing in the United States.

In the research article that emerged, "Pastel Injustice: The Corporate Use of Pinkwashing for Profit," we reviewed the literature on the environmental causes of breast cancer and developed a critical analysis of pinkwashing practices in the United States. In drafting this research article, I drew on my sociological training in a range of political and sociological theories and my experience writing critically about policies and regulations and working collaboratively on research projects. Those skills, when combined with Mia's to-the-point writing style and her capacity to organize complex ideas into manageable concepts, allowed our research paper to become both sociologically informed and accessible to a general audience.

In our article, we argue that companies selling pink-ribbon products or engaging in fundraising efforts while manufacturing toxic chemicals or selling products with known carcinogens are guilty of environmental injustice targeting women. We suggest that consumption oriented practices (most notably, the purchasing of pink-ribbon products) that raise funds for research actually divert attention away from the causes of breast cancer and from the diversity of experiences of women with breast cancer. We also expose that the corporations who were the biggest players in breast cancer awareness and fundraising heavily supported the notion of "the cure" for breast cancer, a practice that entirely obscures questions of the environmental causes of breast cancer. The article concludes by suggesting ways in which the mainstream understanding of breast cancer might be altered. First, we suggest environmental policy reforms that more effectively regulate the types of chemicals suspected of contributing to increasing rates of breast cancer. Second, we note that businesses could change the reality of breast cancer by embracing the notion of prevention, seeking to create safer products with fewer chemicals and steering philanthropic donations to research efforts that search for "the cause" rather than "the cure." Finally, we suggest cultural changes encouraging women to experience a wide range of emotions and responses to breast cancer diagnoses (rather than just expecting women to embrace the identity of a valiant "survivor"). This ideological shift would help generate the type of breast cancer culture in which women might begin to critique consumerist practices and demand more stringent health protections and regulations.

Following the publication of this article in the journal *Environmental Justice* (Lubitow & Davis, 2011), Mia and I had many opportunities to speak publicly about the conflicts of interest inherent in the corporate sponsorship of breast cancer fundraising. We were invited to speak on "The Stupid Cancer Show" radio program whose listeners are dealing with cancer diagnoses. I also spoke at many sociological conferences and other public venues about the trappings of pinkwashing. We were asked to write author guest blogs for a number of health organizations, including *The Story of Stuff* and the *Mom's Rising* blogs. The article's findings were also picked up in a range of print media, including *Forbes.com*, *The Orlando Sentinel*, *Science Daily*, and the *United Press International*. Working and speaking together as a sociologist-activist team allowed Mia and I to stand on firm academic ground when discussing the problems associated with pinkwashing while encouraging individuals and organizations to become involved in efforts to raise awareness and generate social change.

Most memorably, an excerpt of the article was published on *Forbes.com* and generated a written response from Avon (the breast cancer awareness-raising giant, whose cosmetic products contain ingredients linked to breast cancer) in which the company refuted our arguments. We were able to engage in a public dialogue with the company, calling on them to make changes to their corporate practices. Our written response concluded, "It is our sincere hope that Avon and other companies steer clear of pinkwashing and that Avon uses its considerable power and brand recognition to be a true leader in prevention, as well as in early detection and the search for the cure." Although Avon refused to alter their practices, the research article served to open up new discussions on many websites and mobilized many people to join efforts to hold entities like Avon and Susan G. Komen more accountable. We are hopeful that our work will form the foundation of future research that develops a critical stance on philanthropic efforts to address breast cancer.

Our article and the subsequent dialogue with Avon provide a great example of the benefits of collaborative writing that brings real-world experience in line with sociological investigation. Although I could surely have written an academic research article that critically analyzed pinkwashing by myself, pairing my perspective with Mia's hands-on activist approach allowed the resulting research to be accessible, compelling, and easily translatable into action. Our work together allowed us to raise awareness of corporate pinkwashing, generated fascinating discussions, and served to further the efforts of the organizations whose work had inspired us in the first place.

My training as a sociologist has been vital to my efforts to advance social change. The discipline has allowed me to recognize the structural and political aspects of many of our most pressing social problems. This knowledge and understanding has continually inspired me to seek new ways to ameliorate the injustices I have learned about during my education as a sociologist. The relationships that can develop when combining academic questions with activist work are rewarding and inspiring. They can also contribute to real-world outcomes. Our article brought the issue of pinkwashing to a much larger audience. I believe that the growing public awareness and the accompanying potential for new research the article produced will continue to influence our understanding of breast cancer culture and how to change it.

References

Campaign for Safe Cosmetics (CSC). (2012, August 14). FDA Regulations. Retrieved from http://safecosmetics.org/article.php?list=type&type=75

Gray, J. (2010). State of the evidence: The connection between breast cancer and the environment. San Francisco, CA: Breast Cancer Fund. Retrieved from http://www.breastcancerfund.org/assets/pdfs/publications/state-of-the-evidence-2010.pdf

Kay, G. (2005). *Dying to be beautiful: The fight for safe cosmetics.* Columbus: Ohio State University Press.

Knopf-Newman, M. J. (2004). Public eyes: Investigating the causes of breast cancer. In R. Stein (Ed.), *New perspectives on environmental justice: Gender, sexuality, and activism* (pp. 161–176). Brunswick, NJ: Rutgers University Press.

Lubitow, A., & Davis, M. (2011). "Pastel Injustice: The Corporate Use of Pinkwashing for Profit." *Environmental Justice, 4*(2), 139–144.

Malkan, S. (2007). *Not just a pretty face: The ugly side of the beauty industry.* Gabriola Island, British Columbia: New Society Publishers.

Honor Killings: Murder of Mores, Mores of Murder

Mazhar Bağlı
Yıldırım Beyazıt University, Ankara

Prof. Dr. Mazhar Bağlı began his academic career in Tokat Gaziosmanpaşa University, Turkey in 1993 and was in the Sociology Department in Diyarbakır Dicle University in southeastern Turkey from 1999 to 2011. He conducted field research on specific problems of Diyarbakır and participated in many TV programs to discuss his findings. He also worked as a social policy consultant for political parties, public institutions, and research institutes. Dr. Bağlı has received national and international academic attention, particularly for his work on chastity and honor killings. He is presently a faculty member at Yıldırım Beyazıt University in Ankara.

I began working at the Dicle University in the southeastern region of Turkey in 1999. This area has a stronger traditional social structure than other regions in Turkey. Male-dominated relationships are more prevalent in this region, with one example being that the employment rates between men and women are very uneven. To illustrate, the female employment rate in the public workforce is only approximately 15%, while it is 85% for males. Additionally, the property ownership in the region for females is only 2%. And thus, the region reflects a male-oriented structure and socio-cultural characteristics.

When I was working in the region, honor killings had become increasingly common, though little research had been conducted on this disturbing social problem. An honor killing is the cultural tradition of killing a woman believed to have profaned her honor, and thus staining the reputation of everyone related to her.

Honor is considered to be stained when: a woman elopes with her lover, a married woman commits adultery, a divorced woman lives together with a man without being legally married, or a single woman has a relationship with her boyfriend out of wedlock or runs away with her boyfriend without permission of her family and without being married. Honor is evaluated as a virtue only measured by the skin/flesh of the woman and, in fact, is one of the most severe examples of gender inequality globally. Honor killing is highly discriminatory, as it applies only to women. It never applies to a man who has committed similar acts.

As I aimed to expose and challenge this sexist and inhumane practice by conducting my own research about this serious issue, I found that the clearest information on honor killings could be gained by examining the criminals who committed these crimes. I gained the support of TUBİTAK (The Scientific and Technological Research Council of Turkey), one of the most prestigious institutions in Turkey, to carry out my research. All financial costs of the project were provided by the Council, as was assistance in navigating the bureaucracy in order to obtain my interviews.

After receiving the necessary permissions from authorities, I interviewed 190 "honor" killers in 44 prisons across Turkey, gaining the most comprehensive information on the subject to date. The most striking result of this research was that prior understandings about the subject do not accurately reflect the truth. Previously, honor killings were assumed to be committed by people belonging to low socioeconomic groups, as well as to a certain region and specific ethnic group. Honestly, in the beginning I, too, had been expecting to see a distinctive characteristic of the killers that could separate them from others, but I could not. Throughout the interviews, I learned that these killers are not obviously different than the common man who we see around us every day (this inference is based on the sample frame I utilized in this study, which reflects no discrepancy with the social characteristics of men who don't commit honor killings). Moreover, it became clear that the inclination of researchers and the public to attribute the killer's actions to their being different from others both deepens the existing problem and leads to a lack of information on the subject. The false conception that perpetrators are clearly different from others led to the faulty understanding that this was an isolated problem. My research, however, revealed that the perpetrators existed in a much broader societal context.

I set out to use my sociological research to help rid society of incorrect assumptions of where and by whom honor killings are perpetrated. I often use a metaphor about the identification of the sex of newly hatched chicks to help my students better understand the power of the sociological eye. On first glance, young chicks do not have a clear sign that reveals their sex. Only those who have expertise and experience in the field of veterinary medicine are able to differentiate between the sexes. This ability of being able to identify a chick's gender as male or female, soon after it is hatched is, of course, not a gift but the fruits of vast experience and a learning process. Similarly, sociology gives us this kind of insight to understand society. It is through our trained eye, experience, and research that we can identify societal traits in ways that others cannot.

The research that I conducted on honor killings revealed a very complex network of relationships and involved very dramatic stories, the types of intricacies sociology is best positioned to uncover! According to my findings, 47% of the perpetrators do not regret their crimes and many family members of the perpetrators approve of their crimes. Among the killers, 27% received approval from their first-degree relatives (parents and siblings) and 44% received approval from their second-degree relatives (grandparents, uncles, aunts, cousins; even more distant relatives).

Therefore, with such a high level of positive reaction from their social circles, my finding was that imposing heavy penalties on the killers to stop the honor killings did not act as a deterrent. In fact, when I asked the question directly: "Do the punishments being heavier act as a deterrent?" only 14% of the perpetrators answered "yes." In addition, 25% of the perpetrators stated that the punishments which they were given were unfair and they should not be sentenced for honor killings. The notion of deterrence is based on rational choice theory, which predicts that individuals will engage in a cost-benefit calculation. In that theory, it follows that when punishment increases, individuals will increasingly refrain from the crime in order to protect their own best interest. However, in the case of honor killings, the particular honor code of the region complicates this calculation and supersedes rational acts. In other words, members of this society in question are highly likely to cross the rationality line in response to the societal value system around this issue.

Honor killings are highly influenced by societal culture (specific to moral code) that is gender specific. The moral code of the society encourages male individuals to commit these killings and assigns the status of "honor" to those who do so, thus undermining the cost-benefit theory of deterrence. From another perspective, such a way of thinking is based mainly on a high level of gender discrimination in Turkish society. It appears that the killings are committed based on the idea that women (and not men) must live up to an "honor" code, a code attached to rules around their body. This type of thinking is especially embedded in the social structures of the more traditional communities in society, in which the cultural pressure is quite strong. As expected, rural areas are more likely to be marked with such cultural pressures. One major aspect of the honor code is the protection of sexual purity for women. Women's sexual purity is linked to the honor of men and the family and, accordingly, women are subjected to men's decisions and their approval. Women have to conform to men's arbitrary rules. Perhaps the most poignant and disturbing finding from this research was that 41% of the perpetrators answered "yes" to the question: "If you faced the same situation, would you conduct that crime again?"

Clearly, the social environment of the men who commit honor killings influences their actions. The movie *Face Off* (1997) that John Woo directed may give us some tips about how sociology can help us understand how social situations influence people's behavior. When Archer takes on the face of Troy to bring down a terrorist group and those around him expect him to act like Troy, he starts to behave like Troy. Likewise, sociologists must always try to understand situations from every perspective, stepping out of our own comfort zone sometimes in order to better understand why people act in the ways they do. These men, who are expected to uphold norms of gender discrimination and honor in their community, quite readily state that they would kill again.

According to traditional Turkish culture, women should be under the control of men and their "honor" should be protected as a matter of life and death. A sociologist, just like Archer, should look from the perspective of the groups they study in order to understand why people act in certain ways in particular social environments. In other words, sociologists may have to put themselves in Troy's shoes or, in the case of my research, in the shoes of those who perpetrate honor killings, in order to understand behavior in relation to social contexts.

When I made my findings public, I was invited to appear on several TV programs to discuss honor killings. Political parties in Turkey also asked me for my guidance on how to deal with honor killings and other social issues. As well, newspapers began asking me to write articles on honor killings and other regional issues and social inclinations. I also received invitations to make presentations at academic conferences held abroad. I believe that this study is making an important contribution to the collective mind and conscience, which hopefully will culminate in changes to the social policies that allow for a culture with honor killings.

As a sociologist, I have helped provide people with a new perspective on honor killings and other social issues. In the process, I have helped debunk ideas that those who commit honor killings are unlike other members of society. My findings have revealed that honor killings are committed by otherwise ordinary members of society, a society that promotes unequal treatment of women. This finding may be disturbing, but it also provides us with the understanding necessary in order to begin to effectively address this social problem. To protect women from such horrors, we must promote gender equality throughout society.

References

Woo, J. (Director). (1997). *Face off* [Motion picture]. United States: Paramount Pictures.

Speaking Out for Social Justice: Sociology and Cultural Transformation

Brian Klocke
State University of New York Plattsburgh

Brian Klocke is Assistant Professor of Sociology at SUNY Plattsburgh. His sociological research intersects with media studies, criminal justice, and political science. His most recent publications include a book chapter on the media coverage of the Occupy Wall Street Movement in the context of neoliberalism; a chapter on practicing moral panics research (with Glenn Muschert); and an article on the response of journalists to a professor scandal. Dr. Klocke was on the editorial team of SSSP's *Agenda for Social Justice: Solutions 2012*. He is a member of the National Organization of Men Against Sexism and advises the student group No More!

My path to becoming a sociology professor was somewhat of a circuitous one. As a small-town Iowa farm boy, I followed in my brother's and sister's footsteps as first-generation college students. I began undergraduate study in computer engineering at Iowa State University, at the suggestion of my high school guidance counselor. However, it was not what I was passionate about doing. I ended up with a BS in Psychology, with a minor in Design Studies. Still not finding my inspiration, I acquired an MS in College Student Personnel Work and had an early career in student activities and residential life. Being a residence hall director of 4 buildings and 12 resident assistants was the start of my development of a sociological imagination (Mills, 1959). I reflected about how personal biographies and socialization intersect with social norms and culture within institutions to shape group behavior, from the banal and benign, to the life threatening, such as attempted suicides and alcohol poisoning that I had to respond to decisively and quickly in my job. Ultimately, it was not fulfilling, because I wanted to be less reactive and more proactive about making the world a better place.

Before embarking on my trip to the University of Colorado for a PhD in Sociology, I had only completed 3 sociology classes. What drew me to sociology from this limited exposure was the idea of integrating theory and practice with an acute understanding of the intersections between the structural constraints put forth by society and our own ability as individuals, especially in collaboration with others, to affect social change. One of the historical founders of the discipline of sociology, wrote, "The philosophers have only interpreted the world, in various ways; the point is to change it" (Marx, 1845). Inspired by this quote, a few fellow students in my doctoral program and I teamed together to write *The Better World Handbook: From Good Intentions to Everyday Actions* (Jones, Haenfler, Johnson, & Klocke, 2001) before obtaining our PhDs. We were determined to use our studies not only to research abstract sociological ideas but also to put them into concrete social practice. And we wanted to teach others to do the same. The book has been used in many sociology classrooms and by community groups across the United States. Students enjoy it because it offers simple and effective actions that can be implemented in one's daily life to make a difference on numerous social problems. Kevin Danaher, the cofounder of Global Exchange and also a Sociology PhD, described our book as "a 'blueprint' for creating conscious global citizens" (Jones et al., 2001—book cover).

I had long been involved in social justice movements, which taught me things that I could not discover in the classroom. But I also found that my higher education courses taught me how to think more deeply and critically about my social experiences and the social experiences of people I met from other genders (yes there are more than two), racial and ethnic groups, sexual orientations, religions, social classes, physical and cognitive abilities, and more. My study of feminist theory in my graduate program led me to participate in the department's Diversity Committee and to join the department's Feminist Scholars in Sociology (FSS) group. On the Diversity

Committee, I cowrote a grant with a Latina colleague, through which we developed simulation exercises to facilitate undergraduates' cocurricular learning about sexism, classism, racism, and heterosexism so they could start to understand more deeply what was abstractly addressed in sociology classrooms. The interactive exercises were used in campus workshops, giving participants a common tangible experience to draw from when discussing sociological concepts such as institutionalized oppression, discrimination, privilege, social stratification, and social stigma. This helped them experience the issues sociology highlights rather than just hearing about them through a lecture.

Through the FSS, I met the Chair of the National Organization for Men Against Sexism, which is an organization that "advocates a perspective that is pro-feminist, gay affirmative, anti-racist, dedicated to enhancing men's lives, and committed to justice on a broad range of social issues, including class, age, religion, and physical abilities" (nomas.org mission statement). In graduate school, I became a member of the National Council of NOMAS and chair of the Globalization Task Force. I also used my sociological skills as a member of the Colorado Progressive Coalition, whose mission is to organize for low-income, minority, immigrant, LGBT, and youth oriented concerns, and to battle corporate and wealthy interests actively working to maintain or increase systems of oppression.[1] My experiences as a member of these organizations and in peace and global justice movements have helped me further understand the social dynamics of white privilege and male privilege, while also creating a strong foundation for the main ways that I currently put sociology into practice through teaching, advising, and campus activism promoting social justice.

Former American Sociological Association President Michael Burawoy called for "public sociology" that would "transcend the academy and engage wider audiences . . . and challenge the world as we know it, exposing the gap between what is and what could be" (Burawoy, 2004). It is in this spirit that outside the classroom I have been an ongoing participant in the annual Take Back the Night event, an advisor to the student club No More!, and an associate and ally of the Gender and Women's Studies Department. Through these groups, we work towards transforming the campus, the community, and the broader culture of masculinity, to proactively end all forms of sexual and gendered violence. No More!'s mission is "to create a campus and community free of violence by increasing male participation in ending sexual and relationship violence" (The Constitution of No More!). My collaboration with Gender and Women's Studies and Sociology colleagues has helped the group expand and grow in influence

---

[1] http://progressivecoalition.org/

on campus and to transform the lives of men and women as they engage in social action and sociological and feminist study of social problems. No More! facilitates peer education exercises in college classrooms, as well as campus workshops, video discussions, nationally recognized speaker presentations open to the public, and fundraising for the local Violence Intervention Project. In October 2012, for example, No More! collaborated with the Student Activities office to bring documentary filmmaker and anti-sexist activist Byron Hurt to campus to a standing room only crowd of 600 people. The leadership of No More! is often Sociology and/or Gender and Women's Studies majors and minors. The club has brought much awareness to the campus, was runner up for the best club of the year, and has had increasing numbers of students getting involved, as well as taking action in their personal lives.

My work with NOMAS and No More! has caught the attention of the media and has helped us spread our message of ending all forms of sexism and transforming violent masculinity. I was invited by *Huffington Post Live* this year to discuss issues I raised in an article I wrote for the NOMAS newsletter, titled "Roles of Men with Feminism and Feminist Theory" (Klocke, 2001). Unfortunately, on the short notice, I was not able to participate but they posted the article to their website for viewers to read. This provocative piece that I wrote 12 years ago continues to make the rounds through the blogosphere and has been cited in the Sri Lanka *Daily News,* London's *Guardian* newspaper, and Canada's largest daily newspaper, the *Toronto Star.* The club No More! has also written letters published in the campus newspaper criticizing the sexism present in its articles. Their community activism has also been covered in the campus and local newspapers.

One instance where No More! received strong media coverage was for their campaign, in conjunction with the student club Center for Women's Concerns (CWC), addressing the infamous *Girls Gone Wild* (GGW) tour. The GGW video producers' tour bus came to town the weekend of Take Back the Night (an annual event to speak out against sexual violence and sexism) and sponsored a show at a local bar encouraging men "to meet thousands of wild college girls who will do anything to be voted the Hottest Girl in America." Students from CWC and No More! handed out information about sexual assault at the event, were interviewed by local media, and participated in a Take Back the Night march past the event. The secretary of No More! was quoted in *Cardinal Points* (Bilik, 2011), saying "It's a poor choice of entertainment to bring to their club. It perpetuates sexism and violence against women [whom] are seen as objects." We were not able to talk the bar owner out of sponsoring the event, but students raised awareness about the issues by putting them in their broader social context as sociologists in action are called to do.

These students, as sociologists in action, have stood up, spoken out, and broken the silence of the long night, revoking their tacit approval of violence against women and other marginalized groups. They dared to not just imagine a better world but acted to bring it about, one step at a time. They marched through the streets, past the local bar sponsoring *Girls Gone Wild,* chanting "Hey Hey, Ho Ho, Patriarchy has Got to Go!," as others, including some men, came out of their houses and joined in, silent no more. Sociology offers a unique perspective to understanding how culture, social institutions, and social structures reproduce inequality; this perspective avoids victim blaming and shows the importance of collective action and social movements to transform social systems into ones that restrict harm and enable the common good.

References

Bilik, G. (2011, April 14). Wild controversy: 'Girls Gone Wild' tour bus stops in Plattsburgh tonight, *Cardinal Points online.*

Burawoy, M. (2004). 2004 annual Meeting Public Sociologies. *An Invitation to Public Sociology* [Brochure]. Washington, DC: American Sociological Association.

Jones, E., Haenfler, R., Johnson, B., & Klocke, B. (2001). *The better world handbook: From good intentions to everyday actions.* Gabriola Island, Canada: New Society Publishers.

Klocke, B. (2001). Roles of men with feminism and feminist theory. *Brother* (newsletter of the National Organization for Men Against Sexism—NOMAS), *19*, n 2a.

Marx, K. (1845). *Theses on Feuerbach: Thesis 11.* Retrieved from http://www.marxists.org/archive/marx/works/1845/theses/index.htm

Mills, C. W. (1959). *The sociological imagination.* London: Oxford University Press.

On Becoming a Public Sociologist: Amplifying Women's Voices in the Quest for Environmental Justice

Tracy Perkins
University of California, Santa Cruz

Tracy Perkins is a PhD candidate in the Department of Sociology at the University of California, Santa Cruz. She developed and directs *Voices from the Valley* (formerly *25 Stories from the Central Valley*), which uses photography, theater, and a website (www.voicesfromthevalley.org)

to educate students and the general public about environmental justice advocacy in California's San Joaquin Valley. Tracy has worked for Hesperian Health Guides, International Accountability Project, International Rivers, the UC Berkeley Labor Center, and Amigos de las Américas and sits on the board of directors at Greenaction for Health and Environmental Justice.

When I was a teenager, I wanted to change the world. As so many others have discovered before me, however, I found this easier said than done. This quest has taken me to distant lands and back home again, from volunteer organizations to nonprofits, and from unions to academia. Now, I devote most of my time to political issues that reside in the intersections between environmentalism, civil rights, and poverty. Much of this work involves trying to find an appropriate way to work across differences of race, class, language, and national origin, and to be an ally to people most directly impacted by global social problems.

When I first began considering a career in academia, I was full of doubts. At that time, academic writing seemed to me to be written to exclude non-academics and have little connection to the real world, and I wanted to see if there was another way to do it. How could I create a research project that would meet my career goals and also contribute to an improved world? How could I best be of service?

With the collaboration and guidance of many activists, faculty, family and friends,[2] I led the creation of a project called *Voices from the Valley*[3] to help share the life experiences of the people whom I interviewed for my master's thesis—the people most directly impacted by pollution. I wanted to give something back to the women who generously opened their lives up to me and also to find ways to support their work to reduce pollution levels in their communities. Sharing their experiences in a public format was one way to do both.

Our inaugural event at the University of California, Davis, featured the first exhibit of my photos of San Joaquin Valley environmental justice problems and advocates and a moving, interactive performance by Kairos Theater Ensemble. When I look back on that event, one moment stands out in particular. One of the invited activists shared her life story on stage and saw the actors perform it for her and the rest of the audience. She told

---

[2] For a complete list of funders and collaborators, see the project website at: http://www.voicesfrom thevalley.org.

[3] Originally called *25 Stories from the Central Valley*.

us about overcoming great hardship as she crossed into the United States from Mexico, as well as in her life in this country afterward. She described her early and continuing activism as a personal triumph over difficult circumstances. After the actors concluded the scene, which they performed only moments after hearing her story, the director asked if anyone in the audience wanted to share their reflections. One person likened the activist to Rocky, the fictional boxer who achieves greatness from humble beginnings, and the rest of the audience laughed and applauded appreciatively. At the hotel breakfast the next day the activists were still talking about it and calling their friend "Rocky" in loving jest.

How do you evaluate moments like that? What did it mean to the women who saw their lives reenacted on stage or honored through photographs in a gallery space? What might everyone else have learned from bearing witness to their struggles? To be honest, I don't know. Some people in the audience were seeing life experiences similar to their own depicted on stage for the first time, others were learning about issues previously unknown to them, and still others saw how problems they had only read about affected real people. Many were shocked by what they saw and later told me they "didn't know things like this still happened."

Since this project began, the women I interviewed have been part of many different struggles, some of which they won, and some of which they lost. Together, with their male peers and political allies, these advocates helped pass a law to establish a human right to clean drinking water in California, the first of its kind in the nation.[4] They helped fight off legislation that would have brought California's Global Warming Solutions Act of 2006 to a standstill and later sued the state over one of the same law's key provisions.[5] They built community gardens[6] and campaigned against a carcinogenic soil fumigant that was then withdrawn from the market. They saw one of their own appointed to a position within the California Environmental Protection Agency and another to the state's Agricultural Labor Relations Board. I hope *Voices from the Valley* helps honor their struggles, celebrate their accomplishments, and educate the broader public about the vital issues on which they work.

---

[4] Assembly Bill 685, The Human Right to Water Act. See Plevin (2012) and the UN News Center (2012) for more information.

[5] See Terry-Cobo (2011) for more information about the lawsuit.

[6] See California Department of Parks and Recreation (2011) for a description of one of these community gardens.

Like sociology itself, the stories featured in *Voices from the Valley* directly confront the deeply engrained American belief that individuals are exclusively responsible for their own successes and failures in life. They also speak to women's changing role in society by showing them as fully engaged in the political realm. The separation of men into the public sphere of politics and women into the private sphere of the home is still pervasive enough that examples of women actively engaging in politics remain important to share.

But what is it that leads women into the public sphere of environmental justice advocacy? Scholars and journalists have often focused on the role of motherhood in making this leap. They often describe politically inexperienced mothers who become environmental justice activists in order to protect their children and families from environmental threats. However, most of the women I interviewed had political experience before becoming environmental justice activists. They also had broad social justice motivations for their political action that went beyond a desire to protect their children and families, if indeed they had children at all (Perkins, 2012). This matters because depicting women activists primarily as mothers can reinforce stereotypes about women, even though it may also help their immediate goal of limiting pollution by showing them in a sympathetic light that conforms to traditional gender roles. If I had created *Voices from the Valley* without simultaneously conducting a rigorous academic research project that led me to question the conventional wisdom about women environmental justice advocates, I likely would have featured children and motherhood much more heavily on the website and in the photo exhibit. Instead, these themes are present but do not dominate.

There are endless possibilities of how sociological work can combine with the arts and the media to contribute to social change, directly or indirectly. Nonetheless, academics and our community partners cannot solve the ills of the world through a single project. After our inaugural event, the activists were celebrated but then went home the next day to communities still plagued by contaminated drinking water, air pollution, pesticide drift, and health problems. The academics by and large went home to relatively safe and clean communities. Still, I can't help but think that something special has happened through this project. We created what Émile Durkheim might have called moments of collective effervescence that help keep us moving forward, together, in our long, painstaking efforts to make a better world.

Since our first event, my collaborators and I have organized several other theatrical events and photo exhibits. I have also found ways to extend the impact of the project through writing,[7] teaching, public speaking, social

---

[7] See "Images from the Central Valley" by Perkins and Sze (2011) in *Boom: A Journal of California.*

media, and continued development of the project website. The website now features a digital photo exhibit; an interactive photo and oral history collage; a searchable, curated San Joaquin Valley environmental justice news feed and archive; a slideshow of the theater events; a collection of teaching assignments and activities for use in college classrooms; an environmental justice syllabus collection; a map of the San Joaquin Valley towns where I took photos and collected stories; and a list of groups working toward environmental justice in the San Joaquin Valley with links to their websites and social media channels. Since the beginning of the project, I have also been invited to sit on the board of directors of Greenaction for Health and Environmental Justice, one of the nonprofits with which I collaborated on *Voices from the Valley.* Greenaction provides on-the-ground support to communities battling incinerators, hazardous waste sites, nuclear facilities, and a host of other environmental and cultural threats. I am happy to have this new way to give back to the communities in which my research takes place.

As my goal of doing community-engaged research has come to fruition, I have also begun to better value the role of traditional research in social change. The complexity of humanity's intellectual history, and the way that scholarship sometimes follows and sometimes leads change, was opaque to me when I began graduate school but is now becoming increasingly clear.

Change doesn't happen overnight, but it does happen. I often look to the oral histories I collected for this project as a reminder to be patient and to keep up my efforts over the long haul. For example, San Joaquin Valley native Debbie Reyes took the long view when she told me about her many years of activism:

> I used to think, "This place will never change," you know? But I've seen a tremendous change from the first year I got back, thirteen years ago, to now. Then, the Ku Klux Klan was standing on the corner of a gay pride parade; now we have Rally in the Valley, which is like a peace march. We had the Environmental Justice Network Conference. We're having the Uncaging the Valley prisons conference, Black and Brown Unity Marchers. And now, here I'm sitting at a table with folks that are working to create change in the state to regulate pesticide spraying in communities. So inside I was going, "Yeah, finally!" It's taken 25 years but here we are.

> —*Fresno, CA. 2007*

By the time I am Debbie's age, I hope I can look back and see that the world is a safer, cleaner place and know that I played a small part, along with so many others, in making it happen. I work towards a better world through my teaching, research, writing, and community work. Public sociology provides me with a community of kindred spirits traveling similar paths and helps me keep the faith when the future looks bleak.

References

California Department of Parks and Recreation. (2011, October 10). Colonel Allensworth State Historical Park and local residents of Allensworth come together for mutual benefit. Retrieved from http://www.parks.ca.gov/pages/712/files/2011Community%20Garden%20Program.pdf

Plevin, R. (2012, October 2). California takes historic step in safe water for all. *Vida en el Valle.* Retrieved from http://www.vidaenelvalle.com/2012/10/02/1331243/california-takes-historic-step.html

Perkins, T. (2012). Women's pathways into activism: Rethinking the women's environmental justice narrative in California's San Joaquin Valley. *Organization & Environment, 25*(1),76–94.

Perkins, T., & Sze, J. (2011). Images from the central valley. *Boom: A Journal of California, 1*(1), 70–80.

Terry-Cobo, S. (2011, February 9). Lawsuit by low-income groups may delay climate law. *California Watch.* Retrieved from http://californiawatch.org/dailyreport/lawsuit-low-income-groups-may-delay-climate-law-8582

UN News Center. (2012, September 28). California law on human right to water sets example for others—UN expert. Retrieved from http://www.un.org/apps/news/story.asp?NewsID=43118&Cr=water+and+sanitation&Cr1=#.UPskR6HjkwG

Talking the Talk and Walking the Walk: Linking Research and Action on Domestic Violence

Margaret Abraham
Hofstra University

Margaret Abraham is Professor of Sociology and Special Advisor to the Provost for Diversity Initiatives at Hofstra University, New York. She is Vice President for Research of the International Sociological Association (2010–2014). As an action researcher committed to bringing about social change, she frequently writes, speaks publicly, teaches courses, facilitates workshops, and consults on national projects related to domestic violence. Her teaching and research interests include gender, ethnicity, globalization, immigration, and domestic violence, and she is a widely published and an award winning author, an activist, a mother, and a community worker. She is particularly interested in violence against women in South Asian communities in the United States.

My first formal introduction to sociology was as a student in high school in India and it was to be the start of a long-term relationship with the discipline that has lasted over three decades. I was initially attracted to sociology because it taught me how to critically examine social phenomena that are frequently taken for granted and also helped explain the larger historical, social, economic, and political contexts of the world we live in. What sustains my commitment to sociology is the dynamic nature of the field and the incredible opportunity that it offers to combine sociological theory and practice for social transformation.

Particularly exciting for me are the ways that being grounded in sociology, while also drawing on other disciplines, enables me to combine teaching, research, and activism on social justice issues to help bring about social change. Perhaps as you are reading this you may be thinking that I am getting a bit carried away in my passion for sociology and its transformative potential for the public good without really explaining why and how. So I'll try to share with you the trailer version of how I came to be a sociologist in action in addressing the pressing issue of domestic violence.

My research was the first sociological study of domestic violence in an immigrant community frequently called a "model minority" in the United States—specifically the South Asian immigrant community. My research interest on marital violence among South Asian immigrants started in 1989 when I began teaching courses on family issues from a cross-cultural perspective and discussing issues of domestic violence with friends who were volunteers at a women's shelter. The sheer enormity of the problem led me to begin a serious review of the literature on domestic violence. What became increasingly clear was that while there was considerable scholarship on domestic violence, there was little research on its prevalence among ethnic minorities. Around the same time, through the media and several talks I attended, I learned of South Asian organizations that were addressing the problem of domestic violence within South Asian communities in the United States. These included Manavi in New Jersey, Apna Ghar in Chicago, Sakhi in New York, SEWAA in Philadelphia, Sneha in Connecticut, and Maitri and Narika in California, with many more organizations to emerge in the years to come.

My entrée in the field of domestic violence was primarily as a researcher. In the early stages of this research, however, I found myself being asked by some South Asian activists whether my work as a sociologist would be accessible to a larger audience than academics and how it would help abused South Asian women and immigrant communities in bringing about social change. This question, together with discussions with academics, friends, and activists, influenced me to critically reflect on my roles as a sociologist and as a South Asian immigrant woman working in the United

States. Over the years I have increasingly come to see myself as a sociologist engaged in action research, committed to bridging the gap between scholarship and activism in addressing social justice issues.

There are four main ways in which I have been engaged in action research that I will discuss here: as a scholar, public speaker, domestic violence expert, and teacher.

As a scholar, my research on domestic violence in the South Asian Diaspora in the United States contributed to expanding the scholarship in new ways. I introduced the term SAWO (South Asian Women's Organizations) in a paper presentation at the Eastern Sociological Society meetings in 1993, and it is a term used widely today. My research resulted in the first book length monograph on domestic violence among the South Asian Diaspora in the United States called *Speaking the Unspeakable: Marital Violence Among South Asian Immigrants in the United States* (Abraham, 2000). *Speaking the Unspeakable* was based on in-depth interviews with abused immigrant women and surveys and participation observation with SAWOs committed to ending domestic violence.

This research pointed to the need to reconceptualize the problem of domestic violence. While early analyses of domestic violence examined differences in power, privilege, and control, my research emphasized that these forces cannot be understood, relevant to immigrant populations, without taking into account the intersections of citizenship, ethnicity, language, religion, race, class, and gender at the individual, interpersonal, and institutional levels. Researching SAWOs and working closely with Sakhi for South Asian Women in New York also provided important sociological insights into the complex linkages between ideology, structure, goals, strategies, decision making, and outcomes for South Asian Women's organizations addressing violence against ethnic minority women.

My research sought to effectively capture the subtleties of culture and structure and the varying situational contexts that frequently elude large-scale data collection. For me, our understanding of violence would be incomplete without an account of the experiences of those who are often deemed "invisible others" because of their ethnicity, race, class, and legal status.

Drawing on an intersectional analysis and looking to explore outcomes of power for abused South Asian women, my intent was to show how each individual woman's oppression is closely interlocked with cultural and structural oppression in the United States. In addition, it drew attention to the pivotal role played by SAWOs in defining domestic violence in the South Asian community as a social problem.

The second way that I have been engaged in action research, moving toward becoming a sociologist in action, has been as a public speaker.

Some of the South Asian women's organizations encouraged me to speak about marital violence at various public forums. I have spoken at universities, community events, fundraisers, events sponsored by law enforcement agencies, and to medical organizations. Public speaking on domestic violence allows me an important avenue to share my ongoing research with a broader audience than academics. It helps shift domestic violence from being a private problem to a public issue, following the works of C. Wright Mills. My interactions with abused South Asian women, with activists and the various audiences at my public talks have been extremely informative and empowering, both from a sociological and a personal perspective. They have reinforced the value of disseminating our research beyond academia to increase public awareness of social problems and creating avenues for social change.

Stemming from my research and public speaking, the media have picked up on the topic (and on my work), thus increasing the visibility of the problem and the work being done by community-based organizations in addressing domestic violence. Some of these media outlets have included: *India Abroad*, *The New York Times*, *The Chicago Tribune*, *News India-Times*, *Malayalam Pathram*, *Newsday*, and *CNN*.

The third way that I have been able to offer my services is as a domestic violence expert in cases where abused South Asian immigrant women have sought recourse through the judicial system. The opportunity to address groups of lawyers and judges about domestic violence has allowed me to draw on my research and that of other scholars and community activists. In doing so, I hope to increase their understanding of the complex cultural and structural factors facing abused South Asian immigrant women so that they might better address the multiple barriers that these women encounter navigating the courts. I was particularly fortunate to speak to a large audience of judges in 2001 at the New York State Judicial Committee on Women in the Courts: "Courts' Response to Violence Against Women: Progress and Future."

I have also testified in courts, providing written documentation and oral input, and have been involved on Advisory Boards on projects funded by the National Institute for Justice (NIJ). I have also served as a consultant on an NIJ funded project conducted by National Center for State Courts (NCSC) on *Serving Limited English Proficient (LEP) Battered Women: A National Survey of the Courts' Capacity to Provide Protection Orders 2006*.[8] The report was shared with site participants and put online. Information on this project was included in a press release and regular NCSC press publications

---

[8] The NIJ report can be found at http://cdm16501.contentdm.oclc.org/cdm/ref/collection/accessfair/id/26.

targeting key constituents, justices, judges, court administrators, court managers, and court staff. I believe that this report also contributed to the momentum to address LEP issues in the courts. For instance, starting in 2012, the NCSC and the Center for Court Innovation are collaborating to strengthen language access services in the court system, creating new trainings for community based interpreters and new tools to enhance the court's capacity on language access.

Finally, I have been able to link my research interests with my teaching through a seminar on violence against women. I believe that the importance of our research is matched by the value of our teaching, and teaching such courses is an integral part of action research. The course examines the different sociological perspectives on violence, with a special emphasis on domestic violence. Students explore the different manifestations of violence against women from historical, cultural, and contemporary perspectives. Through this course, my students and I learn from each other about how sociology offers important ways to examine, understand, and influence the world we live in. I have also spoken at different universities, and I am always gratified when it is students and student organizations that have played an instrumental role in bringing me to their university to discuss the ways that we can work together to address the problem of domestic violence and violence against women.

Over the years, I have been lucky to have an opportunity to think about the possibilities of how to further and more effectively partner with the broader public in the struggle for social justice. I feel very fortunate, albeit at times a little overwhelmed, that my action research has allowed me as a sociologist to contribute to the discourse on domestic violence while simultaneously providing an important avenue to apply it more concretely in the struggle to end violence against women. For me, as a sociologist, it is important to talk the talk and walk the walk! I know we can make a difference through our action research, and I hope that many of you students and future sociologists will engage in social justice issues and offer us new ways to link research and action for a more just world!

References

Abraham, M. (2000). *Speaking the unspeakable: Marital violence among South Asian immigrants in the United States*. New Brunswick, NJ: Rutgers University Press.

Abraham, M. (2001). *Courts' response to violence against women: Progress and future*. Address given to the New York State Judicial Committee on Women in the Courts.

Transforming Rape Culture on a College Campus: Using Peer Advocacy for Social Change

Linda J. Olson
Castleton State College

Linda J. Olson earned her PhD from the University of New Hampshire and is currently a Professor of Sociology and Women's and Gender Studies at Castleton State College in Vermont. She has won numerous awards for her teaching and activism. She is also the President of the Vermont State Colleges Faculty Federation—Local 3180.[9]

C. Wright Mills had a deep understanding of how our personal lives are touched and shaped by outside social forces; that our biographies are intertwined with our history. Indeed, this appreciation of the connection between our private troubles and public issues is the essence of what Mills defined as the sociological imagination (Mills, 1959). Feminists in the second wave of the feminist movement[10] had a similar appreciation for these connections as evidenced in the slogan "The Personal is Political." Most of the scholarship and activism I have engaged in over the past 20 years has been informed by these assumptions.

I have been collaborating with students about issues such as sexual assault, harassment, stalking, and relationship violence since I started at Castleton State College in 1995. This collaboration is apparent in the work I have done in the creation of both the CHANGE Initiative (Creating, Honoring, Advocating and Nurturing Gender Equity) and PAC (Peer Advocates for CHANGE). The CHANGE Initiative was formed in 2008 to promote gender equity, and PAC, the student activist and advocacy branch of CHANGE, began in 2009. CHANGE and PAC use a model of engagement which draws on and fosters the sociological imagination, enabling students to see how their individual experiences are caught up in larger

---

[9] This piece is dedicated to CHANGE Coordinators Jaklyn VanManen and Amy Bremel as well as all the Castleton PAC students.

[10] The second wave of the feminist movement took place in the 1960s and 1970s. They fought to attain legal rights in areas such as access to education, jobs, and reproductive rights. The focus of the first wave of the feminist movement was suffrage. We are currently in the third wave of the feminist movement, which seeks to overcome the shortcomings of the second wave; specifically by incorporating diversity and rejecting the idea that there is one universal notion of "feminism."

social forces. PAC student Jojo Barrale gained insight into her own biography by placing herself in her history:

> I have gotten so much out of PAC by being a member because it has helped me realize some very important personal things about my life. I also enjoy doing programming and knowing that I have helped spread awareness around this campus.

Through CHANGE and PAC, students are working to actively change campus culture to reduce sexual and relationship violence while also creating a matrix of support for survivors of these issues.

Rape Culture and Campus Life: Defining the Scope of the Problem

In a recent study, the National Institute of Justice estimated that one-fifth to one-fourth of women are the victims of completed or attempted rape while in college (Fisher, Cullen, & Turner, 2000). Young women between the ages of 16 and 24 experience the highest rates of violence from intimate partners (Seely, 2007, p. 191). Research on sexual assault on college campuses indicates that most of the rapes and attempted rapes that occur can be attributed to a small percentage of men who engage in predatory behavior and offend multiple times (Lisak & Miller, 2002; Lisak, 2010). Despite the fact that very few men commit acts that meet the legal definition of rape, I contend that there is a climate that can only be described as a "rape culture" on college campuses.

A rape culture normalizes sexual violence (Buchwald, Fletcher, & Roth, 1993). We see this in advertisements, video games, movies, and music videos, to name a few sources. As a result, we don't take sexual violence seriously as a crime, or we tend to blame the victim for this type of violence. Rape is the only crime where the victim's actions are scrutinized as much as, or sometimes even more than, the perpetrator's. We ask questions such as what was she wearing, why was she drinking, why was she out so late, why was she in his room? We don't do this for any other crime.

A rape culture also causes people to remain silent when they witness these crimes. A horrific example of this bystander mentality is the recent rape of a 16 year old in Steubenville, Ohio. The girl was incapacitated, and her recently convicted rapists carried her unconscious body from party to party for six hours. Others not only watched but posted the events online. Postings included tweets such as "The song of the night is 'Rape Me' by Nirvana" and, in response to reports that the men urinated on their unconscious victim, "Some girls deserve to be peed on." A 12 minute video was also released on YouTube of a young man laughing and joking about the unconscious state of the victim stating things like: "She's deader than OJ Simpson's ex-wife; she's deader than Kaylee Anthony." The video is disturbing enough, but in the background you hear the laughter and encouragement of several other young men, many of whom talk about what happened to the victim as rape. This mentality is the outcome of a rape culture.

"CHANGE"ing Campus Culture

The educational programming we use in the CHANGE Initiative targets bystanders, those who stand by in silence. It has been shown that bystanders can effectively deter crimes, such as rape, not only through direct interventions but also by reporting crimes to authorities. Ultimately, a climate that does not accept such crimes is created. This environment can dissuade criminals, such as rapists, from committing a crime by convincing them that they are in a "highly risky" situation (Banyard, Plante, & Moynihan, 2005).

The goal of our programming is twofold: We want to tackle the rape culture by dispelling myths about sexual violence and give our students the language for intervention when they see a potentially dangerous situation. I also encourage my PAC students to establish their own gender equity programming.

This programming encompasses a number of issues, including national campaigns such as the Hands are not for Hurting campaign and Take Back the Night, which focus on relationship and sexual violence; the You are Loved campaign, which supports the LGBTQ population; and other sex positive programming. It is important that students not see us as just the "antirape" group. The sex positive programming, for example, stresses there is nothing wrong with sex as long as it is safe and consensual. In fact, our most popular program is our "got consent?" campaign. This campaign explains what consent is and is not. During this program students can also win the highly coveted t-shirts that say "got consent?" on the front and "Without consent it's not sex" on the back.

CHANGE has also expanded its programming to emphasize healthy relationships and has started offering some of this programming to younger populations. For example, one of our PAC students worked with a teacher at a local middle school to rework the national Hands are not for Hurting campaign to make it age appropriate for that population. Another student did a similar project with a program called Mentor Connector, which works with at-risk K–12 students. Our rationale is that the younger people are when they learn about healthy relationships the less likely they will be to tolerate unhealthy ones.

Our programs are designed to change a culture that tolerates sexual violence and relationship violence. To determine its effectiveness, one must assess whether or not the programs are changing the attitudes and perceptions that contribute to the problem. In 2010, two years after our program began, Castleton student Courtney Pitts and I conducted a study using the Rape Myth Acceptance Survey. Students who had gone through the CHANGE programming were much less likely to believe in rape myths. In fact, whether or not the students had completed the program accounted for the largest difference in student acceptance of rape myths, even compared to gender, year in school, major, or other variables. CHANGE students were also more likely to have the language for intervention in a potentially dangerous situation, and indicated that they would be more likely to intervene on behalf of someone else. This is the good news; our program is changing campus culture.

Creating a Matrix of Support

Besides reducing problems such as sexual and relationship violence, CHANGE also aims to create a supportive climate for those who are already survivors. We want to create a campus where victims feel they can come forward and report what happened to them and where survivors have access to the continuing support they need. To create a matrix of support, it is important to bring all constituencies on board—administrators, faculty, staff, student leaders, and the larger community. It is also important that we make the administration understand that if we are effective in creating this matrix, sexual assaults will actually go up officially because more will feel comfortable reporting.

The educational outreach we do is one way to create this climate, because education establishes the foundation for empathy for survivors. Also, our Peer Advocates have gone through 25 hours of training to make them an invaluable resource for survivors. PAC students are on call 24 hours a day, 7 days a week to answer questions, provide resources, and provide support. The training they go through includes tackling the rape culture; the construction of masculinity and femininity; research on sexual assault on college campuses; the power and control wheel for relationship violence;[11] what a rape kit examination entails; and empathic listening. They are trained to advocate for students in all capacities, from the campus

---

[11] The power and control wheel is a tool developed by the Domestic Abuse Intervention Project in Duluth, MN. The wheel is used to help people understand the patterns of relationship violence. You can find this and other resources at http://www.theduluthmodel.org.

courts to assisting a student in attaining a relief from abuse order to supporting them through a rape exam.

Looking Ahead

We still have work to do on these issues at Castleton, but I have seen dramatic changes on campus. When we started CHANGE in 2008, I did most of the work with the help of a dedicated work study student, Jaklyn VanManen. When it was time for her to graduate, we convinced the administration that the work she was doing was so valuable that they created a part-time position for her after graduation, and eventually a full time Coordinator position with full benefits. Jaklyn has since moved on to graduate school, but we have been so fortunate to have found an equally dedicated CHANGE Coordinator in Amy Bremel. The work of these two women, combined with the considerable efforts of committed students, has created a sustainable initiative that will live on. This initiative illustrates the kind of engagement that the sociological imagination can foster. I have always believed, as C. Wright Mills did, that a group of committed and educated individuals can create real social change. CHANGE and PAC have worked diligently to dismantle the rape culture on campus while creating a supportive climate for survivors so they know they are not alone. It has been a privilege playing a role in this effort, and I continue to be inspired by the passion and dedication of my students.

References

Banyard, V. L., Plante, E. G., & Moynihan, M. (2005). *Rape prevention through bystander education: Bringing a broader community perspective to sexual violence prevention*. Durham: University of New Hampshire.

Buchwald, E., Fletcher, P., & Roth, M. (1993). *Transforming a rape culture*. Minneapolis, MN: Milkweed Editions.

Fisher, B., Cullen, F., & Turner, M. (2000). *The sexual victimization of college women*. Washington, DC: National Institute of Justice and the Bureau of Justice Statistics.

Lisak, D., & Miller, P. M.. (2002). Repeat rape and multiple offending among undetected rapists. *Violence and Victims, 17*, 73–84.

Lisak, D. (2010). Behind the torment of rape victims lies a dark fear: Reply to the commentaries. *Violence Against Women, 16*(12), 1372–1374.

Mills, C. W. (1959). *The sociological imagination*. New York: Oxford University Press.

Seely, M. (2007). *Fight like a girl: How to be a fearless feminist*. New York: New York University Press.

Discussion Questions

1. What is "pinkwashing"? Describe how Amy Lubitow used sociological tools to combat it. How did her collaboration with activist Mia Davis make her work more effective?

2. According to Lubitow, why might some companies be more interested in helping create a cure for cancer than in preventing it? How can you help in the effort to expose pinkwashing?

3. What were Mazhar Bağlı's key findings about those who perpetrate honor killings? How do they indicate that honor killings are a societal, rather than an individual problem? What implications do they have for those who wish to create policies that will reduce the number of honor killings?

4. How does the widespread acceptance of honor killings in a society, as detailed by Bağlı, highlight the impact of gender socialization on both the society and on individual men and women in that society? Provide an example of how gender socialization impacts gender inequality (a) on your campus and (b) in U.S. society.

5. How did sociology help Brian Klocke move from being reactive to proactive about addressing social problems? What is one social problem you would like to use sociological tools to try to address? Why?

6. Klocke is a member of the National Organization of Men Against Sexism. What is your reaction when you hear the name of this organization? Why? Do you consider yourself a feminist? Why or why not?

7. According to Tracy Perkins, how can depicting female environmental activists primarily as mothers reinforce gender stereotypes? How did she avoid doing so herself? How can social science research help you counter gender stereotypes in your field of interest?

8. How has Perkins used theatre and other visual mediums to bring attention to the effort of environmental activists in the San Joaquin Valley? How have these means of expression helped spread her social scientific findings? How are they examples of public sociology?

9. What are some of the ways Margaret Abraham has brought attention to domestic abuse among South Asian immigrants? Can you imagine doing the same for the ethnic group(s) to which you belong? Why or why not?

10. According to Abraham, how might it be particularly difficult for immigrant women of color, with limited English proficiency, to escape from domestic violence? Imagine you are a sociologist who has been asked to formulate three social policies to address domestic violence among these groups of women. What policies would you suggest?

11. What are some of the outcomes of the rape culture that Linda Olson describes in her piece? Do you see signs of a rape culture on your campus? If so, describe them. If not, describe how your campus has been able to effectively diminish the prevailing rape culture in the larger society. Did reading Olson's

piece change your perspective on the influence of culture on the prevalence of rape in (a) the larger society and (b) your campus? Why or why not? What can *you* do to counter a rape culture?

12. Why is it important for programs to measure their effectiveness? According to Olson, how did CHANGE measure the program's impact? What were their findings?

Resources

ASA Sex and Gender Section

American Sociological Association section encouraging research and curriculum development on gender and sexuality. Includes the section newsletter and good resources and links.

http://www2.asanet.org/sectionsexgend

Equality Now

Works to achieve legal and systemic change that addresses violence and discrimination against women and girls around the world. Offers actions, campaigns, issue briefs, and resources.

http://www.equalitynow.org

Feminist Majority Foundation

Dedicated to women's equality, the organization utilizes research and action to empower women economically, socially, and politically. Believes that feminists—women and men, girls and boys—are the majority, but that this majority must be empowered. Offers an events calendar, a news room, reports and resources, actions, a research center, and a career center.

http://www.feminist.org

Honour Based Violence Awareness Network

An international digital resource center working to advance understanding of honor based violence and forced marriage through research, documentation, information, and trainings. Offers webinars, videos, research reports, trainings, and useful links.

http://hbv-awareness.com

Institute for Women's Policy Research

Conducts research and disseminates its findings to address the needs of women, promote public dialog, and strengthen families, communities, and societies. Focus areas include: employment, education, and economic change; democracy and society; poverty, welfare, and income security; work and family; and health and safety. Offers newsletters, resources, a data center, and research publications.

http://www.iwpr.org

National Committee on Pay Equity

Coalition of women's and civil rights organizations, labor unions, and other key constituents working to eliminate sex- and race-based wage discrimination and to achieve pay equity. Works toward closing the wage gap that still exists between women and men. Offers pay equity data and reports, an action center, and an equal pay day campaign.

http://www.pay-equity.org

National Organization for Women

The largest organization of feminist activists in the United States, founded in 1966. Takes action to bring about equality for all women and promotes gender equality and justice in the United States. Website offers actions, campaigns, issue areas, university chapters, and resources.

http://now.org

National Women's Law Center

Works to expand, protect, and promote opportunity and advancement for women and girls through research, analysis, and advocacy. Conducts campaigns and public awareness efforts to educate and mobilize the public to press for policy changes to improve women's lives. Resources include webinars, videos, fact sheets, reports, toolkits, legal briefs and testimony, and a take action center.

http://www.nwlc.org

Think Before You Pink

Breast Cancer Action organization working to expose companies who at once run pink-ribbon campaigns to help fight breast cancer while at the same time producing the very products linked to causing breast cancer. Offers campaigns and educational resources.

http://thinkbeforeyoupink.org

Title IX

Explains what Title IX is and focuses on ten areas in which Title IX has made a difference. Offers videos, legal case reviews, news articles, and links about Title IX.

http://www.titleix.info

Women's Policy, Inc.

Nonpartisan organization working to ensure that policymakers at the federal, state, and local levels make informed decisions on key women's issues. Researches relevant issues and produces legislative analysis, issue summaries, and impact assessments.

http://www.womenspolicy.org/site/PageServer

Women's Studies/Women's Issues Resource Sites

Selective, annotated listing of websites containing resources and information about women's studies and women's issues. Resources are broken into broad categories.

http://userpages.umbc.edu/~korenman/wmst/links.html

4

Sexuality

O ur sexuality, how we express ourselves sexually, and to whom we are
attracted, has a wide range of implications for our lives. As we write
these words, 14 nations across the globe and 16 states and the District of
Columbia in the United States have legalized gay marriage. The U.S. Federal
government now recognizes same-sex marriages and confers federal marriage benefits to same-sex married couples. Still, there are large areas of
the world in which those who are not heterosexual are at risk. Ironically,
in a world where sexual images are used to sell many products, discomfort
often accompanies discussions about sexuality. Sexual issues, from sexual
orientation to sexual diseases, still tend to be hard for many people to talk
about and often lead to stigmatization. The pieces in this chapter deal with
issues of sexuality in a straightforward way and show how sociologists can
help address issues of inequality related to sexuality.

Crystal Jackson starts off this chapter with "Being an Academic Ally:
Gender Justice for Sex Workers." In her piece, Jackson describes how
engaging in participatory activist research with advocates for sex workers
allowed her "both to engage as an ally and to gain sociological insight into
how social institutions and norms shape the struggles of sex workers." As
Jackson explains, she was interested in researching sex workers "because of
the stereotypes held in the mainstream about who sex workers are and the
types of work that they do," and she also realized that she was fortunate
enough to have gained the trust of this community through her previous
work as an ally. Through her work, Jackson challenges the myths that help
strengthen the oppression of sex workers. She also works directly with local
service agencies addressing rape and domestic violence to ensure that sex
workers, too, can benefit from these services that are often unavailable to

them. In doing so, Jackson helps give voice to a largely silenced minority group.

Juan Battle and Antonio (Jay) Pastrana have also helped shine a light on a marginalized group: LGBT people of color. In "Disrupting a Narrative: Developing a New Discourse of Empowerment for LGBT People of Color," they describe how they became committed to conducting research on this group in a way that "disrupts" the existing narrative that pathologizes LGBT people. They work closely with members of this community to conduct research from the perspective of LGBT people of color. In doing so, they also keep in mind that members of this group have multiple identities that can "be fluid, relational, and dependent on the social context." Together, they developed the Social Justice Sexuality (SJS) Survey, a multi-year study that reached almost 5,000 individuals across the United States. Their research has been influential in the ongoing work of organizations supporting LGBT people of color, through informing understandings of needs and challenges, supporting policy and advocacy initiatives, and providing key data for campaigns for civil rights.

In the next piece, "Indian Blood: Two-Spirit Cultural Dissolution, Mixed-Race Identity, and Sexuality—A Journey of Return," Andrew Jolivette describes the research he conducted to better understand and to help end the "health disparities and sexual discrimination faced by LGBTQ mixed-race Native Americans." Jolivette worked with a community-based organization, the Native American AIDS Project (NAAP) and shared his own relevant experiences with his respondents. In doing so, he stresses his desire to conduct research *with* rather than on the community he studies. Through his research, Jolivette discovered that "mixed-blood American Indian queer people are experiencing ruptures in their social and cultural support networks that under normal circumstances would serve as protective factors against external discrimination." He is now using his findings to work with community partners toward creating new programs to address the needs of mixed-blood people who are also LGBTQ.

Jennifer Reed describes how she used social scientific evidence and her experience with political activism to influence policy decisions in "Sex Work and Sex Trafficking: Influencing State Policy on a Complex Social Issue." Reed maintains that not all sex work is akin to that forced on people through human trafficking. She cites research that shows that most teenagers engaged in sex work do not have pimps who force them to sell their bodies. Instead, they are struggling to support themselves without a safety net. Reed determined that a proposed bill on sex trafficking in Nevada would harm rather than help many sex workers. So she devised a plan to work with others to share this information with policy makers.

She coordinated with other activists, used social media to get her message out, met personally with legislators, and shared social scientific findings with the Nevada State Legislature. Reed's efforts helped lead to a substantial revision of the bill on sex trafficking and the removal of parts of the proposed bill that would have harmed many sex workers.

In "From Damaged Goods to Empowered Patients," Adina Nack shares her story of how her own diagnosis with a cervical human papillomavirus (HPV) infection led her to recognize, firsthand, the stigma associated with women who have sexually transmitted infections (STIs) and the need to address this social issue. It also prompted her to take action by conducting a study of women with genital herpes or HPV that resulted in a number of articles and her book *Damaged Goods: Women Living With Incurable Sexually Transmitted Diseases* (2008). Being willing to publicize her own HPV status has helped Nack enable others to see the connection between the personal troubles of women with STIs and the societal issues of sexism and the stigmatization of women. She states, "If 'knowledge is power,' then I hope that my research, writing projects, and applied collaborations empower not only STI patients but also increase the chances that those who struggle with stigmatizing illnesses can enjoy healthier and happier lives." Nack argues "that destigmatizing STIs, in all social venues, requires us to challenge traditional or sexist norms about sexual relationships and sexual health." In the process, she has given both hope and a voice to women with STIs.

Being an Academic Ally: Gender Justice for Sex Workers

Crystal A. Jackson
John Jay College of Criminal Justice

Crystal A. Jackson is an Assistant Professor of Sociology at the John Jay College of Criminal Justice. She studies the law, work, and culture of sexual labor. Her current research analyzes U.S. sex worker rights activism as a form of labor activism. Jackson is coauthor of *The State of Sex: Tourism, Sex, and Sin in the New American Heartland* (2010), an ethnographic exploration of the only legal sale of sex in the United States—Nevada's legal, rural brothels.

In July 2006, I sat at the registration desk of the first National Sex Worker Rights Conference, hosted by Desiree Alliance, a newly formed organization. My friend and I, both feminist students at the University of Nevada, Las Vegas (UNLV), checked in sex workers, activists, academics, and harm-reduction workers—with many of the registrants fitting more than one of these categories. Meeting leading activists like sexologist Carol Queen and long-time sex worker rights activist Carol Leigh (a.k.a. Scarlot Harlot) left us starstruck. But as a newbie to sex worker rights activism, I was still learning about the people included under the umbrella term "sex work." It turns out that there is a wide range of jobs, some criminalized, some legal, from selling sex to erotic dancing to professional domination service, just to name a few. Often, sex workers work indoors and arrange "dates" online. The people who work in this industry are quite diverse: cisgender and trans-gender women; cisgender men;[1] gay, straight, bi, and queer; white, black, Asian American, Latina/o; and a diverse age range, including students. It was one of the most diverse conferences I have ever attended.

I first became involved with the Desiree Alliance after one of the cofounders reached out to those of us in the sociology department at UNLV who study sexual labor. Because I worked so closely with her, I was listed as a founding member. (I also suspect that she felt that including allies with a university affiliation helped legitimate their cause.) For the 2006 confer-ence, I helped with local arrangements, found an LGBTQ bar and dance club for the after-party and fundraiser, and volunteered in any way I could. I didn't want to be a part of the Desiree Alliance because I identify as a sex worker but because I have friends who are erotic dancers, escorts, and adult film performers. I proudly wore a "Sluts Unite" shirt that I bought at the conference, until it frayed years later.

Flash forward to 2010 when I was in search of a dissertation topic. Having studied legal brothels, strip club regulations, and adult film, I knew I would focus on some aspect of sexual labor, stigma, and the law. I bounced ideas around with my advisor: Should I study the experiences of transgender women who sell sex? Should I build on our previous research on Nevada's legal brothel industry? I kept coming back to the sex workers rights movement and the Desiree Alliance.

I was inspired to do research on sex worker rights activists because of the stereotypes held in the mainstream about who sex workers are and the types of work that they do. Also, from a methodological standpoint, I was lucky enough to have access to a group of people traditionally wary of academics. In fact, several sex workers and sex worker rights activists

---

[1] "Cisgender" and "transgender" and terms used to designate gender identity. Cisgender people identify with the gender assigned to them at birth. Transgender people have a different gender identity than the one assigned to them at birth.

have shared stories with me about giving interviews to scholars, only to find their words twisted to match the popular cultural "prostitution mythology"[2] that all sex workers are victims, or that they all go into sexual labor because of current or previous abuse, or current drug use. I wanted to use my research to provide a more holistic voice, representing the sex workers as the diverse group of people they are.

As part of my dissertation research, I interviewed Audacia Ray, head of the Red Umbrella Project, an organization that provides media and legislative training for sex workers—in addition to hosting a monthly cultural event where sex workers share their stories. Ray shared her hesitancy to take part in academic interviews, saying, "I don't talk to that many researchers these days. I used to do this much more often. But now it's just like, I never see the end result, not just with researchers, but people who are making documentaries, all these projects that I've been interviewed for over the years. I've never seen the end result and I don't know how they help us." This worried me. How can I be both an activist and "utilize" my activist friends for my individual scholarly pursuits? What does it even mean to be an *academic* ally to a social issue or organization?

In activist circles, an ally is a member of the dominant group who recognizes their unearned privilege and actively supports the efforts and struggles of the oppressed group. For example, as a white woman, I engage in antiracism work. Another example is the multitude of straight allies who engage in LGBTQ rights efforts. As an academic ally, I decided to use a method called participatory activist research. Participatory activist research means I can take an explicitly political stance for gender justice through scholarship.[3] It is my hope that the research I conduct will have a positive real world impact for the group I am studying.

According to feminist sociologist Nancy Naples, participatory activist researchers engage *with* the organizations they study, not just as outsiders looking in but as members of that group.[4] Participating in the Desiree Alliance has allowed me both to engage as an ally and to gain sociological insight into how social institutions and norms shape the struggles of sex workers. Instead of viewing the exchange of money for sexual services as a form of violence against women, I have come to understand the unique connections between gender, class, race, the law, sexuality, and work. I see too often how outlawing prostitution and stereotyping sex workers

---

[2] See Ronald Weitzer, "The Mythology of Prostitution: Advocacy Research and Public Policy." *Sexuality Research and Social Policy*, 2010, 7(1): 15–29.

[3] For more on participatory activist research, see Nancy Naples, *Feminism and Method: Ethnography, Discourse Analysis, and Activist Research*, 2003, New York, NY: Routledge. Naples credits standpoint theorists like Dorothy Smith (1987), Patricia Hill Collins (1990) and Donna Haraway (1988, 1987).

[4] Ibid.

actually encourages and abets the physical and sexual violence that sex workers experience at the hands of police, managers, and clients. Who is left to report to when a police officer rapes them?

As an academic ally, I have spoken on radio shows, lobbied local policy makers, written op-eds, and helped train interpersonal violence crisis response service providers in the city. Though little legal change has resulted at this point, I don't consider my efforts to be a failure. In fact, I feel in some ways this makes my research that much more sociologically relevant and politically important as I continue to help provide voice to a group whose voice generally goes unheard.

I have also done several Sex Work/er 101 trainings for local rape and domestic violence crisis hotline advocates. This was something not previously available to them, and something that advocates (some of whom are also my friends) asked me for, and thus we are working together toward creating real social change. Sex workers report being turned away from domestic violence shelters just for being a sex worker, because the shelter does not want to deal with a "pimp," regardless of if the person actually has a manager, or if that manager was the perpetrator.[5] Sex workers who have experienced a sexual assault (whether on the job or not) are uncomfortable accessing institutional assistance.[6] They fear being arrested, or if undocumented, being deported rather than helped.

Sociologist Ronald Weitzer found that the majority of social service providers work from an "oppression paradigm" when assisting sex workers.[7] I present an hour-long workshop to give advocates an alternative to the oppression paradigm when working with interpersonal violence victims/survivors who engage in sexual labor. During my workshops, we speak about the social stigma around sexual labor and why it is important to recognize and honor the term the person identifies with—which may not

---

[5] For more on how institutions ignore or harm sex workers, see two reports on youth's experiences with police, hospitals, schools, and shelters. "Denied Help!: How Youth in the Sex Trade & Street Economy are Turned Away from Systems Meant to Help Us and What We are Doing to Fight Back," *Young Women's Empowerment Project (YWEP)*, 2012, http://ywepchicago. files.wordpress.com/2012/09/bad-encounter-line-report-2012.pdf and "The Commercial Sexual Exploitation of Children in New York City, Volume One, The CSEC Population in New York City: Size, Characteristics, and Needs," R. Curtis, K. Terry, M. Dank, K. Dombrowski, and B. Khan, and submitted to the National Institute of Justice, http://www.courtinnovation.org/sites/default/files/ CSEC_NYC_Volume1.pdf. Both report that youth who sell sex also experience sexual violence from police (CSEC, p. 90), and that "youth in the sex trade and street economy experience institutional violence from healthcare providers almost as often as from police" (YWEP, p. 16). Also see *Sex Work: Writings by Women in the Sex Industry*, eds. F. Delacoste and P. Alexander, 1988, San Francisco, CA: Cleiss Press and *Regulating Sex: The Politics of Intimacy and Identity*, eds. Elizabeth Bernstein and Laurie Schaffner, 2005, New York: Routledge.

[6] Ibid.

[7] Weitzer ibid.

be "sex worker." We breakdown myths, such as the assumption that sex workers have high rates of sexually transmitted infections and HIV. And we discuss why sexual assault should NOT be assumed to be part of the job. We discuss best practices for overcoming these common cultural myths in order to help the person who has experienced domestic/dating violence or rape. Without a formal study, there is no way to assess whether or not these trainings have an impact on advocacy services. But as an academic ally, I hope that my activism helps reduce institutionalized discrimination against sex workers.

As scholars continue to debate sexual labor as a social problem, as a form of deviance, and as an issue of gender justice, sex workers themselves are organizing for legal change and, sometimes, reaching out to scholars or becoming scholars themselves. As a feminist scholar and participatory activist researcher, I have been able to connect my research with a more general public and with social service providers. In this way, I hope to be helping to create a path toward social change and, ultimately, legal change for sex workers in the United States.

Disrupting a Narrative: Developing a New Discourse of Empowerment for LGBT People of Color

Juan Battle
City University of New York

Antonio (Jay) Pastrana
City University or New York

Juan Battle is a Professor of Sociology, Public Health, and Urban Education at the Graduate Center of the City University of New York (CUNY). He is also the Coordinator of the Africana Studies Certificate Program. With over 60 grants and publications—including books, book chapters, academic articles, and encyclopedia entries—his research focuses on race, sexuality, and social justice.

Antonio (Jay) Pastrana is an Assistant Professor of Sociology at John Jay College of Criminal Justice of the City University of New York (CUNY). His research interests include the intersection of race, sexualities, and social movements. In particular, he examines how race-based marginalization and intersectionality issues affect the lives of lesbian, gay, bisexual, and transgender (LGBT) populations in the United States.

For almost 15 years, Juan and Jay have engaged in research that explores a range of theories, issues, and topics related to lesbian, gay, bisexual, and transgender (LGBT) people of color. Over these years, we have worked closely with local, regional, and national organizations in order to make information and research accessible to a wide audience, from students and other academics to activists, artists, philanthropists, and policy makers. Throughout, we use key sociological insights as well as a variety of tools of inquiry in order to disrupt the existing narrative and develop a new discourse about the lived experiences of LGBT people of color in the United States.

Realizing one's personal position in the larger social structures that surround us is fundamental to what the field of sociology has come to understand as the sociological imagination (Mills, 1959). As researchers, Juan and Jay came to understand how narratives—not only the stories that everyday people tell each other but also the more formal bodies of knowledge that are often (mis)represented by research literature—shape, frame, and often limit the ways in which LGBT people of color are reflected in larger social structures like government, education, religion, the economy, and healthcare. These (mis)representations and myths often result in lopsided views of what it means to be a person whose existence is at the intersection of social identities, in this case the intersections of race and sexuality. As an element of a larger body of knowledge known as critical race theory, intersectionality acknowledges the power of narrative and how it can be used to document how various social identities come together in very specific ways (Crenshaw, 1992). It also helps shift the line of inquiry by shining a light on experiences that rarely get reported by knowledge producers (those with the power in the dominant social structures), especially as it relates to race, sexuality, and power relations.

Narratives indeed influence much of the inquiry that sociologists explore. For example, for a project he was working on in the mid 1990s, Juan was interviewing a 19-year-old young black man at Rikers Island—a local jail in New York City. During the interview, the young man proclaimed that, when it came to sexuality, the only thing researchers wanted to do with people of color was to watch them screw and then see how long it took for them to die. Juan was very affected by this observation . . . and possibly by its accuracy. Therefore, on that day, Juan made a promise to himself that he would one day develop a study of LGBT people of color where their lives and experiences would be celebrated and not pathologized.

Yes, issues such as HIV, depression, social isolation, and more may uniquely affect the lives of LGBT people of color; therefore, those issues should be distinctively studied with that population in mind. However, when research(ers) only study a certain group—for example, LGBT people of color—with a pathological assumption, they (inadvertently) perpetuate the very pathology they intend to ameliorate.

Not only can one-sided narratives influence sociological inquiry, so too can a paucity of them. In 2000, as a policy analyst for the National Gay and Lesbian Task Force, one of the largest national LGBT rights organizations in the United States, Jay started collecting narratives of people of color, particularly Asians and Pacific Islanders, blacks, Latina/os, and Native Americans. These semistructured, one-on-one interviews, which lasted anywhere from 35 minutes to two hours, centered the experiences of people of color as insiders and outsiders of LGBT social movements in the United States. Several important sociological observations emerged from these narratives. First, the issues of importance for this population are not necessarily the same issues that the larger LGBT social movement privileges. Though there was general agreement that marriage and inclusion in the military—two issues that are part of the dominant narrative of LGBT rights in this country today—are important, LGBT people of color also included racial and economic justice as vital components to their experience. Second, though LGBT people of color identify and acknowledge the fact that they live intersectional lives, sometimes one identity status is more salient than others. This reflects how identity itself can sometimes be fluid, relational, and dependent on the social context. Finally, and significantly, there was always an agreement that basic knowledge about LGBT people of color is scant.

In 2008, building on the lessons learned from the jailhouse critique and from the LGBT people of color narratives, Juan and Jay together launched the Social Justice Sexuality Project, a multiyear knowledge-based approach to gathering data on LGBT people of color. At the heart of this project is the self-administered Social Justice Sexuality (SJS) Survey, which examines five themes: family formations and dynamics; civic engagement; spirituality and religion; sexual, racial, and ethnic identity; and mental and overall health.

Community buy-in is important for large-scale research endeavors. Various partnerships made it possible for the SJS project to gather data at a wide range of venues such as LGBT people of color pride marches, parades, picnics, religious gatherings, festivals, rodeos, seniors' events, and small house parties across the United States. Given the checkered historical legacy of scientific research with people of color and LGBT populations, these partnerships were important in order to gain access to, and establish legitimacy with, LGBT communities of color and event planners. Some groups and organizations that worked closely with the SJS project included CenterLink[8], a coalition of LGBT community centers across the nation; the International Federation of Black Prides, a group that culls together information about LGBT events catering to black and Latina/o populations;

---

[8] For a list of organizations that partnered with us throughout this project, please visit www .socialjusticesexuality.com.

and the National Queer Asian Pacific Islander Alliance, a federation of LGBT Asian American, South Asian, Southeast Asian, and Pacific Islander organizations. By fostering and continuing relationships with community-based organizations and affinity groups, the SJS team was able to include the community in the process of research. Nearly 5,000 surveys were collected between January and December 2010, from all 50 states, as well as Washington, D.C., and Puerto Rico.

Data analyses from the survey continue to reveal important and useful findings about LGBT people of color in the United States today. For example, our sample included Asian and Pacific Islander, black, and Latina/o LGBT people who were out to people in different settings. We found that having family support, feeling connected to the LGBT community and to other LGBT people, and believing that sexual orientation is an important part of one's identity each has a significant impact on predicting how many people Asian and Pacific Islander, black, and Latina/o LGBTs are out to in their lives.

Additionally, when examining the Latina/o sample, we found that family support was the most important variable in predicting positive health and mental health outcomes. However, for black participants in the sample, family and spirituality were key predictors of favorable social outcomes. Though too numerous to list here, additional differences were also found when examining various racial, gender (e.g., men vs. women), and age cohorts (e.g., younger vs. older respondents), as well as their intersections.

As sociologists in action, we continue to engage with various audiences in order to develop this new discourse on LGBT people of color, which resists using a lens of pathology. These efforts include ongoing collaborations, presentations, and discussions not only at colleges, universities, and other community-based settings but also with policy makers and related stakeholders. For example, the SJS Project worked with Gay Men's Health Crisis (GMHC), one of the largest HIV and AIDS services organizations in the country, in order to better understand the life experiences of what is known as the house and ball community, which is largely comprised of black and Latina/o youth who gather together and compete with one another in events that feature dancing, vogueing, and modeling competitions. In 2010, GMHC was presenting the 20th Annual House of Latex Ball and the SJS project collected surveys from participants, which ultimately helped the organization better serve the health needs of black and Latina/o youth who are part of the larger house and ball community across the country. Later that year, the National Black Justice Coalition (NBJC)—the national civil rights organization dedicated to empowering black LGBT people—invited us to participate in the "OUT on the Hill, Black LGBT Leadership Summit," an inaugural event held at the White House and

Capitol Hill in Washington, D.C. This event included detailed policy briefings with the LGBT liaison to President Barack Obama. During that time, we also gained attention from a meeting held as part of the Congressional Black Caucus convening.

Related to social movement building, the SJS data were cited and used by the Movement Advancement Project (MAP), an independent think tank that conducts policy research on LGBT people and their families. The SJS Project was able to contribute to a 2011 MAP report about LGBT families and social inequality. We have also worked closely with Proyecto Igualdad, a LGBT Latina/o rights program at Lambda Legal, an organization dedicated to achieving civil rights for LGBT people through litigation and public policy work. For each of these nationally and internationally recognized organizations, the SJS Project was able to provide data pertinent to the work that each does on behalf of LGBT people of color. Central to these efforts is increasing the knowledge of basic demographic characteristics without couching it in terms of pathology. These partnerships have underscored the importance and utility of social science research in collecting basic demographic data that can, in turn, be useful in developing strategies for future programmatic agendas with regard to social movement building and to the overall health and wellbeing of LGBT people of color.

These types of interactions with community-based organizations, policy makers, and other stakeholders occurred throughout all stages of the SJS Project and they continue to this day.

Working within a population that is often understudied or underserved continues to show us just how relevant and vital social scientific inquiry can be for others. As sociologists in action, we each believe that collaborating directly with community partners is essential to the research process. In this way, we ensure that our work has direct relevance and is readily accessible. Along the way, we have forged long-lasting relationships with community leaders across the country and this, too, is quite rewarding. In sum, being sociologists in action means that we get to witness how our work positively impacts others while also advancing knowledge about the everyday lives of LGBT people of color.

References

Mills, C. W. (1959/2000). *The sociological imagination.* New York: Oxford University Press.

Crenshaw, K. (1992). Whose story is it, anyway? Feminist and antiracist appropriations of Anita Hill. In T. Morrison (Ed.), *Race-ing justice, engendering power: Essays on Anita Hill, Clarence Thomas, and the construction of social reality* (pp. 402–440). New York: Pantheon Books.

Indian Blood: Two-Spirit Cultural Dissolution, Mixed-Race Identity, and Sexuality—A Journey of Return

Andrew Jolivette
San Francisco State University

Andrew Jolivette is Associate Professor and Chair of American Indian Studies at San Francisco State University. He is the author of three books, *Obama and the Biracial Factor: The Battle for a New American Majority* (2012); *Louisiana Creoles: Cultural Recovery and Mixed-Race Native American Identity* (2007); and *Cultural Representation in Native America* (2006). He is currently writing two new books, *Indian Blood: Decolonizing Gender, Sexuality and Mixed-Race Identity in the Face of HIV* and the *Research Justice Reader.* Jolivette serves on the boards of the Data Center for Research Justice, the GLBT Historical Society & Museum, and Speak Out's Institute for Democratic Education and Culture. He is a former IHART Fellow and an Indigenous Peoples' Representative on the Global Forum on HIV and the Law.

"You know, I've been to places where I've met people, like myself on the reservation [who also attended boarding schools] but obviously didn't like themselves enough because they didn't want to do nothing for themselves. But, um . . . I got beat up. I got the shit beat out of me so bad you wouldn't even recognize me it was so bad. I got kicked in the face about 25 times by this guy with boots on. Just totally beat up on the reservation, nobody came to help, nobody helped me . . . After leaving I got into a relationship but then I started using again. So it was like, you know what? You're gonna go back to the reservation and end up back where you were, go back down hill—sobriety. That's why I came here. I needed to get the sobriety. And that was the main thing. Because what was up there for me was no longer [working]."

"HIV and AIDS is something that I have learned to live with. It's also something that a part of me feels happened for a reason. I wasn't sure if I should disclose my status in this way here today. I spoke with a colleague about it and he said, "How will disclosing impact you? Will it benefit you? Are you giving anything up?" I thought to myself, as a gay man of color, I have a responsibility to disclose. This is a very personal decision, but in indigenous communities and in communities of color we lack faces to make this pandemic real. If you've never known someone living with AIDS, now you do. You know my story and in sharing it I hope that others will know that they can live with this. They can have a career, a family. They too can find love again. Over the past three [eleven] years I have learned AIDS is not me. I am me. AIDS is only one other part of my life."

Rafael Diaz, author of *Latino Gay Men and HIV* (1997) has said, "so many people when they disclose or talk about their HIV status say, 'I'm HIV positive.'" Importantly, Diaz points out that when someone has cancer they don't say, "I am cancer." They say "I have cancer." A simple state of mind can mean so much in terms of our well-being as marginalized communities within the capitalist bureaucracy of the public health system in the United States. The quotation that opens this chapter comes from a mixed-race, gay, American Indian man. His story is not an uncommon one. For American Indian people today, HIV/AIDS, gender, sexuality, and mixed-race identity intersect in complex and traumatic ways in the absence of community support, cultural buffers, and stress-coping mechanisms to combat colonial oppression.

This is my story too. The second quote that opens the chapter is from a keynote talk I delivered at San Francisco State University (SFSU) on World AIDS Day in 2005. As I reflect back on the past 8 years since I first delivered this talk, disclosing my HIV/AIDS positive status to my colleagues and students at SFSU, a great deal has happened. I think about the scars this experience may have left on my life. I think about the traumas that have existed in my communities for more than five centuries in the Americas. I open with my own story because I deeply believe in the practice of research justice. Research justice is about seeking solidarity with research participants. It is about working with—not on—research participants to weave a narrative, a set of life histories captured in one of many moments in time. In fact, to understand the very nature of the colonial haunting that has displaced, removed, relocated, and perpetrated mass acts of genocide (i.e., kidnapping, boarding school abuse, sexual assaults, murder, forced sterilization, etc.) against indigenous peoples, researchers must understand the significance of what Linda Tuhiwai Smith (1999) has termed "indigenous methodologies." Smith argues that for most indigenous peoples research is considered a "dirty word," due to the history of abuse and historical lack of access and power to write about our own communities. Thus, to build a research relationship based on solidarity and justice one must consider research as a ceremony which brings a higher level of trust and buy-in from the community.[9]

---

[9] The concept of research as ceremony is articulated by Cree scholar Shawn Wilson in his book, *Research is Ceremony: Indigenous Research Methods* (2008), Fernwood Publishing.

My research on sexuality and HIV/AIDS with indigenous and mixed-race communities has been life-changing, not only for the participants but also for me personally. The project I describe here was conducted in equal partnership with the Native American AIDS Project (NAAP) and is focused on ending the invisibility of health disparities and sexual discrimination faced by LGBTQ mixed-race Native Americans. National studies show that mixed-race men have the 2nd highest rates of HIV infection for those between the ages of 15 and 22 (Valleroy et al., 2000). Couple this with the fact that American Indians have the highest rate of interracial marriage, and this was the ideal group to work with on issues of sexual discrimination and stress coping among mixed-race queer people in the United States (Lee & Edmonston, 2005). Fifty participants of mixed-race took part in the four focus groups I conducted, and each also completed a demographic profile survey to address issues of indigenous stress coping mechanisms, mental health disparities, and HIV/AIDS risk among mixed-race American Indian gay men and transgender people. The ages of participants ranged from 22 to 67 years. The surveys showed that this population faces high levels of racial and gender discrimination along with extreme experiences of reported sexual violence. The focus group data reveals a pattern of inter-connected psychological and social risk factors for HIV/AIDS transmission within this population.

Through my research, I have learned that mixed-blood American Indian queer people are experiencing ruptures in their social and cultural support networks that under normal circumstances would serve as protective factors against external discrimination. This is in part due to decline of the spiritual, socioeconomic, and cultural significance of two-spirit individuals. Two-spirits in many, but not all, tribal communities are individuals who histori-cally practiced gender balance between male and female genders. In some tribal societies such as the Zuni,[10] two-spirits were not seen as "homosexual," "transgender," or "gay" as they might be seen in a contemporary context. Two-spirits were often religious and ceremonial leaders who held a special place in tribal life because they represented a balance of gender identity and therefore were seen as special keepers of knowledge. Attacks on the prac-tice of two-spirits by European religious leaders during colonization caused dissolution of the traditional roles two-spirits play in all facets of tribal life from the religious to the economic. This occurs in rural, reservation settings where the elders who held the traditional knowledge have died, leaving new, colonial, and nonindigenous views in their place; it is also apparent in urban settings where youth are removed from traditional kinship networks.

---

[10] See Will Roscoe's, *Changing Ones: Third and Fourth Genders in Native North America*, Palgrave, 2000.

As discrimination against two-spirits increases, there is a breakdown in traditional values, beliefs, and practices that leads to detrimental experiences with intergenerational trauma. These traumas within the context of the mixed-blood American Indian queer or two-spirit experience are manifested through racial and gender discrimination, sexual violence, and mixed-race cognitive dissonance (mental confusion or disagreement between one's self-identification and how society views the individual (i.e., I may see myself as a mixed-race American Indian, and society may see me as monoracial, causing me to suffer mental anxiety)). If these traumas are left unaddressed from a traditional two-spirit cultural ethic where queer people's sexuality is accepted and respected, we can expect weak stress coping mechanisms within urban Indian kinship networks.

My research leads me to conclude that the only way to reduce these traumas is through a return to a two-spirit cultural ethic of community support, intergenerational mentoring, and ceremonial healing. The only way to address HIV/AIDS disparities among mixed-blood LGBTQ and two-spirit American Indians (MLGBTQ-2s) is for the community to take action themselves in naming their own stories and working to shift policies and practices that don't reflect their lived experiences. Since the completion of this study, I have been actively working with the Native American Health Center in Oakland, California, to create more programs that will bring greater visibility to mixed-blood people who are also LGBTQ/two-spirit. Over the past year, I have presented this work at the Center for Gender and Sexuality Research, the Center for Biomedical Ethics at Stanford University, and the National Sexuality Institute for policy makers and graduate students across the United States and from Australia, Europe, Latin America, and Asia. These presentations have inspired other researchers to create projects that speak to the need for research to be action-oriented and not simply based on creating new theories. As a mixed-blood, Afro-Latin/French Creole (French, black/West African, American Indian [Opelousa/Atakapa], and Spanish) researcher, the stories of the two-spirit, gay, transgender, bisexual, and queer participants resonated with my own life experiences in profound ways. I attempted to seek a level of solidarity and community by sharing my own story before each of the focus group discussions I conducted, to set some context as to who I am and why I was writing about the critical intersections of gender, sexuality, mixed-race identity, and HIV/AIDS in American Indian communities.

The quote that opens this chapter reveals the ways that violence within tribal contexts has become endemic. These are a result of colonial perspectives (perspectives that forced LGBTQ people to "act like" heterosexuals or to simply deny their sexual and gender identities that were quite different from those practices within European societies at the time of first contact in the Americas) that shift the important role of two-spirits to that of a deviant, unworthy of community acceptance or protection. The following sentiment from a focus group respondent highlights how the literal and symbolic death of old ways have left two-spirits without an effective kinship network of community support, "Because what was up there [on the reservation] for me was no longer [working]. You know there was like—a mile of death up there, really serious death up there." This experience is not unique to the reservations, however. Many of the respondents expressed their difficulty with finding a community of support in the urban environment and affirmed the importance of organizations like NAAP[11] that can serve as surrogate kinship support networks.

It is important to understand the difficulty that people of two-spirit backgrounds experience over their lifetime. These experiences of discrimination and historical trauma are compounded by the oppression directed toward American Indians who are often miscategorized racially or seen as a small population with no statistical relevance in public health research. Several participant comments demonstrate how two-spirit cultural dissolution, coupled with intergenerational trauma and discrimination based on sexual orientation, impacted their behavior growing up.

> Well I was initiated into the club at seven, by one of my cousins. And then one of my brother's friends when I was in high school, one of the macho gang guys like had his way with me. I was like a good Mormon boy, I wasn't gonna do anything. I already knew I was gay. Everybody knew I was gay. But I was a good little Mormon then, I didn't do anything, I didn't . . . People at church never said anything. People at school never said anything. But people where we lived, they knew. Cause my brother was like, "He's gay. He's a sissy." Cause no one would know, outwardly . . . In my white shirt, and my tie, and my little slacks and my book of Mormon. Nope I never did anything bad. I was babysitting his sister, his little sister, and I was coming back from school through the field. And he caught me behind the barn . . . He did things that I actually did like . . . But I didn't want to do because I was a gay Mormon boy. (Indian Blood Focus Group Participant, 2012)

This man's comment about being called "gay" and a "sissy" demonstrates how deeply the individuals in my study were impacted by society's negative view of people who are LGBTQ and how the pressure to fit into society can cause people to practice sexual behaviors that may

---

[11] The Native American AIDS Project (NAAP), founded in 1994, is the only Native-specific HIV organization in California. We provide culturally-specific HIV prevention and CARE services to Native Americans in the state of California. Staff and volunteers come from diverse communities with an indigenous understanding of cultural issues. NAAP embraces the entire community: youth, elders, men and women, gay, straight, two-spirited, sober, and actively using. All services draw upon Native cultural, spiritual, behavioral, and medical traditions to communicate HIV prevention messages and provide linkages to vital care services.

not be healthy for them, especially at such a young age. Therefore, in an effort to address the intersecting oppressions for mixed-race gay men and transgender people in the American Indian community I have set out—on the recommendation and consultation of the community—to construct a community-action intervention model. The goal is to pair elder two-spirit people with younger two-spirits to buffer social stigma, while also providing an intergenerational pathway for indigenous leaders to create an urban Indian kinship network to foster better community coping mechanisms. The ultimate goal of this community-based intervention would be to include a Ceremony of Return (an idea passed to me by a community member) to welcome back two-spirit people into our circle as cultural and spiritual leaders. Moving forward, it will be crucial that we not limit our definition of two-spirit and we maintain a universal definition. This will allow us to bring greater awareness and visibility to both the history and contemporary issues facing two-spirit identified people, including those within the wide range of sexual orientations.

Since the completion of this study there have been community gatherings and reports at several venues to expand on the idea of creating this intervention model. At the present moment, the Circle of Healing Project has been identified as an ideal location to implement the project. Other activities of Circle of Healing include an interactive digital storytelling program. Video stories of two-spirit and LGBTQ American Indians are screened annually at events such as National Native American HIV/AIDS Awareness day. I have also been invited to speak on this topic at several venues in the community, and many people have been inspired to become more active in programs like the Circle of Healing program and HIV/AIDS prevention work as a result of these talks across the United States.

My work as a sociologist in action on issues of sexuality and racial justice has allowed me to work with organizations like the Native American AIDS Project, the DataCenter for Research Justice, Speak Out, and the Native American Health Center's Circle of Healing program in multiple ways. This work allows me to act not simply as an outside researcher but as a member of the community with a vested interest in the transformation of HIV/AIDS, public health, and ethnic studies to practice an intersectional approach to action oriented research rather than the more standard one-dimensional approach. In fact, I am currently in the process of editing a book, the *Research Justice Reader,* in collaboration with the Data Center in Oakland, California. I serve as Vice-Chair of the Data Center board, and in building on this relationship of centering action research as an act of radical love, we hope that stories in the reader (like those shared in this project in the Native American community) will lead to more studies of community-designed, implemented and owned research for the betterment of society.

124   Sociologists in Action on Inequalities

References

Diaz, R. M. (1997). *Latino gay men and HIV: Culture, sexuality, and risk behavior.* New York: Routledge.

Lee, S., & Edmonston, B. (2005). New marriages, new families: U.S. racial and Hispanic intermarriage, *Population Bulletin, 60,* 2.

Smith, L. T. (1999). *Decolonizing methodologies: Research and indigenous peoples.* London: Zed Books.

Valleroy, L. A., MacKellar, D. A., Karon, J. M., Rosen, D. H., McFarland, W., Shehan, D. A., . . . Janssen, R. S. (2000). HIV prevalence and associated risks in young men who have sex with men. *Journal of the American Medical Association, 284*(2), 198–204.

Sex Work and Sex Trafficking: Influencing State Policy on a Complex Social Issue

Jennifer J. Reed
University of Nevada-Las Vegas

Jennifer J. Reed is a doctoral candidate in sociology at the University of Nevada-Las Vegas. After camping out on the lawn of the Nevada Legislature with her son to protest proposed budget cuts to education in 2011, she was elected as a Nevada delegate to the 2012 Democratic National Convention. Jennifer's experience as a teenage mother in Appalachian Ohio began her quest to understand the intersections of gender, sexuality, and economic injustices. She is a proud mom, grandma, and avid social justice activist.

To me, a sociologist in action applies scholarly knowledge from the social sciences to help solve real world problems. As a teen mom who is now a young grandmother, I strive to leave the world a better place for my kids and grandkids. One of the avenues I have found toward working to change the world for the better is to start in my own community by promoting good, evidence-based policy. An important tool for shaping public policy is sociological research. All research simply starts with a question. I like to think of it as a mystery to be solved, which makes it fun. It is even more exciting to use findings from scientifically valid research to help build meaningful policy and contribute to social justice.

Human sex trafficking is a complex issue that has been a popular topic of newly proposed laws in the United States and globally. Human trafficking can be defined as being put in a situation of economic exploitation that you can't escape. In the United States, media commonly equate all human trafficking with sex trafficking. Although many people are actually trafficked for domestic, farm, or factory work, the common narrative of "save the child sex slaves" paints a haunting picture that creates a powerful emotional reaction. People are understandably driven to want to stop a violent, abusive trafficker or "pimp" from profiting from forcing or manipulating our youth, usually believed to be young girls, to trade sex for money. While anyone under age 18 who exchanges sex for money or other resources is considered trafficked by the U.S. federal definition, the term *trafficking* has also been used to promote certain political agendas to end prostitution altogether by those who believe no woman, even an adult, would ever choose to engage in sex work.

When the main Nevada sex trafficking bill, Assembly Bill 67—also known as "AB67" for short—was introduced into the 2013 state legislature, I was a doctoral student in sociology at the University of Nevada-Las Vegas (UNLV). Because I moved to Vegas in 2008 to study gender and sexuality, I had been following the local media campaign leading up to its introduction. I was working with Dr. Barb Brents who is well-known for her research on the sex industries, particularly studies about the safety of legal brothels in Nevada (Brents & Hausbeck, 2005; Brents, Jackson, & Hausbeck, 2010). Nevada is the only state in the United States that has legal prostitution, which is permitted only in regulated brothels located in mostly isolated rural parts of the state. While many people believe that prostitution is legal in "Sin City" Las Vegas, it is actually illegal, although it can be tough to tell with the illusion of sex sold everywhere you look. (As my friend Angie says about Vegas: "There is a butt on every cab.")

Given the reputation of Las Vegas as an adult playground and Nevada as the one U.S. state where legal prostitution remains, when new sex trafficking laws are suggested to regulate Nevada's sex industries, it raises red flags with those who are aware of the history of the U.S. sex trafficking debates. While we can all agree that situations of forced sexual labor must be seriously addressed, the term sex trafficking has been used by some feminist and evangelical groups to promote general antiprostitution and antisex work ideology (Bromfield & Capous-Desyllas, 2012; Weitzer, 2007). From an abolitionist (or prohibitionist) perspective, all prostitution is sex trafficking and should be abolished. Frequently, pornography is asserted as the cause of sex trafficking. On the other hand, from those who come from a sex workers' rights perspective, prostitution and other forms of sex work are seen as viable options that women (and other genders) can choose in order to survive or make a living. Sex work is perceived as a legitimate form of work, and situations of sex trafficking are understood as labor abuses that violate the right to work in safe conditions.

Given the different historical understandings of trafficking, I was paying attention to the neighboring state's recent proposed sex trafficking law, Californians Against Sexual Exploitation (CASE) Act—"Prop 35"— during the fall of 2012. With the help of colleagues in California, I became aware of some parts of Prop 35 that I believe went too far and could result in violating—rather than protecting—a person's rights. This gave me an idea of what to look for when the wording of the proposed Nevada sex trafficking law AB67 was publicly released in January 2013. I carefully read through the unusually long 39 pages of the bill. (Really, 39 pages?) I was quickly convinced of the need to influence this policy outcome when I came across overly broad and vague definitions and targets as well as parts that went too far. For example, the definition of "sexual conduct" used to define prostitution included "any intrusion, however slight, of any part of a person's body" (Nev. A.B. 67, as introduced). Laws need to be focused and written clearly or they risk being misused to target certain groups for costly and unnecessary arrest, prosecution, and incarceration. I had only 120 days in the Nevada legislative session, which was about to begin, to help narrow down this "tough on crimes" sex trafficking bill.

I believe that all good policy is based on evidence through empirical research. I wanted to know, therefore, what sociological (or other) research had informed this law? What I uncovered is that, aside from a few individuals who shared distressing stories to support passing the bill, there was no scientifically valid evidence available on the extent of the sex trafficking problem in Nevada (Heineman, MacFarlane, & Brents, 2012). Why was the bill being introduced with no empirical evidence supporting the need for it? While the Nevada Attorney General officially introduced the bill, I also knew from experience that a politician rarely writes his or her own legislation. My next question then, was who did, indeed, write the bill? I discovered that the bill was brought to Nevada by the policy project director of a national level antitrafficking organization, Polaris Project. Why was an out-of-state group bringing this bill to Nevada?

My next question was, who were my allies and who did I want to influence? As a sociologist in action, building and maintaining relationships with people is essential. I was already a volunteer with the Las Vegas chapter of the Sex Workers Outreach Project (SWOP), so I spoke to members about the issue. I coordinated with the legislative director from the American Civil Liberties Union (ACLU) of Nevada who also linked me with representatives from the Clark County (Las Vegas) and Washoe County (Reno) Public Defenders Offices. With the help of a tech-savvy friend, I built a basic educational website. I created a twitter account specific to the issue in addition to my personal account. I had found twitter to be an invaluable social media tool to amplify one's political voice over the previous two years. I shared my opinion about AB67 on the Nevada State Legislature interactive website and asked others to contribute. I looked up which state representatives were members of the legislative committees that would hear and vote on AB67. I e-mailed those legislators, showed up at public events to meet them, and made appointments to speak with some key committee members at their offices.

I drove eight long hours through the desert from Las Vegas to the state capital of Carson City to testify at the first AB67 legislative hearing on February 20th. I had learned from participating as an activist against the 2011 proposed education budget cuts that it makes the optimal impression to show up in person. On the morning of the first hearing, I was one of only a handful of people in a packed room who signed in to testify against AB67. After all, who is actually *for* sex trafficking? A long line of people testified in support of the bill. I couldn't help but wonder, at 39 pages long, how many people actually read it? Most recited the same few basic talking points provided by outside organizations. At one point, a person got on her knees and quoted Bible scripture while another offered to give money to the state to lock up the evil traffickers. When my turn came, I shared the results of two years of extensive research in two cities that found that the relationship between teen prostitutes and those who benefit from their sexual labor is far more complex than the AB67 policy as written suggested. According to Marcus et al. (2012), 90% (N = 246) in New York City and 86% (N = 108) in Atlantic City of youth engaged in the sex trades reported having *no pimp*. They concluded

> In short, these young people exchange sex for money not because they are being held and trafficked as "sex slaves" but because they have drug habits, are attempting to survive on the streets on their own, are escaping from difficult family situations, and exist at the lowest stratum of a socioeconomic and cultural system that is failing them. (Marcus et al., 2012, p. 164)

Where was the social safety net and alternative resources for these youth? In addition, I emphasized that there was no systematic state or local data on human sex trafficking in Nevada. Where was the evidence to support the existence of a vast human sex trafficking ring as alluded to in earlier testimony? As a sociologist in action, it is important to show up and speak up with your critical perspective, even if your voice shakes, even when you feel like giving up because you feel too small to make a difference (perhaps, especially then). I received a number of requests after that to provide input on the other side of the sex trafficking legislation as originally proposed.

At the end of the 2013 Nevada legislative session, AB67 passed after being revised several times so that the final version was much more focused at only 32 pages, rather than 39. Some important concrete changes that were made include: (1) Sex trafficking of an adult was narrowed to just situations where threats, violence, force, or other abuse is used to cause the person to engage in prostitution; and (2) exceptions were made to maintain legal prostitution in regulated Nevada brothels. The intent of the law was clearly stated on legislative record to only apply to situations of forced sexual labor where another person profits, and not to arrest homeless street kids as pimps who are simply working together trading sex for survival. The Senate committee chair stated that legislators would watch closely for how the new sex trafficking law is used and revisit it as needed in the next state legislative session. In the meantime, a sociological study has resumed on youth in the sex trades in Las Vegas using the research design from New York City and Atlantic City (Marcus et al., 2012). As a sociologist in action, it has been personally rewarding to positively impact public policy, and ultimately real people's lives, by applying sociological tools that bring a nuanced understanding to complex social issues.

References

Brents, B. G., & Hausbeck, K. (2005). Violence and legalized brothel prostitution in Nevada: Examining safety, risk, and prostitution policy. *Journal of Interpersonal Violence, 20*(3), 270–295.

Brents, B. G., Jackson, C. A., & Hausbeck, K. (2010). *The state of sex: Tourism, sex, and sin in the new American heartland.* New York: Routledge.

A. B. 67, 77th Reg. Sess. (Nev. 2013). Retrieved from https://nelis.leg.state.nv.us/77th2013/App#/77th2013/Bill/Text/AB67/BD_AB67

Bromfield, N. F., & Capous-Desyllas, M. (2012). Underlying motives, moral agendas, and unlikely partnerships: The formulation of the U.S. Trafficking in Victims Protection Act through the data and voices of key policy players. *Advances in Social Work, 13*(2), 243–261.

Heineman, J., MacFarlane, R., & Brents, B. G. (2012). Sex industry and sex workers in Nevada. In D. N. Shalin (Ed.), *The social health of Nevada: Leading indicators and quality of life in the Silver State.* Las Vegas: UNLV Center for Democratic Culture. Retrieved from http://cdclv.unlv.edu/healthnv_2012/sexindustry.pdf

Marcus, A., Riggs, R., Horning, A., Rivera, S., Curtis R., & Thompson, E. (2012). Is child to adult as victim is to criminal? Social Policy and street-based sex work in the USA. *Sexuality Research and Social Policy, 9*(2), 153–166.

Weitzer, R. (2007). The social construction of sex trafficking: Ideology and institutionalization of a moral crusade. *Politics and Society, 35*(3), 447–475.

From Damaged Goods to Empowered Patients

Adina Nack

California Lutheran University

Adina Nack, PhD, has been active in sexual health education and research since 1994. Author of the book *Damaged Goods? Women Living With Incurable Sexually Transmitted Diseases* (2008), Nack has won awards for her research, teaching, activism, and public policy work. Currently she is a Professor of Sociology at California Lutheran University where she also serves as director of the Center for Equality and Justice. Nack lives in Ventura County with her daughter and her husband, José Marichal, to whom she is indebted for his support in working to publicly destigmatize sexually transmitted infections. Visit her online at www.adinanack.com.

As a 20-year-old, being diagnosed with a cervical human papillomavirus (HPV) infection did not, at first, seem like a positive "turning-point moment" (Strauss, 1959) in my life. I had no idea that my illness experiences would inspire me to pursue a sexual health education career and ultimately become the foundation for my first sociological study. Back then, I thought that this virus heralded the end of my sex life and maybe marked the end of my fertility. Perhaps most jarring was that this illness made it hard to see myself as a "good girl" . . . someone who could someday become a "good" wife and a "good" mother.

Shuffling out of the procedure room after receiving cryosurgery[12] from my gynecologist, I felt like damaged goods—not just physically but psychologically and socially. Like most Americans, I had been socialized to believe that women who contracted sexually transmitted infections (STIs) were sluts: dirty, promiscuous, irresponsible, stupid sluts. Depressed and considering a lifetime of celibacy, I continued my undergraduate education and found myself gravitating toward women's studies and sociology courses.

Feminists often say, "The personal is political,"[13] which pairs nicely with C. Wright Mills' (1959) assertion that the sociological imagination

---

[12] The medical application of liquid nitrogen to freeze/kill HPV-infected cells.

[13] This statement is often traced back to Carol Hanisch's essay, "The Personal Is Political," originally published in the Redstockings collection Feminist Revolution (New York, NY: Random House, 1979), 204–205.

allows us to view our "personal troubles" within social contexts to reframe them as "public issues." Thanks to my supportive parents and their class privilege—as a family who could afford the best medical treatments—I could put my HPV concerns behind me before beginning graduate school, but my sociological concerns about sexual health policies and practices lingered.

As a PhD student, I volunteered as a sexual health peer educator and eventually directed my university's sexual health education program. Presenting on STIs/HIV to audiences—from junior high students to college students—I met others who were STI-infected and not finding the emotional support they needed. After trying to start a support group (to which only one woman showed up), I realized there was something sociological going on: Support groups for other stigmatizing conditions were flourishing—from HIV-positive groups to 12-step programs for a variety of addictions. I conducted a survey and found that most female patients feared disclosing their STI diagnosis, even to other similarly infected women in a confidential setting.[14]

I've always liked the idea of being a public sociologist: translating research-based findings that have applied value to nonacademic audiences who can use the new knowledge. So for my dissertation, I identified a real-world problem I thought could benefit from evidence-based and theory-driven research. To get to the social-psychological "heart of the matter," I utilized symbolic interactionism and feminist theories to analyze in-depth interview data. I drew on feminist scholarship about gender norms of sexual behaviors and used symbolic interactionism as a lens through which to focus on how individuals intersubjectively formed meanings about STIs during social interactions with medical practitioners and with significant others.

I interviewed adults with medical diagnoses of genital herpes and/or HPV (human papillomavirus) infections. Trained as an ethnographic researcher, I found that one-on-one, in-depth, semistructured interviews allowed me to provide participants with confidentiality when sharing sensitive illness narratives. But I'm not sure that all of the methodological training in the world could have allowed me to connect with my participants—to gain their trust and create rapport—if my own HPV infection had not provided me with complete membership status in this setting.

I initially focused on writing up my findings to present at academic conferences, with the goal of publishing in academic journals. Most academic

---

[14] See pp. 98–100 in my 2000 article, "Damaged Goods: Women Managing the Stigma of STDs" (Deviant Behavior, 21: 95–121); also pp. 17–19 and Appendix B in my book Damaged Goods? Women Living With Incurable Sexually Transmitted Diseases (Temple University, 2008) for more about how this survey informed my research design.

journals have relatively small audiences of readers, so I was grateful when my first and second articles were reprinted in undergraduate readers for courses like introduction to sociology, deviance, and sexuality. I began to receive e-mails from students who identified with my findings. For example, Anne,[15] a senior at the University of Florida, e-mailed me the following:

> I have just gone through the most emotional/traumatic three years of my life and the title of your article ["Damaged Goods: Women Managing the Stigma of STDs"] is exactly what I have gone through. . . . I am really thankful for the work that you are doing in this field.

She and others told me that they felt like I understood what they'd been going through and wanted to know more about my findings.

A six-stage process of "sexual self-transformation" emerged from my analysis. The first five stages represented a series of problems caused by myths, misinformation, harmful interactions (with medical professionals and significant others), and treatments (that were not always effective, often painful, and sometimes quite expensive). The final destination, the sixth stage of reintegration, represented an elusive but important goal— a new sexual self that was healthier and happier as a result of balancing risk-awareness with desires for intimacy.

Feedback like Anne's inspired me to write up the study as a book that would be accessible to the typical undergraduate student. With this goal, I saw my book[16] as a form of advocacy. Those living with STIs have recommended it to each other on sexual health discussion forums (e.g., the American Social Health Association[17]) and have reviewed it on STI-specific Web sites. One HPV blogger wrote, "I was expecting *Damaged Goods* to be something 'over my head,'" and then went on to say she had found the book to be "a new and enlightening reading, compelling." Nonacademic readers got it; sociological research was helping them understand the social-psychological impacts of being diagnosed with medically incurable (though treatable), highly stigmatizing diseases.

By applying feminist theories, I could explain why female STI patients suffered more than their male counterparts. In my articles and book, I argue that destigmatizing STIs requires us to challenge traditional and sexist norms about sexual relationships and sexual health. College students

---

[15] Pseudonyms are used throughout this piece to protect the confidentiality of those who have written to me.

[16] Adina Nack, Damaged Goods? Women Living With Incurable Sexually Transmitted Diseases (Philadelphia, PA: Temple University Press, 2008).

[17] http://www.ashastd.org/phpBB/viewtopic.php?f=4&t=7017

have given me feedback that they understand my sociological explanations of STIs as "personal troubles" and were also inspired to think about STI stigma as a "public issue":

> I was amazed at how insightful and helpful this book is to not only someone living with HPV or HSV, but also to all of those people who they encounter and are possibly affected by it (significant others, doctors, parents, friends, etc.). . . . The stigma that goes along with this situation is wrong, hurtful, and unfair. Nack's efforts to destigmatize this problem are impressive and encouraging and her words really have something for everyone to benefit from. The jokes need to stop. The ignorant comments need to stop. The stigma needs to stop.[18]

Sociological training helped me see, name, and examine the dangers of mixing morality with medicine; these messages were starting to resonate among undergraduate and graduate students.

To get the word out beyond college classrooms, I had to turn my research into sound bites that could be used by journalists. Translating findings for mainstream media was key to becoming a public sociologist. Writing for nonacademic blogs and participating in a magazine writers' workshop helped me develop these skills, and I sought out opportunities to be featured as a sexual health expert—on TV and radio, and in newspapers and magazines that were reaching local, national, and international audiences. I'm a grassroots activist who believes in the power of interactions. I had to be willing and able to make my research—and myself—accessible to a range of nonacademic audiences.

I publicly disclosed my own STI status in the methods sections of my first academic article because it seemed methodologically important for readers to have a sense of my potential biases. And, for the book, I included my own STI autoethnography as an appendix. TV producers, radio hosts, and reporters were drawn to my research, in part because I was willing to talk openly and my sexual partner was (1) uninfected and (2) willing to talk about our sex life on TV.[19] We've been willing to be "poster children" for HPV because we understand that personal narratives can entice viewers and readers into making sociological explorations of sensitive and controversial topics.

As a medical sociologist, I've worked to promote the individual-level and public health benefits of destigmatizing STIs. Research collaborations and service-learning projects with local organizations—like the HIV/AIDS Coalition of Ventura County, CA, and Planned Parenthood of Santa Barbara, Ventura, and San Luis Obispo Counties, Inc.—have given me

---

[18] http://www.amazon.com/review/RYSNFBWBUDT1U/ref=cm_cr_rdp_perm

[19] First interviewed for a 1999 MTV episode of Sex in the 90s and more recently in a fall 2008 episode of the CBS daytime talk show The Doctors. Clip available on YouTube at http://www. youtube.com/watch?v=su7Hcdt3Irs.

opportunities to work with practitioners to improve sexual health care policies and practices and to advocate for comprehensive sex education.

Embracing a public sociology perspective motivated me to both produce and disseminate knowledge about sexual and reproductive health. I will keep working toward the goal of destigmatizing STIs because it represents not only the ideologically correct position but the position that we must embrace to improve individual-level and public health. If "knowledge is power," then I hope that my research, writing projects, and applied collaborations empower STI patients as well as increase the chances that those who struggle with stigmatizing illnesses can enjoy healthier and happier lives.

References

Mills, C. W. (1959). *The sociological imagination.* New York: Oxford University Press.

Strauss, A. L. (1959). *Mirrors and masks: The search for identity.* Glencoe, Illinois: Free Press.

Discussion Questions

1. What were the reasons Crystal Jackson decided to conduct research on sex worker rights activists? Can you picture yourself doing similar research? Why or why not?

2. What is your reaction to Jackson's perspective on sex workers? Do you agree that "outlawing prostitution and stereotyping sex workers actually encourages and abets the physical and sexual violence that sex workers experience at the hands of police, managers, and clients"? Why or why not?

3. Juan Battle and Jay Pastrana emphasize the importance of attaining the perspective of LGBT people of color and *not* viewing them with a pathological lens. List at least three other groups, throughout history, that have been viewed from a pathological lens by social scientists. How does their treatment relate to issues of power, gender, race, class, or ethnicity in academia and social science?

4. The interviews Jay Pastrana conducted of people of color for the National Gay and Lesbian Task Force revealed two key findings. What were they? Why was Pastranas' focus on LGBT people of color so important?

5. Why, according to Andrew Jolivette, are "mixed-blood American Indian queer people experiencing ruptures in their social and cultural support networks that under normal circumstances would serve as protective factors against external discrimination"? What is his proposed response? Do you think it will be effective? Why or why not?

6. One of the obligations of sociologists is to give voice to marginalized people. How does Jolivette do so through his sociological research? If you had the opportunity to give voice to a marginalized group, which group would you choose? Why? How might you use sociological tools to do so?

7. Jennifer Reed writes that "As a sociologist in action, it has been personally rewarding to positively impact public policy, and ultimately real people's lives, by applying sociological tools that bring a nuanced understanding to complex social issues." Describe how the topic covered in her essay is complex and requires a nuanced understanding. Do you think you have the ability to look at such topics in a nuanced way? Why or why not?

8. Why was Reed effective in her efforts to encourage the Nevada legislature to revise the law on sex trafficking? How can sociology help others (like you) become effective citizens who can influence lawmakers?

9. When you were reading Adina Nack's piece, how did you react when you learned that she is living with an STI? What does this tell you, if anything, about your own socially constructed stigmas around STIs?

10. If you were living with an STI, would you have the courage that Nack has had to be public about it and to speak out to educate others? Why or why not? What would be the danger of not speaking out?

Resources

Advocates for Youth

Helps young people make informed and responsible decisions about their reproductive and sexual health. Website has a large variety of resources, publications, multimedia, and information and includes a Parents' Sex Ed Corner, a Sex Education Resource Center, a Take Action Center, and a Youth Activism section.

http://www.advocatesforyouth.org

American Sexual Health Association

Promotes the sexual health of individuals, families and communities by advocating for policy and educating the public in order to foster healthy sexual behavior. Provides extensive resources on STDs and sexual health, including fact sheets, statistics, publications, videos, curriculum and links.

http://www.ashastd.org

ASA Section on Sexualities

American Sociological Association section encouraging and enhancing research, teaching, and other professional activities in the sociology of sexualities for the development of sociology and the betterment of society. Includes the section newsletter and good resources and links.

http://www2.asanet.org/sectionsex

AVERT

Provides a wide range of information to educate people about HIV and AIDS globally. Website is visited by nearly a million people each week and offers resources, multimedia, ways to connect, campaigns, publications, and more.

http://www.avert.org

Center for Research on Gender and Sexuality

Research center dedicated to studying sexuality from a social justice perspective. Offers a seminar series, a speaker bureau, research and articles, and links and resources.

http://cregs.sfsu.edu

Desiree Alliance

Diverse, sex worker-led network of organizations, communities and individuals across the United States working in harm reduction, direct services, political advocacy and health services for sex workers. Provides leadership for sex workers and supporters to come together to advocate for human, labor and civil rights for all workers in the sex industry. Offers a rich section of resources for further research and action.

www.desireealliance.org

GLAAD

Empowers the LGBT community to share their stories, to hold the media accountable for the words and images they present, and to help grassroots organizations communicate effectively.

Offers an Action Center, a library of resources, campaigns, and sub-population specific resources for people of color, youth, and so forth.

http://www.glaad.org

Global Alliance Against Traffic in Women

Works to ensure that the human rights of all migrating women are respected and protected by authorities and agencies. Advocates for living and working conditions that provide women with more alternatives in their countries of origin and to develop and disseminate information to women about migration, working conditions, and their rights. Offers a variety of papers, reports, and videos.

www.gaatw.org

Kinsey Institute

Located at Indiana University, the Institute promotes interdisciplinary research and scholarship in the fields of human sexuality, gender, and reproduction. Excellent source for research and publications.
http://www.indiana.edu/~kinsey

Media Project

A program of Advocates for Youth, offers entertainment professionals the latest facts, research assistance, script consultation, and story ideas on today's sexual and reproductive health issues, including condoms, pregnancy, HIV/AIDS, and abstinence. Offers facts and figures, news updates, petitions, and resources.
http://www.themediaproject.com

Movement Advancement Project

Independent think tank that provides rigorous research, insight and analysis on equality for lesbian, gay, bisexual and transgender (LGBT) people. Work is focused on policy and issues analysis, as well as LGBT social movement issues. Website has resources for those in the movement, policy and issue briefs, and equality maps.
http://www.lgbtmap.org

PFLAG

Organization of parents, families, friends, and straight allies uniting LGBT people. Committed to advancing equality through support, education and advocacy with over 350 chapters and 200,000 supporters in all 50 states. Offers education and programs, advocacy and action, and chapter resources and information.
www.pflag.org

Sex Etc.

A website about sexual health by teens, for teens. Publishes widely read magazine. Website offers a Sex Ed information and video center, an action center, online forums, and other useful resources.
http://sexetc.org

Sexuality Education Resource Centre

Promotes sexual health through education. Offers resoı information and links, on a variety of topics such as sexual hea.. and relationships, parents and family, aboriginal, LGBT, immigrants anu refugees, and youth.

http://www.serc.mb.ca

Sexuality Information and Education Council of the United States

Takes stands on major sexuality issues confronting society and invites other individuals and organizations to affirm these positions and work for their implementation. Good source for information, education, policy briefs, and actions.

http://www.siecus.org

Social Justice Sexuality Project

One of the largest ever national surveys of Black, Latina/o, and Asian and Pacific Islander, and multiracial lesbian, gay, bisexual, and transgender (LGBT) people. Documents and celebrates the experiences of lesbian, gay, bisexual, and transgender (LGBT) people of color.

http://www.socialjusticesexuality.com

5

Intersections

Race, class, gender, and sexuality intersect within each of us and throughout society to create overlapping patterns of inequality. Our identities incorporate all of these aspects of ourselves. In turn, our status in society relates to all of them as well. For example, as sociologist Patricia Hill Collins (2000) explains, the impact of class, gender, and sexuality on individuals and groups cannot be understood in isolation from the effects of race. She describes the relationship among these identities as *intersectionality*. The pieces in this final section reveal the connections among these various identities and demonstrate how these sociologists in action tackle issues of intersectional inequality.

In, "Social Movements and Activist Sociology," Charles Derber describes his career as an activist and sociologist interested in issues of both racial and class inequality. From his days in the civil rights movement being "taken hostage by some White racists, shot at on a country road when driving with Black activists, and slapped in jail by some white sheriffs with no love for Yankee boys," to organizing a National Student Strike Center against the Vietnam War, to engaging in the Battle of Seattle and anti-sweatshop activism, to his leadership in the Occupy Wall Street movement, Derber has spent his entire life using sociological tools to build social movements. The author of many captivating books on economic and political injustice (and how to effectively fight against them), Derber maintains that his best writing "has been animated and informed by my participation in real world struggles to change socially dominant and violent institutions." This piece is an example of Derber's prowess both as a writer and as a change-maker—and his passion for justice and sociology reverberates throughout the essay.

In "How Refugee Girls Change the World (and How You Can Too)," Laura Boutwell shares how relationships inform her sociology in action and thus have led her to conduct participatory action research with people of different races, ethnicities, classes, religions, and genders. She explains, for instance, how sociology is "about grappling with the relationships between individual lives and larger institutional forces," and it is also about understanding how relationships of inequality are structured in our society. Boutwell came to this understanding first through her work teaching English as a Second Language and later through her work collaborating with refugee girls. Working with these girls, she guided them in their use of creative methods to share their stories and work for justice, an experience that has been life-changing for all involved. Bridging from this experience, Boutwell has more recently worked with her undergraduate students to form a student group working to promote immigrant rights and address anti-immigrant bias.

Next, Nancy Mezey shares how she became interested in sociology and social justice work in "Becoming a Sociologist in Action through Theory and Practice: A Personal Journey." She describes how sociology helps us understand "how the intersections of race, class, gender, and sexuality create a relationship between privilege and disadvantage that shape our public and private worlds." Her journey to understanding these issues began as an undergraduate student when she undertook an internship at a maximum security prison and learned about the obstacles prisoners face as they transition to the "outside." She further developed her sociological eye working in victim services in New York City, and then through her travels with the Peace Corps in Mali, where she worked with local villagers to create community gardens. With each new stage in her career, her understanding of inequalities and intersectionalities grew, and she became more deeply committed to using sociological tools to address these patterns of injustice and make society more equitable. Today she continues this commitment through collaborations with her sociology students and through her work with her campus Institute for Global Understanding.

Michael Stout's essay, "Using Sociology to Increase Citizen Participation in a Medium-Sized Midwestern City," looks at the impact of social capital on levels of civic engagement and the overall society. Whereas bonding social capital brings together people similar to one another, "bridging social capital brings individuals together with others who are different from them in terms of their race, social class, ethnicity, education, religion, age, or gender." Communities with high levels of bridging social capital tend to have higher levels of civic engagement and more relationships across identity groups. Working with public officials in his city, Stout helped them understand these concepts and devise strategies to increase the level of bridging social capital in the area, particularly among the most disadvantaged members of the community. As a testament to how sociology can make a difference in the real world, his city went on to hire its first Director of Public Information and Civic Engagement to respond to some of the issues and needs documented in his research.

In "Knowledgeable Power and Powerful Knowledge: Research and Organizing for Educational and Social Justice," Mark R. Warren describes how encountering sociologists who share his desire to use the tools of the discipline to make society more just motivated him to continue his doctoral studies in sociology. Warren found himself questioning, "Do we really need another study showing the harmful effects of poverty and racism?" So, instead of adding to this existing literature, he decided to dedicate his career to studying, understanding and developing effective strategies for addressing inequalities. Warren explains why he researches and writes his books in collaboration with community organizers and activists working for social justice. Activists have made great use of Warren's books which examine community organizing, white racial justice activists, and organizing for school reform. Each of these important texts provides an excellent example of how "rigorous sociological research" can contribute "to understanding and addressing pressing public issues."

Laurence Cox continues by describing how activist groups can gain power by building alliances in "Learning from Each Other's Struggles." He refers to a social movement as "a process of practical sociology, trying to understand oppression and exploitation to bring about change." An activist himself, Cox uses sociological tools to help social movement leaders learn from their own experience and that of other organizations to form alliances and more effectively address structural injustices in society. For instance, he has helped organize a series of over a dozen meetings, "Grassroots Gathering," that bring together movements across Ireland, all working on different campaigns to address neoliberal politics. These approaches, and others Cox describes, are all about translating theoretical understandings of social movements into practice. Reflecting on the possibilities of sociology in action, Cox describes the very important contributions we can make; he states, sociologists "play a part in the struggle for global and social justice, developing movements' strategic capacity, articulating alternative possibilities, and building alliances that point toward a different kind of society."

"Taking It to the Streets: Addressing Inequalities through the Human Rights Cities Movement," by Shelley K. White and Dottie Stevens, is a powerful example of how sociological tools can be used to influence a city. In this case, White and Stevens describe how Boston became officially designated as a "human rights city." White and her sociology colleagues collaborated with local activists to explore the ways in which human rights frameworks might be useful in addressing issues of inequality in the city. Bridging from this research, sociologists and social activists brought together elected officials, social justice organizations, and other key leaders in Boston to establish Human Rights City: Boston & Beyond. Boston thereby joined dozens of other cities worldwide that are working toward a new model of human rights—one that is based in grassroots, bottom-up approaches to ensuring basic principles of "equity, dignity and nondiscrimination." Boston's new organization has already taken steps to address fundamental human rights in the area, such as reliable water access for all.

References

Collins, P. H. (2000). *Black feminist thought: Knowledge, consciousness, and the politics of empowerment* (2nd ed.). New York: Routledge.

Social Movements and Activist Sociology

Charles Derber
Boston College

Charles Derber is Professor of Sociology at Boston College and has written fifteen books, reviewed in the *NY Times*, the *Washington Post*, the *Boston Globe*, and other leading media. His books, which include *Corporation Nation, The Wilding of America, The Pursuit of Attention, People Before Profit, Greed to Green, Marx's Ghost, The Surplus American,* and *Capitalism: Should You Buy It?* have been translated into five languages. He has also written for the *International Herald Tribune*, the *Boston Globe, Newsday, Tikkun,* and many other periodicals. Derber is a life-long activist who is engaged in peace, environmental, labor, and other social justice movements, including Occupy.

Activism and sociology are intertwined like DNA in my life story. The summer before I decided to go to graduate school in sociology at the University of Chicago, I worked registering African Americans to vote in Mississippi, experiencing the clash between the armed world of Southern segregationists and the courage of black civil rights activists. I was taken hostage by some white racists, shot at on a country road when driving with black activists, and slapped in jail by some white sheriffs with no love for Yankee boys. Going south for civil rights work was my first form of "sociological activism," and I learned more sociology than I had in my entire college career: about race relations, state violence, and social change. I henceforth always saw personal participation in social movements as a moral and intellectual necessity.

There are many types of sociological activism, but mine is all about building social movements. This is not based on nostalgia for the 1960s (although I have some) but on a sociological conviction that social movements are unique—the only social organizations capable of creating major democratic systemic change. Historically, the abolitionist, suffragette, and labor movements have been leading champions of social revolutions. Building social movements is the only true survival strategy for all citizens in a world facing climate change, rampant militarism, and predatory corporate capitalism, but it is a special responsibility for sociologists, whose goal is to analyze social systems and help change them.

This is not to say that sociologists should be propagandists for particular movements. Rigid or "politically correct" thinking makes for terrible pedagogy and anemic activism. Sociological activists should never be in the business of trying to police a politically correct worldview or coerce activism from their students, a violation of both their academic authority and the spirit of critical inquiry that allows both sociology and social movements to succeed.

Sociological activists are typically passionate about both their ideas and their commitments to social change. That makes for good sociology and good social movements. Sociologists should, in fact, acknowledge their values and passionate commitments to movements and justice, a form of honesty that leads to trust and more authentic dialogue on and off campus. There is rarely much learning or action without passion, as long as it does not get converted into propaganda, in which case passion becomes blind and can inhibit necessary exposure to a wide range of clashing theories—including those critical of one's own political worldview.

There are many models of movement-oriented sociological activism, one being the use of one's knowledge and work-based resources to help organize new organizations and visions within social movements. In 1971, after I joined the Brandeis sociology department as an assistant professor, I helped organize a National Student Strike Center against the war, coordinating work around the country to help mobilize all-out resistance to President Nixon's expansion of the war in Indo-China. The Student Strike Center created branches on campuses across the country, coordinating national antiwar protests and helping reframe the antiwar movement as a struggle against global capitalist control. The Strike Center brought together antiwar activists from different campuses and connected them with other movement groups, such as the Black Panthers, a militant anti-capitalist and anti-Vietnam African American organization.

As a professor, I led a faction of "soft activists" seeking dialogue and participatory consensus, while my faculty office mate led a "hard activist" wing, stressing discipline and doctrine. We were both sociological activists but we fought about vision, strategy, and tactics, my faction always arguing for inclusiveness, multiplicity of visions, and nonviolence. Sociologist Alvin Gouldner (1982) described "two Marxisms": the humanist, antiauthoritarian, and free-spirited ideals of the young Marx versus the scientific, authoritative, and deterministic Marx of later years. These are metaphors for divisions in many justice movements—both Marxist and non-Marxist. Despite the "two Marx" divisions in the National Strike Center, it became, for a short period, a sociological nerve center of the national antiwar movement and affirmed my view that sociologists could help mobilize and reframe movements from the inside.

Another activist sociology chapter of my life began with the 1999 Battle of Seattle, where labor, peace, and environmental activists converged in the streets of Seattle to oppose neoliberal corporate globalization. I had been writing about globalization in several books getting public attention; part of a sociological activist career is writing for the public to which social movements must appeal. With the students who accompanied me to Seattle, I founded a new organization, the Global Justice Project (GJP), a campus-wide social justice movement at my new academic home, Boston College.

The best thing the GJP did was partner with the National Labor Center—a leading global anti-sweatshop organization—to bring young female sweatshop workers from Bangladesh and El Salvador to campuses in the Boston area. These girls, often illiterate, told their heart-wrenching stories of working 20-hour days and sleeping under their sewing machines to the American students of their own age, who openly wept, with emotion so raw that it is still vivid in my memory. GJP helped them turn grief into activism. Scores of U.S. students worked with GJP to put pressure on the global corporations and force campuses to insist on worker rights. They sent petitions to CEOs to end sweatshop practices and forced disclosure of their own university investments, insisting on sweat-free caps and sneakers in their campus stores. They demanded their campus join monitoring efforts of factories in poor countries, such as those carried out by the Worker Rights Consortium, a global network of labor and human rights activists. Many built long-term relations with the sweatshop workers they couldn't forget.

GJP still exists and has become one of the student groups helping form the Occupy Movement today, demonstrating that sociological activists can put in place enduring organizations for change. After the financial meltdown of 2008, a new national wave of resistance emerged. In my books of this period, such as *Greed to Green* (2010) and *Marx's Ghost* (2011), I argued that the fragmented identity movements of gender, race, and labor must unite to confront the intertwined triple crises of capitalism, climate change, and militarism.

At just this moment, Boston-area lifetime activists in these very movements were coming to the same conclusion. We created together a new organization called the Majority Agenda Project (MAP) to help build new organic ties between movements running on separate tracks. In 2009 and 2010, MAP brought together labor leaders with climate and peace activists. MAP helped nurture creative collaborations, such as "One Nation," a national movement for capitalist transformation led by the national SEIU (Service Employees International Union) and the NAACP. I'll never forget the huge protest held on October 2010 on the Washington Mall, led by African American unionists. What a sight to see poor blacks and whites in their union shirts, walking and singing together for a "new nation," evoking Martin Luther King's Dream of a multiracial movement for peace and justice. Unions such as SEIU began leading social movement struggles not just for high wages for their members but national protests to protect Social Security, Medicare, Medicaid, and union rights.

In 2011, the Occupy Wall Street movement was born. Its immediate predecessor was the Wisconsin Wave, where thousands of workers, students (including sociology graduate students at the University of Wisconsin, housed right next to the Capitol), farmers, and environmentalists occupied the Wisconsin State House to protest Tea Party Governor Scott Walker's move to eliminate public sector unions. Shortly thereafter, the Occupy Movement exploded on the scene, as activists set up tents in the shadows of the biggest banks in the world. I felt like I had been waiting for Occupy my whole life. It proliferated like spring flowers sprouting through cracks in the sidewalk in every American city, creating a diverse, colorful, and spontaneous community of activists from every progressive movement, now uniting to confront the Wall Street tycoons running the country.

Occupy became my sociological and activist preoccupation. I wrote *Marx's Ghost* (2011) and *The Surplus American* (Derber & Magrass, 2012), two books that offered analysis and theatrical productions for explaining and building the movement. I worked with MAP to offer help to young Occupy activists, sharing history of previous Occupy movements and our thoughts about where to go from here. I devoted entire classes to exploring the economic crisis and how Occupy might be the movement that could unite all the diverse identity groups and bring a new generation of Americans into critical thinking and visionary political activism.

Most sociologists will become better scholars and teachers if they engage in sociological activism. My best writing has been animated and informed by my participation in real-world struggles to change socially dominant and violent institutions. Movement participation is one of the best sociological methodologies for collecting data and building theory.

It is thus hardly surprising that some of the best sociologists, often without academic credentials, are activists who work in the community and outside the academy. Their activism is enriched by their sociological analysis, and these "organic intellectuals" often teach their academic counterparts. The dialogue between these two communities of sociological activists—and their mutual involvement in grass roots movements—not only is the lifeblood of good sociology but one of the great forces of social transformation.

Existential social crises require activist sociologists. The clock is ticking, and we need to be in the trenches. It can be risky and time-consuming but also a source of wonderful connections and deep meaning. If we don't translate our sociological knowledge into action, sociology will fail and society will too. Several years ago, students who watched me get arrested with several other sociology faculty while committing civil disobedience in front of a big bank told me it was the most educational moment of their college experience. Our own actions will always speak more eloquently than our words.

References

Derber, C. (2010). *Greed to green: Solving climate change and remaking the economy*. Boulder, CO: Paradigm Publishers.

Derber, C. (2011). *Marx's ghost: Midnight conversations on changing the world*. Boulder, CO: Paradigm Publishers.

Derber, C., & Magrass, Y. R. (2012). *The surplus American: How the 1% is making us redundant*. Boulder, CO: Paradigm Publishers.

Gouldner, A. (1982). *The two Marxisms: Contradictions and anomalies in the development of theory*. New York: Seabury Press.

How Refugee Girls Change the World (and How You Can Too)

Laura Boutwell
Bridgewater State University

Laura Boutwell, PhD, MSW is Assistant Professor of Social Work at Bridgewater State University and faculty advisor for the campus-based Student Immigrant Movement chapter. Laura's background working with lesbian, gay, bisexual, and transgender youth, youth

of color, and refugee and immigrant youth deeply informs her understanding of and commitment to social justice work. Laura founded
the Virginia-based Imani Naliah Project, a participatory action
research initiative with refugee girls and young women from East
and West African countries. Laura received her PhD in Sociology and
graduate certificate in Women's and Gender Studies from Virginia
Tech.

"If you have come here to help me, you are wasting your time.
But if you have come because your liberation is bound up with
mine, then let us work together."

—*Aboriginal activists group, Queensland, 1970s*

Fast Forward and Rewind: 2011 and 1994

It's 2011. I'm with Maimuno, Rahmo, Kaffiyo, and Fadumo, and
they have just finished an amazing panel discussion of what it means
to be activists and refugee girls. I'm blown away by their brilliance, by
how the audience is hanging on their every word, by the way my heart
swells when I think about the history they just made as the first panel
of girl researchers at the National Women's Studies Association Annual
Conference. Later, a professor tells me that she became teary when
Rahmo talked about how being a researcher is one of the ways that
she is changing the world. The panel was that kind of powerful—and
represented the culmination of three years of research I did with The
Imani Nailah Project, a group of refugee girls from Liberia, Haiti, Sudan,
Somalia, and Burundi.

In this piece, I'm going to tell you more about our project and the Imani
girl researchers, but for now, head back with me to 1994. It's a hot, muggy
summer in the South. I have been learning about social inequalities as an
undergraduate sociology major and feel overwhelmed by how broken the
world seems. I want to be involved and to do my part, but I have no real
idea how. I train as an English as a Second Language volunteer and start
teaching English to a family from Vietnam. I soon find myself around a
kitchen table with the Ma family, trying to figure out how to teach the
English word for love. Even though I didn't know it, this is when I started
becoming a sociologist in action.

Sociology as Relationships

My life changed forever that summer, and it changed because of the relationships I made. For me, being a sociologist in action is all about relationships. Some of these relationships are structural ones. I often turn to conflict theory (Collins & Sanderson, 2010) to help me understand how inequality is perpetuated by power imbalances and global structures that keep racism, sexism, homophobia, transphobia, poverty, and anti-immigrant bias alive. Sociology is about grappling with the relationships between individual lives and larger institutional forces. We learn about structural inequalities and how oppression is perpetuated. We pay careful attention to the relationships between institutional racism and health (Jones, 2000), between the bullying of lesbian, gay, bisexual, and transgender youth and educational outcomes (Kosciw, 2004), between anti-immigrant bias and the national economy (Serrano, 2012), and so on. Sociology in action is also about the relationships in our own lives and how we show up as engaged community members. It isn't about saving "other" people; it is about connecting to a shared humanity, to embodying the truth that "we all belong to each other" (Sen, 2011). Sociology in action is about understanding that, in the face of such glaring inequality and oppression in the world, our liberation is truly bound up together (Aboriginal Activists Group, 1970).

After graduating from college, I began working with refugee youth from Iraq, Vietnam, Bosnia, Liberia, and Togo. I learned about the deep pull of home, the human need to belong, and our incredible capacity to survive. I learned how the United States calls itself a nation of immigrants, yet Americans historically and currently fail to support or honor the newly arrived among us. I learned from 9-year-old Bill, from Liberia, as he struggled with his first experiences with racism. I witnessed Biljana, who had just finished medical school in Bosnia, endure a physically demanding factory job while her dream of being a doctor in the United States disappeared before her eyes. I listened to Fadumo as she wistfully told me that she wished I could speak to her father in Somali, because no one fully understands her dad in the States and his sense of isolation and not being valued is a source of deep pain.

From the Imani Nailah Project
to the Student Immigrant Movement

As a PhD student, I turned to the young people in my life and asked if, together, we could work on a research project to tell the stories of what it is like to be refugee girls in the United States. Together, we started The Imani Nailah Project. Named by the girl researchers, Imani Nailah is a combination of Kiswahili and Arabic and roughly translates as *faith in one who succeeds*. We pursued participatory action research (PAR), which is a kind of research that includes everyone in the study as a researcher (there isn't a "researcher" and a "researched"). Rather than seeing refugees as victims who need to be saved (a very common misunderstanding), PAR recognizes refugees as people who make our communities stronger and more connected.

Imani researchers and I conducted a three-year project on what it means to be a refugee in this country. We combined arts-based research, youth-led focus groups, and individual interviews. Imani researchers helped me come up with the research questions about what it means to be a refugee, to be a girl, to be a Muslim, to be African or Haitian, to live in the United States.

We made salt dough maps and flag posters of our homelands. We made biography collages telling our history. We created an oral history project, asking parents and grandparents questions about life back home and their hopes for the future. We wrote poems. More than anything, we talked. We told each other our stories. We discussed what it means to have people call you an "African bootyscratcher." What it means to have people tell you to "go back where you came from." What it means to long for a home that no longer exists. How it feels to be reduced to the perpetual outsider. How Islam is a part of the rhythm and essence of people's lives. How to handle bullies. What our hopes were for the future. How we made the world a better place. As we engaged in "relational knowledge creation" (Hopkins & Pain, 2007, pp. 291), we drew from our connections with each other to advance a deeper understanding about what it means to be a refugee. Through this kind of research, we all became more empowered to create positive change in our own lives and communities.

After three wonderful years, I said sad goodbyes to the Imani researchers. As I moved many states away, I really missed the life-changing relationships I had formed and wondered what my new place in the world would be. I was hungry to continue my work with young people; I wanted to craft a life deeply engaged in connection and as a sociologist in action. Within a few months as a first-year professor at Bridgewater State University, the next stage of my work as a sociologist in action began to take shape: I worked with students to create a campus chapter of the Massachusetts-based Student Immigrant Movement (SIM).

SIM is a youth-led immigrant rights organization working to secure the rights of all students to live full lives, away from the threat of deportations that break families and communities apart. SIM brings attention to the difficulties many immigrant youth face, as they are often kept out of college by unfair federal and state policies that require undocumented students to pay out-of-state tuition rates without the benefit of any college loans. Here, sociology provides a framework to understand the dangers of anti-immigrant bias, the relationship between racism and dehumanizing myths of immigration, and the power and lasting impact of nationwide youth-led social movements working to ensure equality for all. On our campus, SIM is animated by principles of sociology in action: Members work to raise awareness about anti-immigrant bias and to promote immigrant rights. Our activism has taken form in online petition drives, a "drop the 'I' word" campaign, a myths and facts awareness series, and most recently, a deportation demonstration to bring attention to the 1.5 million immigrants who have been deported in the last 5 years. We do all this out of our commitment to build a more supportive campus climate for immigrants and to bring attention to the injustices currently faced by our immigrant friends, neighbors, family members, and fellow students.

Transformation in Relationships: What Sociology Can Do for You

My life has truly been transformed by Imani, by SIM, by my relationships in communities. These relationships are at the root of my activism, my community work, my research, how I teach, who showed up at my wedding, and at the most basic level, how I show up in the world. As you continue to explore how you will be a sociologist in action (because it really is one of the greatest things in the world to be!), I encourage you to understand the structural relationships that create and sustain inequality—and to spend your life seeking out the authentic, equitable, community-based relationships that will challenge oppression and give your life meaning. Our liberation truly is bound up together.

In closing—and in honor of the Imani researchers who created knowledge—I offer a poem written, in relationship, by two Imani researchers.

How Imani Dreams
by Rahmo Isse and Maimuno Guhad

Every day I walk out the door
to be the change I bring to the world
I carry the voice that speaks the truth
I march until my legs give away
I bust the door down until they'll hear
what I have to say
I am a sister, I am a daughter
I am two countries and an ocean
I am the sunny days my mother spent farming
I am the cloudy days the soldiers came running
I come from pain
I come from resilience
I come from courage
You know, I used to think activists were
People who pounded their fists to change the world
I even thought activism meant tanks and

Molotov cocktails being thrown
And somehow, I even pictured myself standing alone
But now I know
That when I speak the true words
Of being this beautiful refugee girl
That I am an activist and
I can change the world.

References

Collins, R., & Sanderson, S. K. (2010). *Conflict sociology: A sociological classic updated.* Boulder, CO: Paradigm Publishing.

Hopkins, P., & Pain, R. (2007). Geographies of age: Thinking relationally. *Area, 39*(3), 287–294.

Jones, C. P. (2000). Levels of racism: A theoretic framework and a gardener's tale. *American Journal of Public Health, 90*(8), 1212–1215. (PMCID: PMC1446334)

Kosciw, J. G. (2004). *The 2003 National School Climate Survey: The school-related experiences of our nation's lesbian, gay, bisexual and transgender youth.* New York: GLSEN. Retrieved from http://www.glsen.org/binary-data/GLSEN_ATTACHMENTS/file/300–3.PDF

Sen, R. (2011). The 9/11 story I choose to tell: We all belong to each other. *Colorlines: News for Action.* Retrieved from http://colorlines.com/archives/2011/09/my_september_11_story_we_belong_to_each_other.html

Serrano, A. (2012, September 12). Bitter harvest: U.S. farmers blame billion-dollar losses on immigration laws. *Time Magazine,* Retrieved from http://business.time.com/2012/09/21/bitter-harvest-u-s-farmers-blame-billion-dollar-losses-on-immigration-laws/.

Becoming a Sociologist in Action through Theory and Practice: A Personal Journey

Nancy J. Mezey
Monmouth University

Nancy J. Mezey received her PhD from Michigan State University. She is currently Associate Professor of Sociology and the Sociology Program Director and was the former Director of the Institute for Global Understanding at Monmouth University. Her areas of specialization are family, race-class-gender studies, and sexualities. Her 2008 book, *New Choices, New Families: How Lesbians Decide about Motherhood,* uses multiracial feminism to study how lesbians decide to become mothers or remain childfree. Dr. Mezey serves as a Board member for the Society for the Study of Social Problems (SSSP) and is a returned Peace Corps Volunteer where she served in Mali from 1988–1990.

In fall 2011, Monmouth University, where I teach, was granted a visit by Dr. Akosua Adamako Ampofo, the 2011 Sociologists for Women in Society (SWS) Feminist Activist award recipient. During her visit, I marveled at the extent of Dr. Ampofo's activism, particularly working against domestic violence in Ghana. Dr. Ampofo commented that I, too, am an activist. I looked at her quizzically because I have grappled with what I consider to be my lack of activist work over the years. She responded that while my activism has not been as focused as hers, it is activism nonetheless.

Shortly after our conversation, I was asked to write a chapter for this book. I feel privileged to join the ranks of other "sociologists in action." This chapter is my attempt to piece together and share with you my journey of becoming a sociologist in action who draws on the intersections of race, class, gender, and sexuality to analyze and better understand the social world.

During my first semester of college, I took an introductory sociology course focusing on sociological theory. After taking that class, my professor suggested that I do an internship in the Pre-Release Program at a maximum security prison for men located 30 minutes from the college. Every Friday I traveled with a handful of other students to spend the afternoon with men finishing long-term sentences and preparing to be released from the only life they had known for the past 10 to 20 years. I was surprised to find that this was a peer-counseling program in which the counselors—those people who helped the soon-to-be-released inmates figure out how to respond to their new lives on the "outside"—were inmates themselves who were serving long-term sentences, some of them for life. I was equally surprised to find how eloquent and gracious these peer-counselors were. That year, and the three following years during which I continued to volunteer at the prison, shattered my understanding of "criminals" and those imprisoned. I also began to see how the theory from my first semester sociology course helped inform my understanding of the race, class, and gender inequalities that the U.S. prison system embodies and perpetuates. This was quite a revelation for a young White woman from the wealthy suburbs of New York City and was mostly likely what hooked me into declaring a major in sociology.

During my junior year, I decided to study in London. At the time, my sister was serving in the Peace Corps in Mauritania, an impoverished African nation with very little infrastructure, situated in the Sahara Dessert. As the trip from London to Mauritania is not very far, I decided to visit. Although the Mauritanian people my sister introduced me to were incredibly hospitable, generous, and welcoming, I left thinking that I could never live in such a poverty-stricken area with a culture so foreign from my own and with so few of the material comforts, such as electricity and running water, that I am used to.

On my return to the United States, through a connection from my father, I landed a paid internship with Victim Services Agency (VSA) in New York City where I worked with counselors, trainers, police officers, and researchers focused on increasing awareness around domestic violence. Through VSA, I worked in Harlem, travelling with a police officer to low-income housing in which domestic disputes had recently occurred. My job was to speak with women who had called the police and offer them services that VSA provided. I was now a senior in college, and similar to my intellectual awakening during my time volunteering in the prison, the reality of my blindness to, or perhaps worse, my misconceptions of people from different race/class backgrounds, became clear to me. I began to recognize how the lives of the people whom I visited daily—people who were living in impoverished areas, who were first-generation immigrants, or poor African Americans, Latinos, and White Americans—were vastly disadvantaged by systemic and structural factors. In other words, these experiences sparked my sociological imagination.

Although I found my work with VSA rewarding, after I graduated from college I was yearning to travel and to learn fluent Spanish. I decided to join the Peace Corps, and requested to go to Latin America. The Peace Corps, however, had other plans for me and sent me to Mali, West Africa, a country that not only borders Mauritania but whose national language is French. Though disappointed not to learn Spanish, I remained excited about joining the Peace Corps and left for Mali, where I lived for two-and-a-half years in a village along the Niger River.

The Peace Corps was life-changing for me. My job was to help local villagers improve gardening techniques and prepare and market the produce they grew. My first step was to work with local leaders, discussing the importance of creating community gardens and negotiating what land to use. I built relationships across organizations to secure funding, materials, and labor to build fences, dig wells, purchase seed, and nurture the community gardens on a daily basis. Because the area of Mali in which I lived was largely populated by Muslims, I also learned how people peacefully and respectfully practice a religion that is marginalized throughout many parts of the Western world. And because Malian society is segregated by gender, I lived among people who held a very different view of gender than what I was used to experiencing. To make sense of these differences and experiences, I drew on basic concepts I had learned in my sociology classes. For example, I drew on my understanding of social structure, culture, and human agency to think about how Malian society is organized, why people value community over individualism, and how Malians make everyday decisions, particularly given their impoverished economic conditions. My ability to understand Malians' experiences through a sociological lens proved deeply helpful as I worked with communities on improving gardening, as well as socializing with Malian friends and community members. On returning from Mali and drawing on the interests I had developed through my undergraduate and work experiences, I decided to pursue my doctoral degree in sociology. While in graduate school, I began to focus on what sociologists call "structural inequalities," how race, class, gender, and sexuality create systematic and institutionalized barriers and opportunities, and how those barriers and opportunities shape our lives. My dissertation, later published as a book titled *New Choices New Families: How Lesbians Decide about Motherhood,* published by Johns Hopkins University Press in 2008, examined how structural inequalities shape lesbians' mothering decisions.

After receiving my PhD, I began working at Monmouth University, where I developed a minor and then a major in sociology. In building the program, I used many of the organizing skills I had learned both as a sociologist and in the Peace Corps. I met with university leaders, convincing them of the importance of the proposed major. I built relationships across disciplines and departments to secure support, resources, and staffing to create new courses, transform existing ones, and place qualified professors in the classroom. In the process, I was able to build a sociology major that incorporates a significant focus on structural inequalities.

In developing the sociology program, I also worked with students to create the Sociology Club. The club focuses on bringing speakers to campus, sponsoring events, and developing projects that highlight social inequalities and change. Drawing on my own experience, we invited several of the previously incarcerated men who I met while volunteering at the prison as an undergraduate student to come to speak to our campus. Meeting with the men encouraged my students to think about race/class/gender inequalities in new ways, similar to how this experience had affected me when I was a student. In addition, club members started a fundraiser for a local organization servicing homeless people living with HIV/AIDS. The students were so taken by the program that they started volunteering weekly, helping run the afternoon lunch program. In doing so, the students assisted an organization that helps transform the lives of individuals and works to rebuild an economically disadvantaged community. Most recently, the Sociology Club started an annual program called, "Stratified Streets: A Visual Tour of Inequality." For our first trip, we took a restorative justice tour of Philadelphia, studying large murals designed and painted by incarcerated men and posted on buildings within communities affected by violence. As a result of this trip, students are hoping to start a similar mural project on campus that speaks to social inequalities affecting their lives. The Club has also participated in political action campaigns by running the "Political Olympics" as part of the university's "Stand Up and Be Counted Campaign," an effort to encourage students to register and vote. The Political Olympics includes a variety of intellectual and physical events that raises awareness about political issues concerning students. They have also helped organize two events aimed at creating a more accepting climate for LGBT students on campus—one that included a panel of LGBT speakers who talked about coming out at work and the other that focused on New Jersey's anti-bullying campaign.

In addition to my work through the Sociology Program, I used my race-class-gender lens as Director of the Institute for Global Understanding (IGU), a grassroots campus organization that raises awareness around global issues. Through IGU and the efforts of many people, our university has developed close ties with both international and local organizations. We have built relationships with the United Nations that encourage us to create programs specifically focusing on social justice and change. For example, we coordinate a program in which university faculty and students conduct studies and help develop technological, health, education, and business initiatives in the village of Macheke, Zimbabwe. In addition, we created a mentorship program in which high school students from a nearby economically disadvantaged community come to campus, are mentored by MU students, and learn about college life. Out of this program, some of the high school students have pursued college careers. Spinning off this program, Monmouth students started a debate team in the same high school. The high school debaters have travelled to tournaments, won trophies, and learned critical thinking and speaking skills that will undoubtedly help them throughout life. IGU also runs a week-long campus-wide Global Understanding Convention that inspires students to consider international careers. While I cannot take responsibility for the success of these programs, I know that my sociological training has helped nurture the programs in which IGU is involved. And, of course, I continue to encourage students to study abroad and join the Peace Corps. Several of our former students are now living overseas, having experiences that are as life-changing for them as they were for me.

My understanding of the social world, as well as my own life, has come directly from my academic studies and practical experiences associated with sociology. What excites me most about sociology is the discipline's commitment to understanding how the intersections of race, class, gender, and sexuality create a relationship between privilege and disadvantage that shape our public and private worlds. I can now say with confidence that my sociological training and knowledge guide everything I do, including my efforts to create positive change in a world organized around social inequalities. In reflecting back over my experiences, first as a student and now as a professor, I realize that for me, being an activist sociologist means using my sociological training to help create and reinforce social systems and cultural beliefs and values that reduce social inequality, as well as inspire others to do the same. If my actions have led to such accomplishments, then I am proud to be considered a "sociologist in action."

Using Sociology to Increase Citizen Participation in a Medium-Sized Midwestern City

Michael Stout
Missouri State University

Dr. Michael Stout is an Associate Professor of Sociology at Missouri State University. His research interests are in the areas of social capital and civic engagement. Professor Stout is the coordinator of the Ozarks Regional Social Capital Study (ORSCS), an ongoing project that tracks levels of social capital and civic engagement in Southwest Missouri. Funded by a local coalition of private, philanthropic, and public contributions, the ORSCS is a valuable source of information for community and civic leaders in the Ozarks.

Public Sociology in the Ozarks

I have always been very active in my community. As an undergraduate sociology major at Temple University in Philadelphia in the late-1990s, I not only learned about many important issues, such as racism, discrimination, segregation, poverty, and economic inequality, but I also was able to experience firsthand how those issues impacted everyday life in the city. The sociological theories and methods I learned have provided me with a toolkit for understanding the underlying dynamics of these issues, and my professors taught me to use my voice to speak out in an informed and effective way. From that point on, I was hooked. I knew I wanted to be a sociologist, and I knew I wanted to work on solving some of society's most pressing issues. As a result of my passion for working to address social problems, I've dedicated my life and my career to engaging important social issues as a sociologist in action.

I currently work in the sociology department at Missouri State University in Springfield, Missouri. Springfield is a mid-size city in the northern part of the Ozarks. It is home to five colleges and two major health care systems and serves as the major metropolitan hub for southwest Missouri. Often referred to as the "Buckle of the Bible Belt," Springfield is home to multiple megachurches, as well as the international headquarters of the Assemblies of God and its national university, Evangel University. For its large population of evangelical Christians, social life typically revolves around attending church and participating in faith-based groups and clubs. Many of Springfield's citizens hold conservative opinions on a range of cultural and social issues. The city is uncommonly homogeneous, with only 8% of its residents being non-white. Additionally, the community faces a wide range of social problems related to its relatively high rates of poverty, alcohol and drug abuse, and its high rates of domestic violence and child abuse.

As a public sociologist, I regularly work with community leaders to identify, define, and solve public issues. So far, the main contribution that I have made in Springfield has been to introduce community leaders to two important sociological concepts, *social capital* and *civic engagement* and to use them in efforts to create public policies and develop programs that empower people.

Social capital refers to networks of social relationships characterized by norms of trust and mutual exchange (e.g., Coleman, 1988; Putnam, 2000) and serves as an indicator of the civic health of communities. According to social capital theory, social networks have value because they provide people with access to important resources, and social scientists have developed surveys to measure social capital and its relationship to other important community indicators, such as education, crime, public heath, political participation, and nonpolitical community participation.

My research primarily looks at the ways in which social capital is related to civic engagement, which can be broadly defined as voluntary participation in organized political activities (e.g., voting, protesting, and membership in a political party) and nonpolitical activities (e.g., volunteering, serving on community committees, and membership in clubs and other voluntary groups). Civic engagement is more common in places with higher levels of social capital, because when citizens know and trust one another it is easier to mobilize them to address public issues. Social capital makes it easier to achieve things that benefit the community as a whole, such as a child-care cooperative among welfare mothers, a microlending group that enables poor people to start businesses, or a system through which farmers can share expensive tools and machinery.

The Ozarks Regional Social Capital Study

Since 2008, I have been the project coordinator of the Ozarks Regional Social Capital Study (ORSCS), an ongoing initiative to collect and share information on social capital and civic engagement in the Ozarks. My work on social capital and civic engagement in the Ozarks serves as a good example of how sociology can have a "real-world" impact. The information that's been collected through the study has helped community leaders make more effective decisions about community and economic development in several ways.

First, it has brought the sociological concepts of social capital and civic engagement to the forefront of policy discussions and introduced community leaders in the Ozarks to a new way of thinking about addressing public issues. For example, according to Brian Fogle, the President of the largest community foundation in Southwest Missouri, the ORSCS "has done a remarkable job in changing our vernacular and dialogue in the community." Similarly, Greg Burris, the City Manager of Springfield, commented that our work has, "literally changed the conversation within our community. We will be using this data to drive our new communication and engagement strategies . . . to move the needle toward greater civic engagement."

Second, measuring social capital shows where it is strong and where it is weak, and it has led to the identification of civic engagement as a public issue. My study showed that the citizens of Springfield and surrounding rural communities in the Ozarks feel alienated from their local leadership, and that they have low levels of trust in national and local government. It also showed that a lower proportion of people in Southwest Missouri are civically engaged compared to the national average. For example, people in this area were less likely than Americans in other geographic areas to report that they have cooperated with neighbors to fix something in their neighborhood, or to have worked on a community project. To make matters worse, we found that all these problems were especially pronounced among groups from low socioeconomic and disadvantaged backgrounds. This is important information for community leaders. As a result of the study, policy makers have made civic engagement a central priority, by establishing programs to increase levels of trust and social capital among low socioeconomic groups in the Ozarks.

Third, studying social capital and civic engagement in the Ozarks has mobilized existing groups and organizations to develop targeted programs in an effort to increase citizen participation in the region. As part of this process, I've called attention to the characteristics of social networks in the Ozarks and introduced community leaders to two key concepts: *bonding* social capital and *bridging* social capital.

Bridging social capital brings individuals together with others who are different from them in terms of their race, social class, ethnicity, education, religion, age, or gender. Bonding social capital brings individuals together with others who are like them. One possible explanation for the lower levels of civic engagement in the Ozarks is that there are high levels of bonding social capital but low levels of bridging social capital. Certainly, civic engagement and political participation require working with different people and diverse groups. So, the idea of a relative lack of bridging social capital in the Ozarks is now part of the community dialogue. Sociological theory has encouraged community leaders to think of the community as mosaics of social networks that could work together on various issues.

Community Impact

My work has had a real impact on policy decisions in the Ozarks. First, in 2012 the City of Springfield, Missouri, hired its first Director of Public Information and Civic Engagement. The job description for the new position, which states that in addition to the more traditional responsibilities of a city Public Information Officer (PIO), the Director of Public Information and Civic Engagement "designs, develops, and implements civic engagement strategies and programs to increase citizen participation and, ultimately, trust in City government" indicates the influence of the social capital study. The Director also "develops mechanisms to measure and track levels of civic engagement over time." This new position illustrates an effort on the part of the City to build social capital and increase civic engagement among the residents of the city.

Second, the ORSCS has informed efforts to address the issue of poverty in the Ozarks. For example, the finding that the least well off citizens are also the least civically engaged has led to the Neighbor for Neighbor (N4N) pilot program, which kicked off in spring 2012. Sponsored by more than 20 community partners representing diverse interests from the public, private, philanthropic, faith-based, and education sectors of the city, the N4N program is a grassroots effort to reduce poverty and increase social capital and civic engagement in two low-income neighborhoods. The project has four goals: (1) "build relationships and increase trust in two Springfield neighborhoods;" (2) "improve the quality of life in the neighborhoods;"

(3) "empower program participants to be agents of change;" and (4) "engage citizens in neighborhoods who feel they have no vote or voice when it comes to important community issues."

Conclusion

My work on social capital in the Ozarks provides an example of how sociology can have a positive impact in the "real world." By using sociological theories and methods, I've worked with community leaders to identify, define, and try to solve pressing issues in the Ozarks. I've come to the realization that, in the process of studying social capital and sharing my findings with community leaders, I've started the process of building new types of social capital. The efforts and policies resulting from this work should lead to higher levels of bridging social capital and increased civic engagement in the Ozarks. Being a sociologist in action has been incredibly rewarding for me, both personally and professionally. I'm making a positive impact on my community, and I'm using my sociological knowledge to empower others. If there's one thing that I've learned as a result of my work, it's that knowledge truly is power.

References

Coleman, J. S. (1988). Social capital in the creation of human capital. *American Journal of Sociology, 94*, S95–S120.

Putnam, R. D. (2000). *Bowling alone: The collapse and revival of American community*. New York: Simon & Schuster.

Knowledgeable Power and Powerful Knowledge: Research and Organizing for Educational and Social Justice

Mark R. Warren
University of Massachusetts Boston

Mark R. Warren is Associate Professor of Public Policy and Public Affairs at the University of Massachusetts Boston. He studies and works with community organizing groups seeking to promote equity and justice in education, community development, and American democratic life. Mark has authored several books, including *Dry Bones*

Rattling: Community Building to Revitalize American Democracy, Fire in the Heart: How White Activists Embrace Racial Justice, and *A Match on Dry Grass: Community Organizing as a Catalyst for School Reform.* Mark cochairs a national network of scholars and community activists designed to promote collaborations that produce research relevant to advancing community needs—the Urban Research-Based Action Network (URBAN).

Early in my graduate school years I attended a meeting of educational sociologists presenting an award to an eminent scholar. He declared, "I am proud to say that no research I have ever conducted has had any direct impact on educational practice." He received a standing ovation and I thought, "This is not the place for me. I'm out of here!"

I almost quit graduate school during my first year as a PhD student in sociology at Harvard University. I came to graduate school like many others thinking that I could contribute to social justice as a sociologist. But I found that most sociologists, while they might care about social justice personally, were not using professional sociology for that purpose. I found mainstream sociology and mainstream sociologists disconnected from the pressing issues facing the people I cared about—poor and working class people and communities of color. They directed their efforts at building theory that responded to sociological traditions but had little direct relevance to transformational politics.

Those who did study poor communities seemed to focus solely on the problems and deficits of these communities. When I thought about what I would do for my dissertation, I would moan to myself, "Do we really need another study showing the harmful effects of poverty and racism?"

In the end, I decided to stay in sociology and write a dissertation focused on analyzing and developing solutions to the issues I cared about: persistent racism, poverty, and educational failure. I knew that sociology provides the tools of critical thinking, research skills, and structural analysis that would best help me conduct social change based research. Fortunately, I found a few other sociologists conducting rigorous sociological research but doing so in a way that contributed to understanding and addressing pressing public issues. These scholars, including Theda Skocpol who became my advisor, showed me that a more engaged or activist form of sociology was possible, and supported me in my research and career.

One other thing bothered me. I felt that mainstream sociology, in its efforts to keep research "objective," had also developed a certain arrogance. Too many sociologists studied people "from above," believing that "regular" people could not contribute to scientific knowledge. That meant that people and communities seemed to be simply fodder for sociological theorizing. That got under my skin. Here's why.

My father was a blue-collar worker, a warehouseman with a high school education. By reading the newspaper cover to cover every day, he knew more about what was going on in the world than most sociologists I met. He thought critically about social and political issues, had been a Teamster Union activist and a fervent supporter of progressive movements everywhere. (You can probably guess what an influence he has been on my life.) Before I went to graduate school, I had worked as a labor and community organizer. I met a range of people in that work and learned a lot from them. Many were smart, sophisticated thinkers who reflected on their practice and developed theories about what worked and what didn't and why. Moreover, I had married a woman who grew up poor and black in London without the chance to go to university. She is the greatest intellectual I know. (She eventually returned to school and received her BA much later in life.)

I recognized that sociologists sometimes have specialized knowledge and research techniques. These are powerful tools that allow us to help make the hidden the visible and, as C. Wright Mills teaches us, to contextualize personal troubles inside the broader context of public issues. But I also knew that "regular" people have knowledge and theory that matter. In my view, public knowledge relevant to societal change would best come from the engagement of diverse perspectives, knowledge, and understandings. So I began a search to develop a form of scholarship that was both a more engaged, or activist, form of scholarship and a more collaborative one.

I knew that I wanted to write my dissertation about effective efforts to engage poor and working people in civic and political participation to address pressing issues in their lives. I was fortunate that Theda Skocpol had just taken a trip to Texas to discuss her research with a large and powerful community organizing network called the Industrial Areas Foundation. She introduced me to the network's director in the Southwest, Ernesto (Ernie) Cortes, and he agreed to have me come down. Within weeks, I was on a plane to a state I had never visited before.

Thus began a profound learning experience for me that changed the way I looked at political organizing and the critical role that religious faith can play in progressive politics. I studied the network through the sociological tools of ethnography. During two years of research, I interviewed over one hundred people, observed scores of meetings and collected and analyzed documents like reports and newspaper articles. I did this in constant dialogue with the organizers and leaders in the network, sharing my research plans and my findings along the way and getting their feedback. Ernie and many of these organizers and leaders were highly sophisticated thinkers, and I learned from my discussions with them as much as I learned from studying their organizing work.

There was some tension in our relationship. As a sociologist and researcher, I was responsible for presenting an independent, fair, and balanced analysis of the network's organizing and that did not always square with their self-understanding. I wrote a particularly controversial section about the failure of one of the network's local groups to participate in a protest against the pardoning of a white skinhead convicted of a racist hate killing. We discussed (and argued) for days over this. In the end, like many organizers, I found that tension can be a good thing. I believe I wrote a much more complex and nuanced account of the event as a result of the intense discussions, and that I became a better sociologist. I think it led many participants in the network to think about the need to confront racism in a more explicit way.

I eventually published a book from my dissertation research called *Dry Bones Rattling* (Warren, 2001). I helped organize a variety of book discussions around the country that brought academics together with community organizers and leaders. I spoke at these events, but also shared the stage with organizers and leaders in the network who were able to tell their stories and share their views too. These were exciting collaborations with rich conversations across the divides that typically separate us.

There is a deep and profound cynicism in the academic world, and I refuse to be part of it. The typical academic story about grassroots efforts goes something like this. "A brave group of people organized against the odds. They had a few victories, but ultimately fell victim to more powerful opponents or to their own internal weaknesses that were the result of the oppressive structures in which they operated. We can applaud them for trying, but nothing can really change."

That's not the story I told in my book. As noted above, I pointed out problems and challenges in the network's work. But I drew out what scholars and organizers could learn from a network that made very successful advances in building participation and leadership in low-income communities of color, forging alliances across race and class lines, and creating real and meaningful reform in a range of policy areas, including housing, job training, and public education. I am humbled to say that even twelve years after the book came out, community organizers and activists still come up to me and tell me how important reading the book has been in helping them with their work. Many learned that protesting injustice, while important, was not enough. They found through my work a way to sink deep roots in low-income communities and build long-term relationships with people to create concrete improvements in their lives, such as better education, safer neighborhoods, opportunities for job training, and more responsive governments.

The PICO organizing network, for example, had done door-to-door neighborhood organizing for a number of years in California cities but struggled with rapid turnover in membership and instability in leadership. Learning from the experience of the Industrial Areas Foundation, the network changed strategy to congregation-based organizing and began to work with leaders and communities with stable connections to faith institutions. As a result, over a number of years. the PICO-affiliated Oakland Communities Organization was able to build a large and powerful organization of parents and community members to develop a long-term campaign to transform the schools serving the city's low-income children from large, impersonal and mostly ineffective institutions to small, community-connected and more successful schools.

Soon after *Dry Bones Rattling* was published, I moved to the Harvard Graduate School of Education where I continued my collaborative research approach. I worked with activists to study how some white people develop a commitment to racial justice activism, and this resulted in my book *Fire in the Heart* (Warren, 2010). Few whites told me they moved toward activism when they read about racism in a book; rather, it was when they had a direct, personal experience witnessing racism. They developed their commitments to activism as they built respectful and meaningful relationships with people of color and learned from them. Many told me that working across racial lines to help create a new kind of community and society based on respect and justice was difficult, but also exciting and deeply meaningful work.

Many young white people are concerned about racism but troubled about their role as white people in confronting racism. I have discussed the book with many groups of white racial justice activists who reflect on the book's findings to help them understand better the critical importance of white people speaking up and acting against racism. I have also worked with multiracial groups who are finding ways to challenge continued prejudice and white privilege behaviors among white people in ways that keep them involved rather than driving them away from the struggle for racial justice.

I next turned my focus toward community organizing for public education. Along with Karen Mapp, another faculty member at Harvard, and a research team of 15 doctoral students, we studied six community organizing groups across the country that had been effective in creating real improvements in the quality and equity of public education. We approached the study in a collaborative fashion, committed to working with groups so that our findings would be relevant and useful to advancing organizing efforts at public education. We published our research in *A Match on Dry Grass* (Warren, Mapp, & the Community Organizing and School Reform Project, 2011). We held a national conference with the organizing groups where 200 parents, young people, educators, and other stakeholders discussed lessons from these and other promising models of community-based approaches to equity and justice in education. After the conference, many of the groups involved strengthened their organizing and went on to achieve important victories. Padres y Jovenes Unidos in Denver, for example, had already launched a campaign to end the school-to-prison pipeline in Denver and replace it with a restorative justice approach to school discipline. Through learning about how to build state-level alliances at the conference and in other venues, they proved able to build a coalition powerful enough to get the Colorado state legislature to pass a "smart school discipline law" that reduced harsh disciplinary practices in public schools across the state.

Our approach to education reform stood in stark contrast to the mainstream approach taken by education researchers at Harvard (and beyond). In the traditional model, education policy is the province of experts and not of the teachers and communities on the ground. In my view, effective change requires the participation of people most affected by educational failure and injustice—families and communities in alliance with educators at the local level. Experts have a critical role to play. But parents, young people, and teachers bring local knowledge and core value commitments to equity and justice. Moreover, by engaging with people on the ground, they come to own research and the resulting policy and practice initiatives so they will actually help implement them.

We need a broad social movement to address deep structures of injustice and move toward equity and social justice. This movement needs to include sociologists and other academics, as well as community organizers, parents, young people, educators, and a broad array of stakeholders. We will have different roles within that movement but we need to find ways to work together and learn from each other. We need to create powerful knowledge and knowledgeable power.

Building these kinds of relationships across the academic/community divide and across lines of race, class, and gender can be challenging. It's exciting work, though, because, if we attempt to build truly respectful, diverse communities, we are working to create the kind of world we want to exist. My wife taught me this: Social justice is not just a "cause" out there to work for. It involves how we live our lives today, how we treat other people, how we build community.

For me, the personal is political in my desire to build relationships with people and collaborate with communities. The academic life can be a lonely one but I am not lonely. Being an activist sociologist and teacher offers me a deeply meaningful life. In the end, what really sustains me and all of us in doing activist sociology, or in being change agents of any kind, are the relationships we build in the lives we lead.

References

Warren, M. R. (2001). *Dry bones rattling: Community building to revitalize American democracy*. New Jersey: Princeton University Press.

Warren, M. R. (2010). *Fire in the heart: How white activists embrace racial justice*. New York: Oxford University Press.

Warren, M. R., Mapp, K. L., & Community Organizing & School Reform Project. (2011). *A match on dry grass: Community organizing as a catalyst for school reform*. New York: Oxford University Press.

Learning from Each Other's Struggles

Laurence Cox
National University of Ireland Maynooth

Laurence Cox completed his BA in European Studies and a PhD in Sociology at Trinity College Dublin (TCD). He has taught at TCD, Waterford, and many activist and adult education settings, and now works at the National University of Ireland Maynooth. Along the way, he has been a busker, kitchen porter, translator, magazine editor, kindergarten organizer, and father. Dr. Cox has been active in many different social movements over the past quarter century and collaborates widely with activists on teaching, research, and writing. His publications include *Understanding European Movements, Marxism and Social Movements, Ireland's New Religious Movements*, and *Buddhism and Ireland*.

Making Connections

The structures of power and inequality that make up society are interlinked and cannot be understood in isolation. The knowledge needed to understand and change them has to be *earned,* in reflecting on our own experience of challenging them and talking to others who have put theory to the test of practice. Social movements, then, are a process of practical sociology, trying to understand oppression and exploitation to bring about change.

Sociology and social movements have always been in dialogue, from Tocqueville, Marx, and Durkheim to Angela Davis, Herbert Marcuse, Frances Piven, and Toni Negri. The experience of patriarchy, the rise of women's movements, and feminist scholarship are not separate processes. The same goes for capitalism, working-class struggles, and Marxist theory; for racism, the struggles of the oppressed, and the rise of Black or postcolonial studies, and for many other forms of power and exploitation.

Below, I describe a series of interlinked projects that I have been involved in with other engaged sociologists and movement thinkers. As a young activist, growing up around human rights, antiapartheid, peace, and ecology movements, I was conscious of movement subcultures—feminist, antiauthoritarian, socialist—grounded in the 1960s and 1970s and still active in the 1980s and 1990s.

My PhD dissertation, on the potential for radical alliances developing these cultures of resistance, was written against the background of the Zapatista uprising in Mexico and submitted in time to see the Seattle protests against an unjust world order validate its conclusions and change the movement landscape across the global North. Writing the thesis went hand-in-hand with editing an activist magazine that made those links in practical ways, and with organizing small gatherings of activists from different movements—around the possibilities of new political alliances, networking independent media, reviving older alternative movements, and creating cross-movement dialogues—part of a wider networking process that enabled a resurgence of social movements in the 2000s.

Knowledge for Social Change

My first full-time job, while still working toward my PhD, was in the rust-belt town of Waterford, Ireland, teaching workers in residential care institutions for young offenders, children with behavioral difficulties, and with other populations. These students introduced me to a whole world of community organizing, which represented (in working-class voices) many of the same grassroots, radical-democratic values that I had found in my research.

I also started to work with graduate students doing research "from and for" their own movements, which helped me think about how movements learn. When movements reinvent the wheel, they easily make strategic mistakes, for example, by appealing to the powerful and wealthy who benefit from the inequalities the movements are challenging. All movement activity costs time, energy, and struggle, but one of the easiest things to change is the movement's own practice, ensuring that participants' efforts do not go to waste—that we are not just acting out our untested *beliefs* about what works, or letting organizational goals become an end in themselves.

Participatory action research (PAR) in movement practice involves activists exploring together what they do, and how they can do it better. It can have different kinds of impact: awareness of *being* a movement (not just delivering services), a wider perspective on social change, clearer articulation of strategic choices, a chance to reflect on the whirl of "things to do," the ability to ask what is working, or a chance to hold discussions that would otherwise not happen. Methodologically, this means treating participants as everyday experts on their own activities and purposes. PAR develops this knowledge, bringing participants together to share the knowledge they have attained through their different standpoints.

Over the past 15 years, I have run a program supporting graduate student activists using PAR with their own movements and taught courses based around this model in the academy and community education settings. Participants are in movements ranging from working-class community organizing to home birth activism and from feminist spirituality to fighting the oil and gas industry. The results have ranged from oral histories via radical education and communication projects to the creation of "lessons learned" tools for other campaigns.

Intersectional Politics

Back in Dublin, I joined other activists calling a "Grassroots Gathering," bringing together different Irish movements opposed to the neoliberal politics of "profit at all costs." In the Gatherings (13 to date) we try to turn theoretical understanding into practice. In a single society, different forms of oppression and injustice are interconnected and need to be challenged together. States, and many NGOs, present these as separate "issues," which can be solved without seriously challenging social structures. But the barriers that prevent such initiatives from transforming situations of exploitation, oppression, and stigma are represented by entrenched social interests, which can only be tackled by large-scale alliances of those affected and other movements for change.

The Gatherings create an understanding that we need to work with each other in order to create effective movements. This is easier said than done, but some key alliances have been made between ecologists, left-wing organizers, and solidarity/peace activists. Community activists were more cautious of whether alliances would benefit their communities, but nevertheless links were made, which have stood the test of time. A sexual attack by one activist on another was met with a feminist uprising, which transformed movement cultures in many ways, contributing to a new wave of feminist groups.

The network has played an important role in resisting the World Economic Forum and the EU's neoliberal policies and in opposing the use of Ireland's Shannon airport for U.S. military and CIA aircraft, among other issues. It has also contributed to supporting community opposition to Shell's gas pipeline at Rossport, NW Ireland, a key battle over environmental destruction and the private appropriation of natural resources.

Most importantly, perhaps, many activists came to act out of the basic social analysis that injustice and oppression are interconnected, and movements must work together to challenge them. When we do, we find we are stronger, and we have a better understanding of how society operates and how to change it. This is sociology in action.

Learning from Each Other's Struggles

Since 2008, Ireland has experienced economic and political crisis. As the state has increasingly attacked social movements and poor and marginalized communities, professionalized advocacy (legal, media, policy, and fund-raising work on behalf of others) has declined, but grassroots organizing by those directly affected has grown. In this context, I and some other sociologists and community educators set up a Master of Arts (MA) geared toward social movements, moving away from existing models and providing advocacy skills for state-funded professionals. It highlights broader questions of power and injustice, tools for radical education and personal transformation within an overarching sense of community education methods and activism as a skilled practice.

This MA in "Community Education, Equality, and Social Activism" is not a simple activist training—the "nuts and bolts" of how to organize a meeting, create a website, or run a protest are widely available—but rather gives activists the chance to step back and reflect on their day-to-day activities and, crucially, to learn from each other's struggles. A history of increasingly separate and professionalized "sectors," structured around government departments dealing with issues such as gender equality, disability, poverty, migration, the environment, and so forth has led to distrust between movements and a tendency to take one particular way of organizing for granted. Spending a year with a small number of other activists is a very powerful—if sometimes bumpy—way of overcoming these barriers and coming to see ourselves as reflective practitioners.

This same double process—of supporting activists as they reflect on their own experience and of bridging the gaps between them—found shape internationally in cofounding the open-access social movement research journal *Interface*. Unlike other social movement research journals, *Interface* is not a space where academics talk "about" movements as experts but a space for dialogue between movement theorists and researchers engaged in social movements. Activists work at every level of the journal, from editing and peer review to writing and distribution.

Interface asks its authors to share their understanding with people involved in *other* movements, in *other* countries, using *different* disciplines or thinking within *different* intellectual/political traditions. Rather than preaching to the choir and debating within an already-agreed framework, it asks participants to create knowledge that "works" beyond its specific context of origin, again focusing on learning from each other's struggles. Now in its ninth issue, *Interface* has become a productive space of encounter between activists and researchers across the world.

Conclusion

Activist sociologists, along with movement thinkers and community educators, play a part in the struggle for global and social justice, developing movements' strategic capacity, articulating alternative possibilities, and building alliances that point toward a different kind of society. In this sociology in action, we gain a wider perspective on our work, make new connections and alliances, see new possibilities for social transformation, and understand the basic fact of intersectionality: "If you are not free, I am not free."

Taking It to the Streets: Addressing Inequalities through the Human Rights Cities Movement

Shelley K. White
Worcester State University

Dottie Stevens
Survivors, Inc.

Shelley K. White is Assistant Professor of Public Health at Worcester State University. She is a sociologist with a Master of Public Health degree who teaches about and researches global and domestic health and inequalities, globalization and development, public policy, human rights, and social movements. Shelley has worked with a number of social justice and human rights organizations, including Free the Children International, the People's Health Movement, and SocMed.

Dottie Stevens has a Master's Degree in Human Services Planning from UMass Boston's College of Public and Community Service. She has served in a number of public positions, including President of the Coalition for Basic Human Needs, President of the Massachusetts Welfare Rights Union, Vice President of the National Welfare Rights Union, and former candidate for Governor of Massachusetts. As a mother of four on welfare, Dottie has spent her life in activism. She is the Coordinator of Survivors Inc. and Editor of *Survival News*.

Do human rights really matter? That is, once the idea of universal human rights has been legally accepted, does life improve for communities? What happens when national governments don't recognize human rights; can communities still ensure that their rights will be protected, respected, and promoted?

As you might imagine, communities and nations around the world struggle with these questions. These are also questions that Dottie and I have struggled with in our own activist work right here in the United States, in our home city of Boston.

The idea of human rights, as a universal concept, was first expressed after World War II, with the creation of the Universal Declaration of Human Rights (UDHR). The UDHR is a beautiful document forwarding the principles of equity, dignity, and nondiscrimination (United Nations, 1948). Unfortunately, as a declaration, it remains an *aspirational* document and does not bind nations to comply. Since the UDHR was adopted in 1948, the United Nations (UN) has created many treaties detailing human rights; they describe economic, social, cultural, political, and civil rights and the special rights that must be protected for children, women, immigrants, people of color, and many others. Unlike the UDHR, these treaties *do* bind nations to uphold human rights, but only once a nation signs the documents and then ratifies them (the latter meaning that the nation incorporates the rights into its legal and policy systems to ensure the rights will be protected, respected, and promoted).[1]

Before even beginning my training as a sociologist, I thought of myself as a human rights activist. I believed deeply in the principles expressed by the human rights framework, having fought wholeheartedly for global

---

[1] To learn more, visit the UN's Office of the High Commissioner for Human Rights (OHCHR) at www.ohchr.org, particularly this factsheet: http://www2.ohchr.org/english/bodies/docs/OHCHR-Fact Sheet30.pdf

children's rights, health rights, disability rights, and others. Thus, while completing my PhD work and continuing my studies of human rights, I jumped when the opportunity presented itself to collaborate on planning a one-day human rights conference to precede the American Sociological Association's (ASA) 2008 conference in Boston. A group of sociologists studying and working on human rights approached my department at Boston College, seeking this collaboration, and many students and professors responded. From the beginning, we aimed for more than just another academic exercise where we discussed human rights; we wanted to actually *do something tangible* to advance human rights. We also wanted our process to be informed and guided by activists and organizers engaged in human rights and social justice struggles on a daily basis. Very early in our process, we reached out to several Boston-based organizations and had several—from unions and workers' organizations to global justice programs and low-income women's groups—join our burgeoning planning committee.

In our meetings, we realized that we first had to ask whether the human rights framework was seen as important in the U.S. context. You see, the United States has had a paradoxical relationship with human rights. While an early champion of the concept, with heroes like Eleanor Roosevelt who led the drafting of the UDHR, the United States has since dragged its feet, having signed and ratified only select human rights treaties (Human Rights Watch, 2009). For instance, when the UN issued two covenants in 1966 that would translate the UDHR into binding documents, the United States didn't sign either until 1977 and only ratified the one focused on civil and political rights (with reservations), not the one ensuring economic, social, and cultural rights (Glendon, 2001). The United States has also refused to ratify the Convention on the Elimination of All Forms of Discrimination against Women (1979), the Convention on the Rights of the Child (1989)—which is signed by all other nations but Somalia—and the Convention on the Rights of Persons with Disabilities (2006), to name a few (Blau & Moncada, 2005).[2] Thus, we wondered if people and groups struggling for justice in the United States even felt connected to the human rights framework.

As part of our planning, three sociology graduate students on the committee—Amy Finnegan, Adam Saltsman, and I—undertook a participatory study, which led us to dialogue with 51 activists and organizers from 42 social justice organizations around Boston (Finnegan, Saltsman, & White, 2010). We asked them whether, and how, they used the human rights

[2] To learn about the treaties, and which nations have signed and ratified, visit the UN's Treaty Collection at: http://treaties.un.org/Pages/Treaties.aspx?id=4

framework to advance their work (which included social justice campaigns focused on environment, peace, LGBTQ, health, housing, labor, education, transportation, and many other issues).

At the end of our interviews, we also introduced the idea of Human Rights Cities and asked whether our interviewees thought this concept could work in the U.S. context. Human Rights Cities (HRCs) are the product of a movement first started in 1997 in Rosario, Argentina, which has spread to a couple dozen cities since. The goal of HRCs is to create a bottom-up, grassroots movement in which communities learn about their human rights, develop a sense of ownership, and then hold their municipal governments accountable to the promise of human rights (Marks, Modrowski, & Lichem, 2008). This is a countermovement to the common critiques of human rights, which include that the UN approach engages only federal-level governments and is often legalistic and otherwise inaccessible to common people (Cranston, 1973; Donnelly, 1989; Evans, 1996; Evans, 2001; Fields, 2003; Forsythe, 1991). Our interviewees were intrigued to learn that Washington, D.C., had recently become the first U.S. city to declare itself a Human Rights City, in 2008, and many expressed enthusiasm for this novel approach (Blau, 2008; Council of District of Columbia, 2008).

Fortunately, one of the activists I had the pleasure to interview was Dottie Stevens. Dottie was a long-time activist with Survivors Inc., a Boston-area organization working on behalf of low-income women. I didn't know it then, but our interview would be the start of a wonderful collaboration, in which I would soon take a back seat, supporting her enthusiastic and successful campaign to make Boston a Human Rights City. You see, after our interviews in the spring of 2008 (which deeply informed our content and approach to the conference), we held our "Boston Human Rights: Ideas and Action" conference in August.[3] We attracted over 150 participants, including sociologists from the ASA conference and activists from the Boston area, creating a rich dialogue about the potential of grassroots human rights movements. Many of our interviewees played key roles in facilitating conference dialogue sessions about the potential of advancing human rights in Boston. Dottie volunteered for this role and sparked an animated discussion among participants, particularly about the promise of the HRC campaign.

Following this conference, Dottie was energized by the group discussions and the keynote address delivered by Shula Koenig, founder of the People's Movement for Human Rights Learning, the international agency sponsoring the HRC network.[4] She formed a relationship with Shula and reached out to several Boston-area organizations engaged in rights-based

---

[3] See: www.bostonhumanrights.org

[4] See: http://www.pdhre.org/

work. By March of 2011, she had also reached out to her representative, Charles Yancey, Dean of the Boston City Council, whom she had known and worked with on antipoverty issues for many years. After calling his office to propose the idea of passing a resolution to make Boston a Human Rights City, she heard back within days that he would support this movement. Councilor Yancey convinced the entire council to pass the resolution (signed April 13, 2011)[5] and he presented it to Survivors Inc. at a conference in April 2011 to create a Steering Committee for Human Rights City Boston!

Several meetings followed in 2011 and 2012, where Dottie and Survivors Inc. took the lead in mobilizing like-minded groups and individuals to expand the steering committee and select key actions to take. I joined as well, contacting individuals whom we interviewed in 2008 along with some new key constituents. I also brought in a sociology undergraduate student as an intern to support these early efforts. Eventually, the committee and its supporters grew to include, among others, Mass Global Action, the Green Rainbow Party, iconic Boston activist Mel King, the Rainbow Coalition, Mass Welfare Rights Union, Dudley Street Neighborhood Initiative, Women's International League for Peace and Freedom, Mass Alliance of HUD Tenants, Results, the Union of Minority Neighborhoods, UMass Boston, Frederick Douglass Peace Garden, and Budget 4 All. Ultimately, we changed our name to Human Rights City Boston & Beyond, as some folks were from other cities and wanted to organize HRCs across Massachusetts.

During early meetings, we discussed the various rights issues facing our Boston-area communities, and the list was long! However, we agreed that we needed to start with a clear focus. Mass Global Action (MGA), an organization challenging the ill effects of economic globalization in Massachusetts, became a key organization on the steering committee. It brought to the committee its work on water rights, focusing on water shut-offs and other water access issues around Boston, and the committee voted to adopt the right to water as our first campaign.

MGA had already been working on a campaign called the Color of Water, documenting how water shut-offs around Boston were disproportionately affecting low income and minority neighborhoods. Human Rights City Boston & Beyond provided the mobilization that this campaign desperately needed, supporting a postcard petition campaign and Right to Water hearings around Boston. We printed 2,000 postcards, declaring that

---

[5] See: http://meetingrecords.cityofboston.gov/sirepub/cache/2/lqumop45w0izrjrpehhegivg/1039505 122013083357563.PDF

Boston was now a human rights city, but that not everyone in Boston had the most basic human right to water. Water bills are higher in Boston than in other U.S. cities and have been escalating in order to pay for cleaning up corporate pollution of Boston Harbor. Meanwhile, protections against water shut-offs are inadequate and shut-offs have been disproportionately impacting marginalized communities. MGA had found that thousands of people are affected each year, and that "for every 1% increase in people of color by city ward, there was a 4% increase in threatened water shut-offs" (Stevens, 2012). The campaign calls for a moratorium on water shut-offs because of inability to pay, as well as meaningful subsidies for low-income rate payers. Dottie and a group of supporters went to the 2012 Boston Marathon, gathering hundreds of signatures on the postcards. Postcards are still being collected, with plans to bring them to Boston's Mayor and the Water Commissioner. In collaboration with MGA, they also held three hearings in East Boston, Dorchester, and Roxbury to gather testimonies of people suffering without stable water access. Finally, they have held workshops about why and how water is being privatized and how to make it a human right. Dottie also featured this issue with an article titled "The Color of Water," published in *Survival News*.[6]

Human Rights City Boston & Beyond has accomplished a lot in its first two years. In addition to the Right to Water project, its members have held dozens of workshops at homeless shelters, organized teach-ins on university campuses, held forums at churches, spoken on Occupy Radio, been interviewed by Boston Neighborhood Network TV, published articles in local newspapers, and had their activities shown on YouTube. At marches and rallies, Dottie and other leaders have participated as keynote speakers, addressing human rights and distributing copies of the UDHR. Finally, through the committee's outreach, other Massachusetts cities such as Cambridge, Weymouth, and Concord are now actively organizing to make their cities HRCs as well. Already, Boston is well on its way to accomplishing the key goals of the HRC movement, providing education about human rights, instilling a grassroots sense of ownership, and holding its city government accountable!

In many ways, I have felt like a very fortunate witness of this HRC process in Boston. Dottie, building on her incredible history of successful activism for marginalized populations, took the spark of this idea and shepherded it forward. However, I am thrilled to have played—along with my graduate school colleagues—an important part in starting this movement and, more broadly, in making sociology matter in the *real world*. Sociology is the study

---

[6] Survival News, Volume 24, No. 1 (Winter/Spring 2012); available through www.survivorsinc.org.

of power in society; we examine who has power and how those who don't have power can organize for change. My long-time commitment to studying and rectifying inequalities in society led me to study human rights, and that study led our small research group to think deeply about what human rights means in the U.S. context. Our dialogues with activists and organizers around Boston formed a unique research project that was participatory and inclusive and, from the beginning, was intentional in moving toward the action(s) that our participants felt were most relevant and important in the Boston context. Had it not been for this combination of partnered planning, sociological research, and informed action, I believe that Boston would not be a Human Rights City today. The potential of this HRC model is just at its beginning stages in Boston, and I am excited to see it continue to unfold!

References

Blau, J. (2008, September 5–8). *Human rights cities in process*. Paper presented at the first International Sociological Association Forum of Sociology: Sociological Research and Public Debate, Barcelona, Spain.

Blau, J., & Moncada, A. (2005). *Human rights: Beyond the liberal vision*. Lanham, MD: Rowman & Littlefield.

Council of the District of Columbia. (2008, December 10). *A ceremonial resolution in the Council of the District of Columbia*. Retrieved from http://www.pdhre .org/DC-HRC-Resolution.pdf

Cranston, M. W. (1973). *What are human rights?* London: Bodley Head.

Donnelly, J. (1989). *Universal human rights in theory and practice*. Ithaca, NY: Cornell University Press.

Evans, T. (1996). *US hegemony and the project of universal human rights*. New York: St. Martin's Press.

Evans, T. (2001). *The politics of human rights: A global perspective*. Sterling, VA: Pluto Press.

Fields, A. B. (2003). *Rethinking human rights for the new millennium*. New York: Palgrave Macmillan.

Finnegan, A. C., Saltsman, A. P., & White, S. K. (2010). Negotiating politics and culture: The utility of human rights for activist organizing in the United States. *Journal of Human Rights Practice, 2*(3), 307–333.

Forsythe, D. P. (1991). *The internationalization of human rights*. Lexington, MA: Lexington Books.

Glendon, M. A. (2001). *A world made new: Eleanor Roosevelt and the Universal Declaration of Human Rights*. New York: Random House.

Human Rights Watch. (2009). *United States ratification of human rights treaties*. Retrieved from http://www.hrw.org/news/2009/07/24/united-states-ratification-international-human-rights-treaties

Marks, S. P., Modrowski, K. A., & Lichem, W. (2008). *Human rights cities: Civic engagement for societal development*. New York: People's Movement for Human Rights Learning.

Stevens, D. (2012, Winter/Spring). The color of water in Boston. *Survival News*, *24*(1), 9.

United Nations. (1948). Universal Declaration of Human Rights. Retrieved from https://www.un.org/en/documents/udhr/

Discussion Questions

1. Charles Derber says that "there is rarely much learning or action without passion." How do your own experiences support or refute this statement?

2. Do you agree with Derber that "if we don't translate our sociological knowledge into action, sociology will fail and society will too"? Why or why not?

3. How did Laura Boutwell and the Imani researchers conduct their project on what it is like to be refugee girls? How do you think the methods of data collection they used helped Boutwell and the participants to collect rich, detailed data?

4. How does Boutwell connect sociology in action to relationships? How do you think you could expand and deepen the relationships in your life by becoming a sociologist in action?

5. Nancy Mezey describes how students in the sociology club at her school are hoping to create a mural project on their campus "that speaks to social inequalities affecting their lives." Imagine that you are in charge of coming up with some ideas for such a project on your campus. On what topics would your murals focus? Why?

6. As Mezey points out, sociology helps us understand "how the intersections of race, class, gender, and sexuality create a relationship between privilege and disadvantage that shape our public and private worlds." Describe an example of this fact from either Mezey's piece or your own life.

7. What is the difference between bonding and bridging social capital? How, as Michael Stout describes, can higher levels of bridging social capital in a community lead to greater community involvement and civic engagement? Do you believe there is a high level of bridging social capital among the students at your college or university? What makes you think so?

8. How are the public officials of Springfield, Missouri, making use of the sociological tools Stout has taught them to use? How might you make use of them to increase civic engagement in your own neighborhood or on your own campus?

9. When Mark Warren wrote up his research findings on the Industrial Areas Foundation (IAF), his work resulted in tension between him and the lead organizer for the IAF. Why? How does Warren's description of this incident help you understand the role of a sociologist studying an organization? How do you think you would have handled this situation? Why?

10. How has Warren's family influenced the topics he chose to study and his collaborative research approach? If you become a professional sociologist, on what topics will you focus, and might this be influenced by your background?

11. According to Laurence Cox, what are some of the impacts of Participatory Action Research (PAR) in movement practice? If you were/are a member of a social movement, how might this type of research benefit your movement?

12. How does Cox help activists understand the basic fact of intersectionality: "If you are not free, I am not free?" Why can it sometimes be very difficult for members of different oppressed groups to work together? Why might groups in power be nervous about efforts to create ties among different activist organizations?

13. Throughout their piece, Shelley White and Dottie Stevens describe *collaborations* with various organizations. Why is the ability to make connections and work with other individuals and groups so important in efforts to understand and improve society? Describe the last time you worked with others to accomplish a goal. What were some of the low and high points of the collaborative effort? What did you learn and gain from the experience?

14. According to White and Stevens, what are the goals of the HRC Movement and what has Human Rights City Boston & Beyond done to accomplish them? How did White and her fellow sociologists use their sociological imagination to help create and steer the movement?

Resources

Ethnicity and Race Tutorial

Intersections of race, ethnicity, class, and inequality domestically and globally. Provides flashcards, good information, and an excellent list of resources and links.

http://anthro.palomar.edu/ethnicity

Free the Children

World's largest network of youth helping youth. Works to empower North American youth through leadership and education and to empower youth in poor regions through development of schools, health, water, sanitation, and microdevelopment. Website offers excellent curriculum, resources and education on children's rights issues, and exciting campaigns such as We are Silent, Halloween for Hunger (We Scare Hunger), and the Year of Education.

http://www.freethechildren.com

Institute on Race and Poverty

Provides resources for students, academics, policy makers, and community organizations seeking to address reform in taxation, housing, and education, with a focus on race and poverty. Particularly useful are their maps, data sets, and studies.

http://www.law.umn.edu/metro/index.html

Institute for Women's Policy Research

Provides research on the economic issues facing women and the needs of women, particularly surrounding employment education, economic change, poverty, welfare, income security, health, and work and family. Provides quick data, publications, newsletters, and guides and tools to educate and work toward change on these issues.

http://www.iwpr.org

Public Agenda

Provides research and tools for advocacy and education on issues cutting across intersections of race, gender, class, and sexuality. User has ability to create data and find information based on selected intersections.

http://www.publicagenda.com

Public Housing in the United States

Good history of public housing in the United States and how policy has been shaped by race and class.

http://en.wikipedia.org/wiki/Public_housing_in_the_United_States#References

United for a Fair Economy

Aims to close the wealth gap, to change tax rules that favor the wealthy, and to focus on the connections between race and class inequality. Works to bring people together from various cultures, races, and classes to work together toward economic justice. Excellent resources on popular economics education, the racial wealth divide, tax fairness, CEO pay, and inequality.

http://faireconomy.org

Index

About the Editors

Shelley K. White, PhD, MPH, is Assistant Professor of Health Sciences and Public Health at Worcester State University. She recently taught in the Sociology Department at Simmons College, where she also coordinated the Simmons World Challenge—an interdisciplinary, student-led learning program which creates actionable solutions to global social justice problems. Shelley's teaching and research focus on health and illness, globalization and development, inequalities, social movements, and social justice. She previously worked in HIV/AIDS policy globally and domestically, and serves on the board of directors of Free the Children and SocMed. She is coeditor of *Sociologists in Action: Sociology, Social Change, and Social Justice* (with Kathleen Odell Korgen and Jonathan White; 2nd Edition, 2014), and her recent publications appear in the *Journal of Human Rights Practice; American Journal of Public Health; Education, Citizenship and Social Justice; Public Health Reports;* and *Critical Public Health.*

Jonathan M. White, PhD, is Associate Professor of Sociology at Bentley University and Director of the Bentley Service Learning Center. He specializes in inequality, globalization, human rights, and public sociology. He has received numerous teaching and humanitarian awards, is founder of Sports for Hunger, and has served on the board of directors of Free the Children, the Graduation Pledge Alliance, Me to We, Youth for Peace, and other civic engagement organizations. He is coauthor of *The Engaged Sociologist: Connecting the Classroom to the Community* (with Kathleen Odell Korgen) (4th Edition, 2013), coeditor of *Sociologists in Action: Sociology, Social Change, and Social Justice* (with Kathleen Odell Korgen and Shelley White; 2nd Edition, 2014), and served as associate editor to *The New York Times* bestseller *Me To We* by children's rights advocates Marc and Craig Kielburger.

Shelley and Jonathan live in Massachusetts and are the proud aunt and uncle of Jared, Kyle, Tyler, Arielle, Cameron, Brianna, Mikayla, Joshua, Jack, Logan, Tyler, Joey, and Brookelyn.

Kathleen Odell Korgen, PhD, is Professor of Sociology at William Paterson University in Wayne, New Jersey. Her primary areas of specialization are race relations, racial identity, and public sociology. Professor Korgen's publications include *The Engaged Sociologist: Connecting the Classroom to the Community* (with Jonathan White) (4th Edition, 2013), *Sociologists in Action: Sociology, Social Change, and Social Justice* (with Jonathan White and Shelley White; 2nd Edition, 2014), *Multiracial Americans and Social Class* (2010), *Contemporary Readings in Sociology* (2008), *Crossing the Racial Divide: Close Friendships Between Black and White Americans* (2002), and *From Black to Biracial* (1999).

⊛SAGE research**methods**

The essential online tool for researchers from the world's leading methods publisher

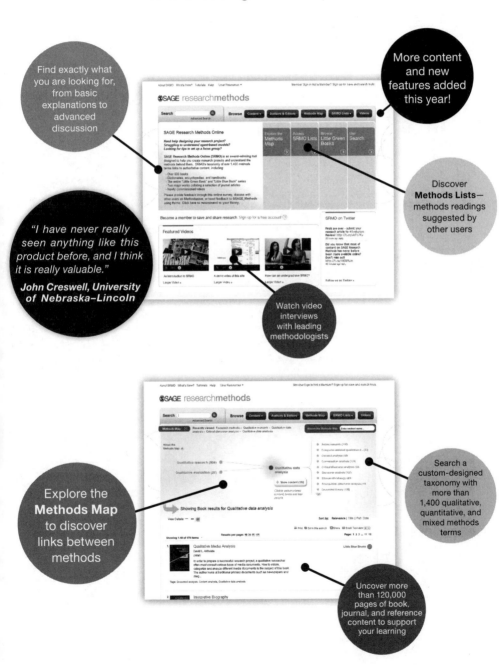

More content and new features added this year!

Find exactly what you are looking for, from basic explanations to advanced discussion

Discover Methods Lists— methods readings suggested by other users

"I have never really seen anything like this product before, and I think it is really valuable."
John Creswell, University of Nebraska–Lincoln

Watch video interviews with leading methodologists

Explore the Methods Map to discover links between methods

Search a custom-designed taxonomy with more than 1,400 qualitative, quantitative, and mixed methods terms

Uncover more than 120,000 pages of book, journal, and reference content to support your learning

Find out more at
www.sageresearchmethods.com